Teacher Resource Book B

VISIONS

Language ✧ Literature ✧ Content

Mary Lou McCloskey

Lydia Stack

Australia ✧ Canada ✧ Mexico ✧ Singapore ✧ United Kingdom ✧ United States

VISIONS TEACHER RESOURCE BOOK B
Mary Lou McCloskey and Lydia Stack

Publisher: *Phyllis Dobbins*
Director of Development: *Anita Raducanu*
Director, ELL Training and Development: *Evelyn Nelson*
Developmental Editor: *Tania Maundrell-Brown*
Associate Developmental Editor: *Yeny Kim*
Associate Developmental Editor: *Kasia Zagorski*
Editorial Assistant: *Audra Longert*
Production Supervisor: *Mike Burggren*
Marketing Manager: *Jim McDonough*
Manufacturing Manager: *Marcia Locke*
Photography Manager: *Sheri Blaney*
Development: *Proof Positive/Farrowlyne Associates, Inc.; Quest Language Systems, LLC*
Design and Production: *Proof Positive/Farrowlyne Associates, Inc.*
Cover Designer: *Studio Montage*
Printer: *West*

Printed in the United States of America.
3 4 5 6 7 8 9 10 08 07 06 05 04

For more information, contact Heinle, 25 Thomson Place, Boston, Massachusetts 02210 USA,
or you can visit our Internet site at http://www.heinle.com

ISBN: 0-8384-5339-2

Contents

LESSON PLANS

TEACHER RESOURCES

READING SUMMARIES (English, Spanish, Hmong, Vietnamese, Chinese, Cambodian, Haitian Creole)

PARENT NEWSLETTERS (English, Spanish, Vietnamese, Hmong, Cantonese, Cambodian, Haitian Creole)

VIDEO SCRIPTS

VIDEO WORKSHEETS

Class ______________________ Date ______________

UNIT 1 Challenges

CHAPTER 1 • The Race, by Jennifer Trujillo, & The Camel Dances, by Arnold Lobel

Chapter Materials

Activity Book: pp. 1–8
Audio: Unit 1, Chapter 1
Student Handbook
Student CD-ROM: Unit 1, Chapter 1
Teacher Resource Book: Lesson Plan, p. 1; Teacher Resources, pp. 35–64; Reading Summaries, pp. 65–66; Activity Book Answer Key
Teacher Resource CD-ROM
Assessment Program: Unit 1, Chapter 1 Quiz, pp. 7–8; Teacher and Student Resources, pp. 115–144
Assessment CD-ROM: Unit 1, Chapter 1 Quiz
Transparencies
The Heinle Newbury House Dictionary/CD-ROM
Web site: http://visions.heinle.com

➤ **See the Teacher's Edition wrap-around for complete teaching suggestions for each section.**

Day 1

- **Unit Opener** (p. 1) 20 MIN.
  Preview the unit reading selections. Complete the "View the Picture" activity.
- **Objectives** (p. 2) 5 MIN.
  Present the chapter objectives.
- **Use Prior Knowledge** (p. 2) 15 MIN.
  Activate prior knowledge about competitions.
- **Build Background** (p. 3) 5 MIN.
  Provide the background information on ballet.
- **Homework:** KWL (TRB, p. 42); Have students complete the first and second columns based on what they learned in class. Students will complete the third column at the end of the chapter.

Day 2

- **Check Homework** 5 MIN.
  OR
- **Warm Up** 5 MIN.
  Write on the board: List 3 types of competitions.
- **Build Vocabulary** (p. 3) 15 MIN.
  Introduce synonyms and using references.
- **Text Structure** (p. 4) 10 MIN.
  Present the text features of a poem and a fable.
- **Reading Strategy** (p. 4) 10 MIN.
  Teach the strategy of making inferences.
- **Reading Selection Opener** (p. 5) 5 MIN.
  Preview the chapter reading selections.
- **Homework:** Activity Book (p. 1)

Day 3

- **Check Homework** 5 MIN.
  OR
- **Warm Up** 5 MIN.
  Write on the board: List 2 things you learned about a poem and 2 things you learned about a fable.
- **Reading Selections** (pp. 6–9) 25 MIN.
  Have students read the selections and use the reading strategy. Teach spelling, capitalization, and punctuation points on TE pp. 6–9.
- **Reading Comprehension** (p. 10) 10 MIN.
  Have students answer the questions.
- **Build Reading Fluency** (p. 10) 5 MIN.
  Teach how to build reading fluency by reading key phrases.
- **Homework:** Activity Book (p. 2)

Day 4

- **Check Homework** 5 MIN.
  OR
- **Warm Up** 5 MIN.
  Write on the board: Complete these sentences:
  a. In "The Race," the rider rode her horse because ______.
  b. In "The Camel Dances," the Camel worked very hard because ______.
- **Listen, Speak, Interact** (p. 11) 15 MIN.
  Have students describe something they like to do.
- **Elements of Literature** (p. 11) 15 MIN.
  Teach how to distinguish sounds of rhyming words.
- **Word Study** (p. 12) 10 MIN.
  Present the suffix *-er* and complete the activity.
- **Homework:** Activity Book (pp. 3–4)

Day 5

- **Check Homework** 5 MIN.
  OR
- **Warm Up** 5 MIN.
  Write on the board: Write a rhyming word for these words:
  a. cat **b.** mouse **c.** deer **d.** bear **e.** shark
- **Grammar Focus** (p. 12) 15 MIN.
  Present past tense verbs.
- **From Reading to Writing** (p. 13) 15 MIN.
  Teach how to write a poem.
- **Across Content Areas** (p. 13) 10 MIN.
  Provide related science content on classifying animals.
- **Homework:** Activity Book (pp. 5–8); Have students complete the third column of the KWL chart from Day 1. Have students study for the Unit 1, Chapter 1 Quiz.

Class ______________________ Date ______________________

UNIT 1 Challenges

CHAPTER 2 • Hatchet, by Gary Paulsen

Chapter Materials

Activity Book: pp. 9–16
Audio: Unit 1, Chapter 2
Student Handbook
Student CD-ROM: Unit 1, Chapter 2
Teacher Resource Book: Lesson Plan, p. 2; Teacher Resources, pp. 35–64; Reading Summaries, pp. 67–68; Activity Book Answer Key
Teacher Resource CD-ROM
Assessment Program: Unit 1, Chapter 2 Quiz, pp. 9–10; Teacher and Student Resources, pp. 115–144
Assessment CD-ROM: Unit 1, Chapter 2 Quiz
Transparencies
The Heinle Newbury House Dictionary/CD-ROM
Web site: http://visions.heinle.com

➤ **See the Teacher's Edition wrap-around for complete teaching suggestions for each section.**

Day 1

- **Unit 1, Chapter 1 Quiz** (Assessment Program, pp. 7–8) 20 MIN.
- **Objectives** (p. 14) 5 MIN.
  Present the chapter objectives.
- **Use Prior Knowledge** (p. 14) 15 MIN.
  Activate prior knowledge about forests.
- **Build Background** (p. 15) 5 MIN.
  Provide background information on fire.
- **Homework:** KWL (TRB, p. 42); Have students complete the first and second columns based on what they learned in class. Students will complete the third column at the end of the chapter.

Day 2

- **Check Homework** 5 min.
  OR
- **Warm Up** 5 MIN.
  Write on the board: Fuel can be a _____, a _____, or a _____.
- **Build Vocabulary** (p. 15) 15 MIN.
  Introduce using context.
- **Text Structure** (p. 16) 10 MIN.
  Present the text features of realistic adventure fiction.
- **Reading Strategy** (p. 16) 10 MIN.
  Teach the strategy of identifying cause and effect.
- **Reading Selection Opener** (p. 17) 5 MIN.
  Preview the chapter reading selection.
- **Homework:** Activity Book (p. 9)

Day 3

- **Check Homework** 5 MIN.
  OR
- **Warm Up** 5 MIN.
  Write on the board: Which one of these things is NOT a feature of realistic adventure fiction?
  a. setting
  b. stanzas
  c. events
  d. problem
- **Reading Selection** (pp. 18–23) 25 MIN.
  Have students read the selection and use the reading strategy. Teach the spelling, capitalization, and punctuation points on TE pp. 18–23.
- **Reading Comprehension** (p. 24) 10 MIN.
  Have students answer the questions.
- **Build Reading Fluency** (p. 24) 5 MIN.
  Teach how to build reading fluency by reading chunks of words.
- **Homework:** Activity Book (p. 10)

Day 4

- **Check Homework** 5 MIN.
  OR
- **Warm Up** 5 MIN.
  Write on the board: List 3 possible reasons why Brian wanted to build a fire.
- **Listen, Speak, Interact** (p. 25) 15 MIN.
  Have students act out events in the story.
- **Elements of Literature** (p. 25) 15 MIN.
  Teach the use of figurative language.
- **Word Study** (p. 26) 10 MIN.
  Present compound words.
- **Homework:** Activity Book (pp. 11–12)

Day 5

- **Check Homework** 5 MIN.
  OR
- **Warm Up** 5 MIN.
  Write on the board: Divide these compound words into two words: classroom, textbook, doorknob. What do the words mean?
- **Grammar Focus** (p. 26) 10 MIN.
  Present the past tense of the verb *be*.
- **From Reading to Writing** (p. 27) 20 MIN.
  Teach how to write a realistic adventure story.
- **Across Content Areas** (p. 27) 10 MIN.
  Introduce related science content on combustion.
- **Homework:** Activity Book (pp. 13–16); Have students complete the third column of the KWL chart from Day 1. Have students study for the Unit 1, Chapter 2 Quiz.

Class ____________________ Date ____________________

UNIT 1 Challenges

CHAPTER 3 • Antarctic Adventure, by Meredith Hooper

Chapter Materials

Activity Book: pp. 17–24
Audio: Unit 1, Chapter 3
Student Handbook
Student CD-ROM: Unit 1, Chapter 3
Teacher Resource Book: Lesson Plan, p. 3; Teacher Resources, pp. 35–64; Reading Summaries, pp. 69–70; Activity Book Answer Key
Teacher Resource CD-ROM
Assessment Program: Unit 1, Chapter 3 Quiz, pp. 11–12; Teacher and Student Resources, pp. 115–144
Assessment CD-ROM: Unit 1, Chapter 3 Quiz
Transparencies
The Heinle Newbury House Dictionary/CD-ROM
Web site: http://visions.heinle.com

See the Teacher's Edition wrap-around for complete teaching suggestions for each section.

Day 1

- **Unit 1, Chapter 2 Quiz** (Assessment Program, pp. 9–10) 20 MIN.
- **Objectives** (p. 28) 5 MIN.
  Present the chapter objectives.
- **Use Prior Knowledge** (p. 28) 15 MIN.
  Activate prior knowledge about directions on a map.
- **Build Background** (p. 29) 5 MIN.
  Provide the background information on Antarctica.
- **Homework:** KWL (TRB, p. 42); Have students complete the first and second columns based on what they learned in class. Students will complete the third column at the end of the chapter.

Day 2

- **Check Homework** 5 MIN.
  OR
- **Warm Up** 5 MIN.
  Write on the board: List 3 words that describe Antarctica.
- **Build Vocabulary** (p. 29) 15 MIN.
  Introduce words about ships.
- **Text Structure** (p. 30) 10 MIN.
  Present the text features of a historical narrative.
- **Reading Strategy** (p. 30) 10 MIN.
  Teach the strategy of predicting.
- **Reading Selection Opener** (p. 31) 5 MIN.
  Preview the chapter reading selection.
- **Homework:** Activity Book (p. 17)

Day 3

- **Check Homework** 5 MIN.
  OR
- **Warm Up** 5 MIN.
  Write on the board: Which genre tells about real people—adventure fiction or historical narrative?
- **Reading Selection** (pp. 32–35) 25 MIN.
  Have students read the selection and use the reading strategy. Teach the spelling, capitalization, and punctuation points on TE pp. 32–35.
- **Reading Comprehension** (p. 36) 10 MIN.
  Have students answer the questions.
- **Build Reading Fluency** (p. 36) 5 MIN.
  Teach how to build reading fluency by using rapid word recognition.
- **Homework:** Activity Book (p. 18)

Day 4

- **Check Homework** 5 MIN.
  OR
- **Warm Up** 5 MIN.
  Write on the board: Write 3 things that you remember about "Antarctic Adventure."
- **Listen, Speak, Interact** (p. 37) 15 MIN.
  Have students retell the order of events.
- **Elements of Literature** (p. 37) 15 MIN.
  Present personification.
- **Word Study** (p. 38) 10 MIN.
  Present adverbs.
- **Homework:** Activity Book (pp. 19–20)

Day 5

- **Check Homework** 5 MIN.
  OR
- **Warm Up** 5 MIN.
  Write on the board: List 3 things that happened to you today in the order that they happened.
- **Grammar Focus** (p. 38) 15 MIN.
  Present *and* to join words.
- **From Reading to Writing** (p. 39) 15 MIN.
  Teach how to write a historical narrative.
- **Across Content Areas** (p. 39) 10 MIN.
  Introduce related social studies content about bodies of land and water.
- **Homework:** Activity Book (pp. 21–24); Have students complete the third column of the KWL chart from Day 1. Have students study for the Unit 1, Chapter 3 Quiz.

Class ______________________________ Date ____________________

UNIT 1 Challenges

CHAPTER 4 • Yang the Youngest, by Lensey Namioka

Chapter Materials

Activity Book: pp. 25–32
Audio: Unit 1, Chapter 4
Student Handbook
Student CD-ROM: Unit 1, Chapter 4
Teacher Resource Book: Lesson Plan, p. 4; Teacher Resources, pp. 35–64; Reading Summaries, pp. 71–72; Activity Book Answer Key
Teacher Resource CD-ROM
Assessment Program: Unit 1, Chapter 4 Quiz, pp. 13–14; Teacher and Student Resources, pp. 115–144
Assessment CD-ROM: Unit 1, Chapter 4 Quiz
Transparencies
The Heinle Newbury House Dictionary/CD-ROM
Web site: http://visions.heinle.com

➤ **See the Teacher's Edition wrap-around for complete teaching suggestions for each section.**

Day 1

- **Unit 1, Chapter 3 Quiz** (Assessment Program, pp. 11–12) 20 MIN.
- **Objectives** (p. 40) 5 MIN.
  Present the chapter objectives.
- **Use Prior Knowledge** (p. 40) 15 MIN.
  Activate prior knowledge about the first day of school.
- **Build Background** (p. 41) 5 MIN.
  Provide the background information on China.
- **Homework:** KWL (TRB, p. 42); Have students complete the first and second columns based on what they learned in class. Students will complete the third column at the end of the chapter.

Day 2

- **Check Homework** 5 MIN.
  OR
- **Warm Up** 5 MIN.
  Write on the board: Write 3 things that you remember about China.
- **Build Vocabulary** (p. 41) 15 MIN.
  Introduce homonyms.
- **Text Structure** (p. 42) 10 MIN.
  Present the text features of a first-person narrative.
- **Reading Strategy** (p. 42) 10 MIN.
  Teach the strategy of comparing a reading with your experiences.
- **Reading Selection Opener** (p. 43) 5 MIN.
  Preview the chapter reading selection.
- **Homework:** Activity Book (p. 25)

Day 3

- **Check Homework** 5 MIN.
  OR
- **Warm Up** 5 MIN.
  Write on the board: Who tells the story in "Yang the Youngest?" Which pronouns does he use to tell it?
- **Reading Selection** (pp. 44–49) 25 MIN.
  Have students read the selection and use the reading strategy. Teach the spelling, capitalization, and punctuation points on TE pp. 44–49.
- **Reading Comprehension** (p. 50) 10 MIN.
  Have students answer the questions.
- **Build Reading Fluency** (p. 50) 5 MIN.
  Teach how to build reading fluency by adjusting reading rate.
- **Homework:** Activity Book (p. 26)

Day 4

- **Check Homework** 5 MIN.
  OR
- **Warm Up** 5 MIN.
  Write on the board: In "Yang the Youngest," a boy from _____ goes to a new school in _____. He doesn't speak _____ very well, and he is lonely. At the end, he meets another boy who might become his _____.
- **Listen, Speak, Interact** (p. 51) 15 MIN.
  Have students identify colloquial speech.
- **Elements of Literature** (p. 51) 15 MIN.
  Teach how to analyze characters.
- **Word Study** (p. 52) 10 MIN.
  Present words with a Latin root.
- **Homework:** Activity Book (pp. 27–28)

Day 5

- **Check Homework** 5 MIN.
  OR
- **Warm Up** 5 MIN.
  Write on the board: Which of these expressions is colloquial speech?
  a. Hello.
  b. Good afternoon.
  c. Hi.
- **Grammar Focus** (p. 52) 15 MIN.
  Present complex sentences with dependent clauses.
- **From Reading to Writing** (p. 53) 15 MIN.
  Teach how to write a first-person narrative.
- **Across Content Areas** (p. 53) 10 MIN.
  Introduce related social studies content on culture.
- **Homework:** Activity Book (pp. 29–32); Have students complete the third column of the KWL chart from Day 1. Have students study for the Unit 1, Chapter 4 Quiz.

Class ______________________ Date ______________________

UNIT 1 Challenges

CHAPTER 5 • The Scholarship Jacket, by Marta Salinas

Chapter Materials

Activity Book: pp. 33–40
Audio: Unit 1, Chapter 5
Student Handbook
Student CD-ROM: Unit 1, Chapter 5
Teacher Resource Book: Lesson Plan, p. 5; Teacher Resources, pp. 35–64; Reading Summaries, pp. 73–74; Activity Book Answer Key
Teacher Resource CD-ROM
Assessment Program: Unit 1, Chapter 5 Quiz, pp. 15–16; Teacher and Student Resources, pp. 115–144
Assessment CD-ROM: Unit 1, Chapter 5 Quiz
Transparencies
The Heinle Newbury House Dictionary/CD-ROM
Web site: http://visions.heinle.com

➤ See the Teacher's Edition wrap-around for complete teaching suggestions for each section.

Day 1

- **Unit 1, Chapter 4 Quiz** (Assessment Program, pp. 13–14) 20 MIN.
- **Objectives** (p. 54) 5 MIN.
  Present the chapter objectives.
- **Use Prior Knowledge** (p. 54) 15 MIN.
  Activate prior knowledge about awards.
- **Build Background** (p. 55) 5 MIN.
  Provide the background information on school traditions.
- **Homework:** KWL (TRB, p. 42); Have students complete the first and second columns based on what they learned in class. Students will complete the third column at the end of the chapter.

Day 2

- **Check Homework** 5 MIN.
  OR
- **Warm Up** 5 MIN.
  Write on the board: What is the initial of your first name? Of your last name? If you aren't sure, reread "Build Background" on page 55 of your book.
- **Build Vocabulary** (p. 55) 15 MIN.
  Introduce words about emotions.
- **Text Structure** (p. 56) 10 MIN.
  Present the text features of a short story.
- **Reading Strategy** (p. 56) 10 MIN.
  Teach the strategy of finding the main idea and details.
- **Reading Selection Opener** (p. 57) 5 min.
  Preview the chapter reading selection.
- **Homework:** Activity Book (p. 33)

Day 3

- **Check Homework** 5 MIN.
  OR
- **Warm Up** 5 MIN.
  Write on the board: When characters speak in a story, it is called ______. The words that people say in a story are put in ______ marks.
- **Reading Selection** (pp. 58–67) 25 MIN.
  Have students read the selection and use the reading strategy. Teach the spelling, capitalization, and punctuation points on TE pp. 58–67.
- **Reading Comprehension** (p. 68) 10 MIN.
  Have students answer the questions.
- **Build Reading Fluency** (p. 68) 5 MIN.
  Teach how to build reading fluency by reading chunks of words silently.
- **Homework:** Activity Book (p. 34)

Day 4

- **Check Homework** 5 MIN.
  OR
- **Warm Up** 5 MIN.
  Write on the board: "The Scholarship Jacket" is told in first-person narration. How do we know this?
- **Listen, Speak, Interact** (p. 69) 15 MIN.
  Have students debate issues.
- **Elements of Literature** (p. 69) 15 MIN.
  Present character motivation.
- **Word Study** (p. 70) 10 MIN.
  Present root words.
- **Homework:** Activity Book (pp. 35–36)

Day 5

- **Check Homework** 5 MIN.
  OR
- **Warm Up** 5 MIN.
  Write on the board: To identify character motivation, ask yourself, "______ did the character say or do this?" Give an example of a character's motivation in "The Scholarship Jacket."
- **Grammar Focus** (p. 70) 15 MIN.
  Present *could* and *couldn't* for past ability.
- **From Reading to Writing** (p. 71) 15 MIN.
  Teach how to write a short story.
- **Across Content Areas** (p. 71) 10 MIN.
  Introduce related science content on nutrition.
- **Homework:** Activity Book (pp. 37–40); Have students complete the third column of the KWL chart from Day 1. Have students study for the Unit 1, Chapter 5 Quiz.

Class ______________________ Date ______________________

UNIT 1 Challenges

APPLY AND EXPAND

End-of-Unit Materials

Student Handbook
CNN Video: Unit 1
Teacher Resource Book: Lesson Plan, p. 6; Teacher Resources, pp. 35–64; Home-School Connection, pp. 119–125; Video Script, pp. 161–162; Video Worksheet, p. 173
Teacher Resource CD-ROM
Assessment Program: Unit 1 Test, pp. 17–22; Teacher and Student Resources, pp. 115–144
Assessment CD-ROM: Unit 1 Test
Transparencies
The Heinle Newbury House Dictionary/CD-ROM
Heinle Reading Library
Web site: http://visions.heinle.com

➤ **See the Teacher's Edition wrap-around for complete teaching suggestions for each section.**

Day 1

- **Unit 1, Chapter 5 Quiz** (Assessment Program, pp. 15–16) 20 MIN.
- **Listening and Speaking Workshop** (pp. 72–73) 25 MIN.
  Introduce the assignment of presenting a television news report. Have students write the report (steps 1–4).
- **Homework:** Have students review and practice their reports to present the next day.

Day 2

- **Listening and Speaking Workshop** (pp. 72–73) 45 MIN.
  Have students practice and present their television news reports to the class (step 5).
- **Homework:** Have students reread "Antarctic Adventure" in preparation for the Viewing Workshop on Day 3.

Day 3

- **Viewing Workshop** (p. 73) 45 MIN.
  Show a video about Shackleton and have students compare and contrast it to the reading.
  Show the Visions CNN video for this unit. Have students do the Video Worksheet.
- **Homework:** Have students write a summary of the similarities and differences between the video and the reading.

Day 4

- **Writer's Workshop** (pp. 74–75) 45 MIN.
  Present the writing assignment of telling how someone faced a challenge. Have students do pre-writing preparation and write a draft (steps 1–2).
  Homework: Have students review their drafts in preparation for revising them on Day 5.

Day 5

- **Writer's Workshop** (pp. 74–75) 45 MIN.
  Have students revise, edit, and publish their writing (steps 3–5).
- **Homework:** Have students take their writing home to share with their family.

Day 6

- **Review and Reteach** 45 MIN.
  In small groups, have students list major points from the unit. Ask students to choose three points that they are least clear on and would like to review. Based on results of chapter quizzes and student feedback, choose points from the unit to reteach to the class.
- **Homework:** Have students study for the Unit 1 Test.

Day 7

- **Unit 1 Test** (Assessment Program, pp. 17–22) 45 MIN.
  After the Unit 1 Test, reassess student learning. Record strong and weak areas based on the unit test. Review weak areas before the Mid-Book Exam.

Class ______________________________ Date ______________

UNIT 2 Changes

CHAPTER 1 • Why Do Leaves Change Color in the Fall?

Chapter Materials

Activity Book: pp. 41–48
Audio: Unit 2, Chapter 1
Student Handbook
Student CD-ROM: Unit 2, Chapter 1
Teacher Resource Book: Lesson Plan, p. 7; Teacher Resources, pp. 35–64; Reading Summaries, pp. 75–76; Activity Book Answer Key
Teacher Resource CD-ROM
Assessment Program: Unit 2, Chapter 1 Quiz, pp. 23–24; Teacher and Student Resources, pp. 115–144
Assessment CD-ROM: Unit 2, Chapter 1
Transparencies
The Heinle Newbury House Dictionary/CD-ROM
Web site: http://visions.heinle.com

➤ **See the Teacher's Edition wrap-around for complete teaching suggestions for each section.**

Day 1

- **Unit Opener** (pp. 78–79) 20 MIN.
  Preview the unit reading selection. Complete the "View the Picture" activity.
- **Objectives** (p. 80) 5 MIN.
  Present the chapter objectives
- **Use Prior Knowledge** (p. 80) 15 MIN.
  Activate prior knowledge about the seasons.
- **Build Background** (p. 81) 5 MIN.
  Provide the background information on North America and climate.
- **Homework:** KWL (TRB, p. 42); Have students complete the first and second columns based on what they learned in class. Students will complete the third column at the end of the chapter.

Day 2

- **Check Homework** 5 MIN.
  OR
- **Warm Up** 5 MIN.
  Write on the board: The northern part of North America has four seasons. They are ______, ______, ______, and ______.
- **Build Vocabulary** (p. 81) 15 MIN.
  Introduce the use of a word wheel.
- **Text Structure** (p. 82) 10 MIN.
  Present the features of a scientific informational text.
- **Reading Strategy** (p. 82) 10 MIN.
  Teach the strategy of making inferences.
- **Reading Selection Opener** (p. 83) 5 MIN.
  Preview the chapter reading selection.
- **Homework:** Activity Book (p. 41)

Day 3

- **Check Homework** 5 MIN.
  OR
- **Warm Up** 5 MIN.
  Write on the board: True or false?
  a. Photosynthesis is a process found in animals.
  b. Photosynthesis turns water and carbon dioxide into sugar.
- **Reading Selection** (pp. 84–87) 25 MIN.
  Have students read the selection and use the reading strategy. Teach spelling, capitalization, and punctuation points on TE pp. 84–87.
- **Reading Comprehension** (p. 88) 10 MIN.
  Have students answer the questions.
- **Build Reading Fluency** (p. 88) 5 MIN.
  Build reading fluency by doing repeated reading.
- **Homework:** Activity Book (p. 42)

Day 4

- **Check Homework** 5 MIN.
  OR
- **Warm Up** 5 MIN.
  Write on the board: Write 3 things that you remember about "Why Do Leaves Change Color in the Fall?"
- **Listen, Speak, Interact** (p. 89) 20 MIN.
  Have students role-play a scientific interview.
- **Elements of Literature** (p. 89) 10 MIN.
  Introduce processes.
- **Word Study** (p. 90) 10 MIN.
  Present the pronunciation of *ph* in context.
- **Homework:** Activity Book (pp. 43–44)

Day 5

- **Check Homework** 5 MIN.
  OR
- **Warm Up** 5 MIN.
  Write on the board: Put these sentences into the order in which they happen.
  The leaves change color.
  The leaves appear and are green.
  The leaves fall from the tree.
  The leaves grow larger.
- **Grammar Focus** (p. 90) 15 MIN.
  Present the simple present tense.
- **From Reading to Writing** (p. 91) 15 MIN.
  Teach how to write a scientific informational text.
- **Across Content Areas** (p. 91) 10 MIN.
  Introduce related science content on trees.
- **Homework:** Activity Book (pp. 45–48); Have students complete the third column of the KWL chart from Day 1. Have students study for the Unit 2, Chapter 1 Quiz.

Class ______________________________ Date ______________________

UNIT 2 Changes

CHAPTER 2 • Elizabeth's Diary, by Patricia Hermes

Chapter Materials

Activity Book: pp. 49–56
Audio: Unit 2, Chapter 2
Student Handbook
Student CD-ROM: Unit 2, Chapter 2
Teacher Resource Book: Lesson Plan, p. 8; Teacher Resources, pp. 35–64; Reading Summaries, pp. 77–78; Activity Book Answer Key
Teacher Resource CD-ROM
Assessment Program: Unit 2, Chapter 2 Quiz, pp. 25–26; Teacher and Student Resources, pp. 115–144
Assessment CD-ROM: Unit 2, Chapter 2
Transparencies
The Heinle Newbury House Dictionary/CD-ROM
Web site: http://visions.heinle.com

➤ **See the Teacher's Edition wrap-around for complete teaching suggestions for each section.**

Day 1

- **Unit 2, Chapter 1 Quiz** (Assessment Program, pp. 23–24) 20 MIN.
- **Objectives** (p. 92) 5 MIN.
  Present the chapter objectives.
- **Use Prior Knowledge** (p. 92) 15 MIN.
  Activate prior knowledge about moving to a new place.
- **Build Background** (p. 93) 5 MIN.
  Provide the background information on Jamestown.
- **Homework:** KWL (TRB, p. 42); Have students complete the first and second columns based on what they learned in class. Students will complete the third column at the end of the chapter.

Day 2

- **Check Homework** 5 MIN.
  OR
- **Warm Up** 5 MIN.
  Write on the board: In the _____ 1607, a group of _____ people traveled by _____ to make new homes in North _____.
- **Build Vocabulary** (p. 93) 15 MIN.
  Introduce making varied word choices.
- **Text Structure** (p. 94) 10 MIN.
  Present the text features of a historical fiction diary.
- **Reading Strategy** (p. 94) 10 MIN.
  Teach the strategy of summarizing.
- **Reading Selection Opener** (p. 95) 5 MIN.
  Preview the chapter reading selection.
- **Homework:** Activity Book (p. 49)

Day 3

- **Check Homework** 5 MIN.
  OR
- **Warm Up** 5 MIN.
  Write on the board: The people in the story are going to a new home. List 3 problems that you think they will have there.
- **Reading Selection** (pp. 96–97) 25 MIN.
  Have students read the selection and use the reading strategy. Teach spelling, capitalization, and punctuation points on TE pp. 96–97.
- **Reading Comprehension** (p. 98) 10 MIN.
  Have students answer the questions.
- **Build Reading Fluency** (p. 98) 5 MIN.
  Teach how to build reading fluency by using rapid word recognition.
- **Homework:** Activity Book (p. 50)

Day 4

- **Check Homework** 5 MIN.
  OR
- **Warm Up** 5 MIN.
  Write on the board: List 2 problems that Elizabeth had in Jamestown.
- **Listen, Speak, Interact** (p. 99) 15 MIN.
  Have students talk about the sequence of events in the story.
- **Elements of Literature** (p. 99) 15 MIN.
  Teach students to identify flashbacks.
- **Word Study** (p. 100) 10 MIN.
  Present the suffix *-ty*.
- **Homework:** Activity Book (pp. 51–52)

Day 5

- **Check Homework** 5 MIN.
  OR
- **Warm Up** 5 MIN.
  Write on the board: Write these numbers as words: 20, 30, 40, 50, 60, 80, 90.
- **Grammar Focus** (p. 100) 15 MIN.
  Present the future tense with *will*.
- **From Reading to Writing** (p. 101) 15 MIN.
  Teach how to write a diary entry.
- **Across Content Areas** (p. 101) 10 MIN.
  Introduce related language arts content on genres.
- **Homework:** Activity Book (pp. 53–56); Have students complete the third column of the KWL chart from Day 1. Have students study for the Unit 2, Chapter 2 Quiz.

Class ______________________________ Date ______________________

UNIT 2 Changes

CHAPTER 3 • And Now Miguel, by Joseph Krumgold

Chapter Materials

Activity Book: pp. 57–64
Audio: Unit 2, Chapter 3
Student Handbook
Student CD-ROM: Unit 2, Chapter 3
Teacher Resource Book: Lesson Plan, p. 9; Teacher Resources, pp. 35–64; Reading Summaries, pp. 79–80; Activity Book Answer Key
Teacher Resource CD-ROM
Assessment Program: Unit 2, Chapter 3 Quiz, pp. 27–28; Teacher and Student Resources, pp. 115–144
Assessment CD-ROM: Unit 2, Chapter 3
Transparencies
The Heinle Newbury House Dictionary/CD-ROM
Web site: http://visions.heinle.com

➤ See the Teacher's Edition wrap-around for complete teaching suggestions for each section.

Day 1

- **Unit 2, Chapter 2 Quiz** (Assessment Program, pp. 25–26) 20 MIN.
- **Objectives** (p. 102) 5 MIN.
  Present the chapter objectives.
- **Use Prior Knowledge** (p. 102) 15 MIN.
  Activate prior knowledge on farm life.
- **Build Background** (p. 103) 5 MIN.
  Provide the background information on the Sangre de Cristo Mountains.
- **Homework:** KWL (TRB, p. 42); Have students complete the first and second columns based on what they learned in class. Students will complete the third column at the end of the chapter.

Day 2

- **Check Homework** 5 MIN.
  OR
- **Warm Up** 5 MIN.
  Write on the board: The Sangre de Cristo Mountains cross two states—_____ and _____.
- **Build Vocabulary** (p. 103) 15 MIN.
  Introduce the LINK strategy.
- **Text Structure** (p. 104) 10 MIN.
  Present the text features of a play.
- **Reading Strategy** (p. 104) 10 MIN.
  Teach the strategy of determining the sequence of events.
- **Reading Selection Opener** (p. 105) 5 MIN.
  Preview the chapter reading selection.
- **Homework:** Activity Book (p. 57)

Day 3

- **Check Homework** 5 MIN.
  OR
- **Warm Up** 5 MIN.
- **Reading Selection** (pp. 106–113) 25 MIN.
  Have students read the selection and use the reading strategy. Teach spelling, capitalization, and punctuation points on TE pp. 106–113.
- **Reading Comprehension** (p. 114) 10 MIN.
  Have students answer the questions.
- **Build Reading Fluency** (p. 114) 5 MIN.
  Teach how to build reading fluency by adjusting your reading rate.
- **Homework:** Activity Book (p. 58)

Day 4

- **Check Homework** 5 MIN.
  OR
- **Warm Up** 5 MIN.
  Write on the board: At first, Miguel's father didn't want him to go to the mountains with the men. Do you think he was right? Write one reason why or why not.
- **Listen, Speak, Interact** (p. 115) 15 MIN.
  Have students perform a scene from the play.
- **Elements of Literature** (p. 115) 15 MIN.
  Introduce scenes in a play.
- **Word Study** (p. 116) 10 MIN.
  Present *its* and *it's*.
  Homework: Activity Book (pp. 59–60)

Day 5

- **Check Homework** 5 MIN.
  OR
- **Warm Up** 5 MIN.
  Write on the board: Write *its* or *it's* in the blanks.
  I got a new bike, but I didn't like _____ color.
  _____ blue, but I wanted a red one.
- **Grammar Focus** (p. 116) 15 MIN.
  Present the future conditional.
- **From Reading to Writing** (p. 117) 15 MIN.
  Teach how to write dialogue for a play.
- **Across Content Areas** (p. 117) 10 MIN.
  Introduce related social studies content on state flags.
- **Homework:** Activity Book (pp. 61–64); Have students complete the third column of the KWL chart from Day 1. Have students study for the Unit 2, Chapter 3 Quiz.

Class ______________________________ Date ______________________________

UNIT 2 Changes

CHAPTER 4 • Tuck Triumphant, by Theodore Taylor

Chapter Materials

Activity Book: pp. 65–72
Audio: Unit 2, Chapter 4
Student Handbook
Student CD-ROM: Unit 2, Chapter 4
Teacher Resource Book: Lesson Plan, p. 10; Teacher Resources, pp. 35–64; Reading Summaries, pp. 81–82; Activity Book Answer Key

Teacher Resource CD-ROM
Assessment Program: Unit 2, Chapter 4 Quiz, pp. 29–30; Teacher and Student Resources, pp. 115–144
Assessment CD-ROM: Unit 2, Chapter 4
Transparencies
The Heinle Newbury House Dictionary/CD-ROM
Web site: http://visions.heinle.com

➤ **See the Teacher's Edition wrap-around for complete teaching suggestions for each section.**

Day 1

- **Unit 1, Chapter 3 Quiz** (Assessment Program, pp. 27–28) 20 MIN.
- **Objectives** (p. 118) 5 MIN.
  Present the chapter objectives.
- **Use Prior Knowledge** (p. 118) 15 MIN.
  Activate prior knowledge about surprises.
- **Build Background** (p. 119) 5 MIN.
  Provide background about the Korean War.
- **Homework:** KWL (TRB, p. 42); Have students complete the first and second columns based on what they learned in class. Students will complete the third column at the end of the chapter.

Day 2

- **Check Homework** 5 MIN.
  OR
- **Warm Up** 5 MIN.
  Write on the board: After the Korean War, Korea was divided into two countries, _____ Korea and _____ Korea.
- **Build Vocabulary** (p. 119) 15 MIN.
  Introduce related words.
- **Text Structure** (p. 120) 10 MIN.
  Present the text features of realistic fiction.
- **Reading Strategy** (p. 120) 10 MIN.
  Teach the strategy of drawing conclusions.
- **Reading Selection Opener** (p. 121) 5 MIN.
  Preview the chapter reading selection.
- **Homework:** Activity Book (p. 65)

Day 3

- **Check Homework** 5 MIN.
  OR
- **Warm Up** 5 MIN.
  Write on the board: In a story, the setting is the _____, the plot is the _____, and the characters are the _____.
- **Reading Selection** (pp. 122–127) 25 MIN.
  Have students read the selection and use the reading strategy. Teach spelling, capitalization, and punctuation points on TE pp. 122–127.
- **Reading Comprehension** (p. 128) 10 MIN.
  Have students answer the questions.
- **Build Reading Fluency** (p. 128) 5 MIN.
  Teach how to build reading fluency by doing choral read aloud.
- **Homework:** Activity Book (p. 66)

Day 4

- **Check Homework** 5 MIN.
  OR
- **Warm Up** 5 MIN.
  Write on the board: Summarize the plot of "Tuck Triumphant" in three sentences.
- **Listen, Speak, Interact** (p. 129) 15 MIN.
  Have students role-play interviewing a newcomer.
- **Elements of Literature** (p. 129) 15 MIN.
  Introduce style in a first-person narrative.
- **Word Study** (p. 130) 10 MIN.
  Present the suffix *-less*.
- **Homework:** Activity Book (pp. 67–68)

Day 5

- **Check Homework** 5 MIN.
  OR
- **Warm Up** 5 MIN.
  Write on the board: Which of these sentences are complete? Which are incomplete? Why?
  a. I was wrong.
  b. Really wrong.
  c. I needed to apologize.
  d. Fast.
- **Grammar Focus** (p. 130) 15 MIN.
  Present the use of adjectives before nouns.
- **From Reading to Writing** (p. 131) 15 MIN.
  Teach how to write a realistic story.
- **Across Content Areas** (p. 131) 10 MIN.
  Introduce related social studies content on types of families.
- **Homework:** Activity Book (pp. 69–72); Have students complete the third column of the KWL chart from Day 1. Have students study for the Unit 2, Chapter 4 Quiz.

Class ______________________________ Date ______________________

UNIT 2 Changes

CHAPTER 5 • The Journal of Jesse Smoke, by Joseph Bruchac, & Ancient Ways, by Elvania Toledo

Chapter Materials

Activity Book: pp. 73–80
Audio: Unit 2, Chapter 5
Student Handbook
Student CD-ROM: Unit 2, Chapter 5
Teacher Resource Book: Lesson Plan, p. 11; Teacher Resources, pp. 35–64; Reading Summaries, pp. 83–84; Activity Book Answer Key
Teacher Resource CD-ROM
Assessment Program: Unit 2, Chapter 5 Quiz, pp. 31–32; Teacher and Student Resources, pp. 115–144
Assessment CD-ROM: Unit 2, Chapter 5
Transparencies
The Heinle Newbury House Dictionary/CD-ROM
Web site: http://visions.heinle.com

➤ **See the Teacher's Edition wrap-around for complete teaching suggestions for each section.**

Day 1

- **Unit 2, Chapter 4 Quiz** (Assessment Program, pp. 29–30) 20 MIN.
- **Objectives** (p. 132) 5 MIN.
  Present the chapter objectives.
- **Use Prior Knowledge** (p. 132) 15 MIN.
  Activate prior knowledge about planning for a trip.
- **Build Background** (p. 133) 5 MIN.
  Provide background on the Trail of Tears.
- **Homework:** KWL (TRB, p. 42); Have students complete the first and second columns based on what they learned in class. Students will complete the third column at the end of the chapter.

Day 2

- **Check Homework** 5 MIN.
  OR
- **Warm Up** 5 MIN.
  Write on the board: Write 2 things that you remember about the Trail of Tears.
- **Build Vocabulary** (p. 133) 15 MIN.
  Introduce finding root words.
- **Text Structure** (p. 134) 10 MIN.
  Present the text features of a historical journal.
- **Reading Strategy** (p. 134) 10 MIN.
  Teach the strategy of understanding the sequence of events.
- **Reading Selection Opener** (p. 135) 5 MIN.
  Preview the chapter reading selections.
- **Homework:** Activity Book (p. 73)

Day 3

- **Check Homework** 5 MIN.
  OR
- **Warm Up** 5 MIN.
  Write on the board: Complete this sentence with the words happens, real, people.
  "The Journal of Jesse Smoke" is a historical fiction journal. This means that it is based on _____ events and _____, but not everything that_____ is true.
- **Reading Selections** (pp. 136–141) 25 MIN.
  Have students read the selections and use the reading strategy. Teach spelling, capitalization, and punctuation points on TE pp. 136–141.
- **Reading Comprehension** (p. 142) 10 MIN.
  Have students answer the questions.
- **Build Reading Fluency** (p. 142) 5 MIN.
  Build reading fluency by reading to memorize.
- **Homework:** Activity Book (p. 74)

Day 4

- **Check Homework** 5 MIN.
  OR
- **Warm Up** 5 MIN.
  Write on the board: List 3 ways that people changed according to Elvania Toledo's poem.
- **Listen, Speak, Interact** (p. 143) 15 MIN.
  Have students identify how language reflects culture and regions.
- **Elements of Literature** (p. 143) 15 MIN.
  Introduce metaphors.
- **Word Study** (p. 144) 10 MIN.
  Present the suffix *-ness*.
- **Homework:** Activity Book (pp. 75–76)

Day 5

- **Check Homework** 5 MIN.
  OR
- **Warm Up** 5 MIN.
  Write on the board: "My heart is an open book" is an example of a _____.
- **Grammar Focus** (p. 144) 15 MIN.
  Present the present continuous tense.
- **From Reading to Writing** (p. 145) 15 MIN.
  Teach how to write a poem.
- **Across Content Areas** (p. 145) 10 MIN.
  Introduce related math content on using rank order.
- **Homework:** Activity Book (pp. 77–80); Have students complete the third column of the KWL chart from Day 1. Have students study for the Unit 2, Chapter 5 Quiz.

Class ______________________ Date ______________________

UNIT 2 Changes

APPLY AND EXPAND

End-of-Unit Materials

Student Handbook
CNN Video: Unit 2
Teacher Resource Book: Lesson Plan, p. 12; Teacher Resources, pp. 35–64; Home-School Connection, pp. 126–132; Video Script, pp. 163–164; Video Worksheet, p. 174
Teacher Resource CD-ROM
Assessment Program: Unit 2 Test, pp. 33–38; Teacher and Student Resources, pp. 115–144
Assessment CD-ROM: Unit 2 Test
Transparencies
The Heinle Newbury House Dictionary/CD-ROM
Heinle Reading Library
Web site: http://visions.heinle.com

➤ **See the Teacher's Edition wrap-around for complete teaching suggestions for each section.**

Day 1

- **Unit 2, Chapter 5 Quiz** (Assessment Program, pp. 31–32) 20 MIN.
- **Listening and Speaking Workshop** (pp. 146–147) 25 MIN.
  Introduce the assignment of preparing, participating in, and reporting an interview. Have students write questions and conduct the interviews (steps 1–2).
- **Homework:** In preparation for Day 2, have students write a summary of their interview.

Day 2

- **Listening and Speaking Workshop** (pp. 146–147) 45 MIN.
  Have students prepare and give their reports to the class (step 3). Then conduct the evaluations (step 4).
- **Homework:** Have students reread "The Journal of Jesse Smoke" and "Elizabeth's Diary" in preparation for the Viewing Workshop on Day 3.

Day 3

- **Viewing Workshop** (p. 147) 45 MIN.
  Show a video about the Cherokees in the 1830s or the English colonists in Virginia. Have students analyze how the video creates its effect. Show the Visions CNN video for this unit. Have students do the Video Worksheet.
- **Homework:** Have students write a paragraph to summarize how the video creates its effect.

Day 4

- **Writer's Workshop** (pp. 148–149) 45 MIN.
  Present the assignment of writing a persuasive letter to the editor. Have students do pre-writing preparation and write a draft (steps 1–2).
- **Homework:** Have students review their drafts in preparation for revising them on Day 5.

Day 5

- **Writer's Workshop** (pp. 148–149) 45 MIN.
  Have students revise, edit, and publish their letters (steps 3–5).
- **Homework:** Have students identify facts and opinions in their letters.

Day 6

- **Review and Reteach** 45 MIN.
  In small groups, have students list major points from the unit. Ask students to choose three points that they are least clear on and would like to review. Based on results of chapter quizzes and student feedback, choose points from the unit to reteach to the class.
- **Homework:** Have students study for the Unit 2 Test.

Day 7

- **Unit 2 Test** (Assessment Program, pp. 33–38) 45 MIN.
  After the Unit 2 Test, reassess student learning. Record strong and weak areas based on the unit test. Review weak areas before the Mid-Book Exam.

Class ______________________ Date ______________________

UNIT 3 Courage

CHAPTER 1 • Life Doesn't Frighten Me, by Maya Angelou

Chapter Materials

Activity Book: pp. 81–92
Audio: Unit 3, Chapter 1
Student Handbook
Student CD-ROM: Unit 3, Chapter 1
Teacher Resource Book: Lesson Plan, p. 13; Teacher Resources, pp. 35–64; Reading Summaries, pp. 85–86; Activity Book Answer Key
Teacher Resource CD-ROM
Assessment Program: Unit 3, Chapter 1 Quiz, pp. 39–40; Teacher and Student Resources, pp. 115–144
Assessment CD-ROM: Unit 3, Chapter 1
Transparencies
The Heinle Newbury House Dictionary/CD-ROM
Web site: http://visions.heinle.com

➤ See the Teacher's Edition wrap-around for complete teaching suggestions for each section.

Day 1

- **Unit Opener** (pp. 152–153) 20 MIN.
  Preview the unit reading selections. Complete the "View the Picture" activity.
- **Objectives** (p. 154) 5 MIN.
  Present the chapter objectives.
- **Use Prior Knowledge** (p. 154) 15 MIN.
  Activate prior knowledge about what frightens you.
- **Build Background** (p. 155) 5 MIN.
  Provide the background information on nursery rhymes.
- **Homework:** KWL (TRB, p. 42); Have students complete the first and second columns based on what they learned in class. Students will complete the third column at the end of the chapter.

Day 2

- **Check Homework** 5 MIN.
  OR
- **Warm Up** 5 MIN.
  Write on the board: If a story is told out loud for many years, it is part of the _____ _____.
- **Build Vocabulary** (p. 155) 15 MIN.
  Introduce new vocabulary.
- **Text Structure** (p. 156) 10 MIN.
  Present the text features of a poem.
- **Reading Strategy** (p. 156) 10 MIN.
  Teach the strategy of using images to understand poetry.
- **Reading Selection Opener** (p. 157) 5 MIN.
  Preview the chapter reading selection.
- **Homework:** Activity Book (p. 81)

Day 3

- **Check Homework** 5 MIN.
  OR
- **Warm Up** 5 MIN.
  Write on the board: An _____ is a picture in your mind. Some words in poems help us form _____.
- **Reading Selection** (pp. 158–161) 25 MIN.
  Have students read the selection and use the reading strategy. Teach spelling, capitalization, and punctuation points on TE pp. 158–161.
- **Reading Comprehension** (p. 162) 10 MIN.
  Have students answer the questions.
- **Build Reading Fluency** (p. 162) 5 MIN.
  Teach how to build reading fluency by doing echo read aloud.
- **Homework:** Activity Book (p. 82)

Day 4

- **Check Homework** 5 MIN.
  OR
- **Warm Up** 5 MIN.
  Write on the board: List 3 things from the poem, "Life Doesn't Frighten Me," that do not frighten Maya Angelou.
- **Listen, Speak, Interact** (p. 163) 15 MIN.
  Have students discuss personal experiences.
- **Elements of Literature** (p. 163) 15 MIN.
  Teach the types of rhyme.
- **Word Study** (p. 164) 10 MIN.
  Present contractions.
- **Homework:** Activity Book (pp. 83–84)

Day 5

- **Check Homework** 5 MIN.
  OR
- **Warm Up** 5 MIN.
  Write on the board:
  a. The words walk and talk are _____ rhymes.
  b. The words need and deep are _____ rhymes.
- **Grammar Focus** (p. 164) 10 MIN.
  Present prepositional phrases of place.
- **From Reading to Writing** (p. 165) 20 MIN.
  Teach how to write a poem.
- **Across Content Areas** (p. 165) 10 MIN.
  Introduce related science content on the respiratory system.
- **Homework:** Activity Book (pp. 85–88); Have students complete the third column of the KWL chart from Day 1. Have students study for the Unit 3, Chapter 1.

Class ______________________ Date ______________________

UNIT 3 Courage

CHAPTER 2 • Matthew A. Henson, by Wade Hudson

Chapter Materials

Activity Book: pp. 89–96
Audio: Unit 3, Chapter 2
Student Handbook
Student CD-ROM: Unit 3, Chapter 2
Teacher Resource Book: Lesson Plan, p. 14; Teacher Resources, pp. 35–64; Reading Summaries, pp. 87–88; Activity Book Answer Key
Teacher Resource CD-ROM
Assessment Program: Unit 3, Chapter 2 Quiz, pp. 41–42; Teacher and Student Resources, pp. 115–144
Assessment CD-ROM: Unit 3, Chapter 2
Transparencies
The Heinle Newbury House Dictionary/CD-ROM
Web site: http://visions.heinle.com

➤ **See the Teacher's Edition wrap-around for complete teaching suggestions for each section.**

Day 1

- **Unit 3, Chapter 1 Quiz** (Assessment Program, pp. 39–40) 20 MIN.
- **Objectives** (p. 166) 5 MIN.
  Present the chapter objectives.
- **Use Prior Knowledge** (p. 166) 15 MIN.
  Activate prior knowledge about making preparations for a trip.
- **Build Background** (p. 167) 5 MIN.
  Provide the background information on the North Pole.
- **Homework:** KWL (TRB, p. 42); Have students complete the first and second columns based on what they learned in class. Students will complete the third column at the end of the chapter.

Day 2

- **Check Homework** 5 MIN.
  OR
- **Warm Up** 5 MIN.
  Write on the board: Write 2 facts about the North Pole.
- **Build Vocabulary** (p. 167) 15 MIN.
  Introduce learning synonyms with reference aids.
- **Text Structure** (p. 168) 10 MIN.
  Present the text features of a biography.
- **Reading Strategy** (p. 168) 10 MIN.
  Teach the strategy of finding the main idea and supporting details.
- **Reading Selection Opener** (p. 169) 5 MIN.
  Preview the chapter reading selection.
- **Homework:** Activity Book (p. 89)

Day 3

- **Check Homework** 5 MIN.
  OR
- **Warm Up** 5 MIN.
  Write on the board: List 3 important features of a biography.
- **Reading Selection** (pp. 170–173) 25 MIN.
  Have students read the selection and use the reading strategy. Teach spelling, capitalization, and punctuation points on TE pp. 170–173.
- **Reading Comprehension** (p. 174) 10 MIN.
  Have students answer the questions.
- **Build Reading Fluency** (p. 174) 5 MIN.
  Teach how to build reading fluency by using repeated reading.
- **Homework:** Activity Book (p. 90)

Day 4

- **Check Homework** 5 MIN.
  OR
- **Warm Up** 5 MIN.
  Write on the board: Who got to the North Pole first, Robert E. Perry or Matthew Henson?
- **Listen, Speak, Interact** (p. 175) 15 MIN.
  Have students role-play an interview with a character.
- **Elements of Literature** (p. 175) 15 MIN.
  Teach chronological order and transitions.
- **Word Study** (p. 176) 10 MIN.
  Present proper nouns.
- **Homework:** Activity Book (pp. 91–92)

Day 5

- **Check Homework** 5 MIN.
  OR
- **Warm Up** 5 MIN.
  Write on the board: Correct the errors in these sentences.
  Rosa is from mexican. She is mexico.
- **Grammar Focus** (p. 176) 15 MIN.
  Present two-word verbs.
- **From Reading to Writing** (p. 177) 15 MIN.
  Teach how to write a short biography.
- **Across Content Areas** (p. 177) 10 MIN.
  Introduce related math content on measuring temperature.
- **Homework:** Activity Book (pp. 93–96); Have students complete the third column of the KWL chart from Day 1. Have students study for the Unit 3, Chapter 2 Quiz.

Class ______________________ Date ______________________

UNIT 3 Courage

CHAPTER 3 • Anne Frank: The Diary of a Young Girl, by Anne Frank

Chapter Materials

Activity Book: pp. 97–104
Audio: Unit 3, Chapter 3
Student Handbook
Student CD-ROM: Unit 3, Chapter 3
Teacher Resource Book: Lesson Plan, p. 15; Teacher Resources, pp. 35–64; Reading Summaries, pp. 89–90; Activity Book Answer Key
Teacher Resource CD-ROM
Assessment Program: Unit 3, Chapter 3 Quiz, pp. 43–44; Teacher and Student Resources, pp. 115–144
Assessment CD-ROM: Unit 3, Chapter 3
Transparencies
The Heinle Newbury House Dictionary/CD-ROM
Web site: http://visions.heinle.com

See the Teacher's Edition wrap-around for complete teaching suggestions for each section.

Day 1

- **Unit 3, Chapter 2 Quiz** (Assessment Program, pp. 41–42) 20 MIN.
- **Objectives** (p. 178) 5 MIN.
  Present the chapter objectives.
- **Use Prior Knowledge** (p. 178) 15 MIN.
  Activate prior knowledge about differences.
- **Build Background** (p. 179) 5 MIN.
  Provide the background information on World War II.
- **Homework:** KWL (TRB, p. 42); Have students complete the first and second columns based on what they learned in class. Students will complete the third column at the end of the chapter.

Day 2

- **Check Homework** 5 MIN.
  OR
- **Warm Up** 5 MIN.
  Write on the board: How do we know about Anne Frank's experiences?
- **Build Vocabulary** (p. 179) 15 MIN.
  Introduce using context.
- **Text Structure** (p. 180) 10 MIN.
  Present the text features of a diary.
- **Reading Strategy** (p. 180) 10 MIN.
  Teach the strategy of using chronology to locate and recall information.
- **Reading Selection Opener** (p. 181) 5 MIN.
  Preview the chapter reading selection.
- **Homework:** Activity Book (p. 97)

Day 3

- **Check Homework** 5 MIN.
  OR
- **Warm Up** 5 MIN.
  Write on the board: List 3 important features of a diary.
- **Reading Selection** (pp. 182–185) 25 MIN.
  Have students read the selection and use the reading strategy. Teach spelling, capitalization, and punctuation points on TE pp. 182–185.
- **Reading Comprehension** (p. 186) 10 MIN.
  Have students answer the questions.
- **Build Reading Fluency** (p. 186) 5 MIN.
  Teach how to build reading fluency by reading chunks of words silently.
- **Homework:** Activity Book (p. 98)

Day 4

- **Check Homework** 5 MIN.
  OR
- **Warm Up** 5 MIN.
  Write on the board: Why did Anne Frank and her family have to hide from the Nazis?
- **Listen, Speak, Interact** (p. 187) 15 MIN.
  Have students act out a dialogue.
- **Elements of Literature** (p. 187) 15 MIN.
  Introduce tone.
- **Word Study** (p. 188) 10 MIN.
  Present the suffix *-ion.*
- **Homework:** Activity Book (pp. 99–100)

Day 5

- **Check Homework** 5 MIN.
  OR
- **Warm Up** 5 MIN.
  Write on the board: _____ is the attitude or feeling that a writer shows in a piece of writing.
- **Grammar Focus** (p. 188) 15 MIN.
  Present the use of conjunctions to form compound sentences.
- **From Reading to Writing** (p. 189) 15 MIN.
  Teach how to write a diary entry.
- **Across Content Areas** (p. 189) 10 MIN.
  Introduce related social studies content on social groups.
- **Homework:** Activity Book (pp. 101–104); Have students complete the third column of the KWL chart from Day 1. Have students study for the Unit 3, Chapter 3 Quiz.

Class ______________________________ Date ______________________

UNIT 3 Courage

CHAPTER 4 • Lance Armstrong: Champion Cyclist, by President George W. Bush

Chapter Materials

Activity Book: pp. 105–112
Audio: Unit 3, Chapter 4
Student Handbook
Student CD-ROM: Unit 3, Chapter 4
Teacher Resource Book: Lesson Plan, p. 16; Teacher Resources, pp. 35–64; Reading Summaries, pp. 91–92; Activity Book Answer Key
Teacher Resource CD-ROM
Assessment Program: Unit 3, Chapter 4 Quiz, pp. 45–46; Teacher and Student Resources, pp. 115–144
Assessment CD-ROM: Unit 3, Chapter 4
Transparencies
The Heinle Newbury House Dictionary/CD-ROM
Web site: http://visions.heinle.com

➤ **See the Teacher's Edition wrap-around for complete teaching suggestions for each section.**

Day 1

- **Unit 3, Chapter 3 Quiz** (Assessment Program, pp. 43–44) 20 MIN.
- **Objectives** (p. 190) 5 MIN.
  Present the chapter objectives.
- **Use Prior Knowledge** (p. 190) 15 MIN.
  Activate prior knowledge about ways to treat disease.
- **Build Background** (p. 191) 5 MIN.
  Provide background on the *Tour de France.*
- **Homework:** KWL (TRB, p. 42); Have students complete the first and second columns based on what they learned in class. Students will complete the third column at the end of the chapter.

Day 2

- **Check Homework** 5 MIN.
  OR
- **Warm Up** 5 MIN.
  Write on the board: Complete this sentence with the correct word(s).
  The Tour de France is a ______.
  a. vacation **b.** school **c.** bicycle race
- **Build Vocabulary** (p. 191) 15 MIN.
  Introduce using multiple reference aids.
- **Text Structure** (p. 192) 10 MIN.
  Present the text features of a speech.
- **Reading Strategy** (p. 192) 10 MIN.
  Teach the strategy of distinguishing fact from opinion.
- **Reading Selection Opener** (p. 193) 5 MIN.
  Preview the chapter reading selection.
- **Homework:** Activity Book (p. 105)

Day 3

- **Check Homework** 5 MIN.
  OR
- **Warm Up** 5 MIN.
  Write on the board: Would you look in a dictionary or a thesaurus to find a synonym for a word? Which would you use to find its pronunciation and meaning?
- **Reading Selection** (pp. 194–197) 25 MIN.
  Have students read the selection and use the reading strategy. Teach spelling, capitalization, and punctuation points on TE pp. 194–197.
- **Reading Comprehension** (p. 198) 10 MIN.
  Have students answer the questions.
- **Build Reading Fluency** (p. 198) 5 MIN.
  Build reading fluency by adjusting your reading rate.
- **Homework:** Activity Book (p. 106)

Day 4

- **Check Homework** 5 MIN.
  OR
- **Warm Up** 5 MIN.
  Write on the board: List 3 things that President Bush said about Lance Armstrong.
- **Listen, Speak, Interact** (p. 199) 15 MIN.
  Have students listen to and discuss a speech.
- **Elements of Literature** (p. 199) 15 MIN.
  Introduce style, tone, and mood.
- **Word Study** (p. 200) 10 MIN.
  Present interpreting figurative language.
- **Homework:** Activity Book (pp. 107–108)

Day 5

- **Check Homework** 5 MIN.
  OR
- **Warm Up** 5 MIN.
  Write on the board: Match these words with their definitions.
  Words: **1.** tone **2.** mood **3.** style
  Definitions:
  a. The way something is written.
  b. The speaker's attitude.
  c. The feeling the audience gets.
- **Grammar Focus** (p. 200) 15 MIN.
  Present superlative adjectives.
- **From Reading to Writing** (p. 201) 15 MIN.
  Teach how to write a speech.
- **Across Content Areas** (p. 201) 10 MIN.
  Introduce related social studies content on reading a chart.
- **Homework:** Activity Book (pp. 109–112); Have students complete the third column of the KWL chart from Day 1. Have students study for the Unit 3, Chapter 4 Quiz.

Class ______________________________ Date ______________

UNIT 3 Courage

CHAPTER 5 • Earthquake, by Huynh Quang Nhuong

Chapter Materials

Activity Book: pp. 113–120
Audio: Unit 3, Chapter 5
Student Handbook
Student CD-ROM: Unit 3, Chapter 5
Teacher Resource Book: Lesson Plan, p. 17; Teacher Resources, pp. 35–64; Reading Summaries, pp. 93–94; Activity Book Answer Key
Teacher Resource CD-ROM
Assessment Program: Unit 3, Chapter 5 Quiz, pp. 47–48; Teacher and Student Resources, pp. 115–144
Assessment CD-ROM: Unit 3, Chapter 5
Transparencies
The Heinle Newbury House Dictionary/CD-ROM
Web site: http://visions.heinle.com

➤ **See the Teacher's Edition wrap-around for complete teaching suggestions for each section.**

Day 1

- **Unit 3, Chapter 4 Quiz** (Assessment Program, pp. 45–46) 20 MIN.
- **Objectives** (p. 202) 5 MIN.
  Present the chapter objectives.
- **Use Prior Knowledge** (p. 202) 15 MIN.
  Activate prior knowledge about qualities of natural disasters.
- **Build Background** (p. 203) 5 MIN.
  Provide the background information on Vietnam.
- **Homework:** KWL (TRB, p. 42); Have students complete the first and second columns based on what they learned in class. Students will complete the third column at the end of the chapter.

Day 2

- **Check Homework** 5 MIN.
  OR
- **Warm Up** 5 MIN.
  Write on the board: List 3 natural disasters.
- **Build Vocabulary** (p. 203) 15 MIN.
  Introduce using the dictionary to find definitions.
- **Text Structure** (p. 204) 10 MIN.
  Present the text features of a memoir.
- **Reading Strategy** (p. 204) 10 MIN.
  Teach the strategy of drawing conclusions and giving support.
- **Reading Selection Opener** (p. 205) 5 MIN.
  Preview the chapter reading selection.
- **Homework:** Activity Book (p. 113)

Day 3

- **Check Homework** 5 MIN.
  OR
- **Warm Up** 5 MIN.
  Write on the board: You are going to read the story "Earthquake." List 2 things that you think will happen in the story.
- **Reading Selection** (pp. 206–211) 25 MIN.
  Have students read the selection and use the reading strategy. Teach spelling, capitalization, and punctuation points on TE pp. 206–211.
- **Reading Comprehension** (p. 212) 10 MIN.
  Have students answer the questions.
- **Build Reading Fluency** (p. 212) 5 MIN.
  Teach how to build reading fluency by using rapid word recognition.
- **Homework:** Activity Book (p. 114)

Day 4

- **Check Homework** 5 MIN.
  OR
- **Warm Up** 5 MIN.
  Write on the board: Imagine that you were in an earthquake. What would you do?
- **Listen, Speak, Interact** (p. 213) 15 MIN.
  Have students discuss emergencies.
- **Elements of Literature** (p. 213) 10 MIN.
  Introduce foreshadowing.
- **Word Study** (p. 214) 15 MIN.
  Present compound words.
- **Homework:** Activity Book (pp. 115–116)

Day 5

- **Check Homework** 5 MIN.
  OR
- **Warm Up** 5 MIN.
  Write on the board: _____ gives clues about what is going to happen in a narrative.
- **Grammar Focus** (p. 214) 15 MIN.
  Present pronoun referents.
- **From Reading to Writing** (p. 215) 15 MIN.
  Teach how to write a memoir.
- **Across Content Areas** (p. 215) 10 MIN.
  Introduce related social studies content on reading a map.
- **Homework:** Activity Book (pp. 117–120); Have students complete the third column of the KWL chart from Day 1. Have students study for the Unit 3, Chapter 5 Quiz.

Class ______________________ Date ______________

UNIT 3 Courage

APPLY AND EXPAND

End-of-Unit Materials

Student Handbook
CNN Video: Unit 3
Teacher Resource Book: Lesson Plan, p. 18; Teacher Resources, pp. 35–64; Home-School Connection, pp. 133–139; Video Script, pp. 165–166; Video Worksheet, p. 175
Teacher Resource CD-ROM
Assessment Program: Unit 3 Test, pp. 49–54; Mid-Book Exam, pp. 55–60; Teacher and Student Resources, pp. 115–144
Assessment CD-ROM: Unit 3 Test, Mid-Book Exam
Transparencies
The Heinle Newbury House Dictionary/CD-ROM
Heinle Reading Library
Web site: http://visions.heinle.com

➤ **See the Teacher's Edition wrap-around for complete teaching suggestions for each section.**

Day 1

- **Unit 3, Chapter 5 Quiz** (Assessment Program, pp. 47–48) 20 MIN.
- **Listening and Speaking Workshop** (pp. 216–217) 25 MIN.
  Introduce the assignment of presenting a biographical narrative. Have students choose their topics and collect their facts (steps 1–2).
- **Homework:** Have students review their facts to make sure that they are correct.

Day 2

- **Listening and Speaking Workshop** (pp. 216–217) 45 MIN.
  Have students prepare and present their biographical narratives (steps 2–6).
- **Homework:** Tell students to reread the reading selection that they will compare and contrast to a video on Day 3.

Day 3

- **Viewing Workshop** (p. 217) 45 MIN.
  Show a video about a person in this unit and have students compare and contrast it to the reading. Show the Visions CNN video for this unit. Have students do the Video Worksheet.
- **Homework:** In preparation for the Writer's Workshop, ask students to look up the word *courage*. Tell them to ask other people what the word means to them.

Day 4

- **Writer's Workshop** (pp. 218–219) 45 MIN.
  Present the writing assignment of writing a response to literature. Have students do research and write a draft (steps 1–2).
- **Homework:** Have students review their drafts in preparation for revising them on Day 5.

Day 5

- **Writer's Workshop** (pp. 218–219) 45 MIN.
  Have students revise, edit, and publish their writing (steps 3–5).
- **Homework:** Have students take their work home and read it to family members.

Day 6

- **Review and Reteach** 45 MIN.
  In small groups, have students list major points from the unit. Ask students to choose three points that they are least clear on and would like to review. Based on results of chapter quizzes and student feedback, choose points from the unit to reteach to the class.
- **Homework:** Have students study for the Unit 3 Test.

Day 7

- **Unit 3 Test** (Assessment Program, pp. 49–54) 45 MIN.
  After the Unit 3 Test, reassess student learning. Record strong and weak areas based on the unit test. Review weak areas before the Mid-Book Exam.
- **Homework:** Have students study for the Mid-Book Exam.

Day 8

- **Mid-Book Exam** (Assessment Program, pp. 55–60) 45 MIN.

Class ________________________ Date ________________________

UNIT 4 Discoveries

CHAPTER 1 • The Library Card, by Jerry Spinelli, & At the Library, by Nikki Grimes

Chapter Materials

Activity Book: pp. 121–128
Audio: Unit 4, Chapter 1
Student Handbook
Student CD-ROM: Unit 4, Chapter 1
Teacher Resource Book: Lesson Plan, p. 19; Teacher Resources, pp. 35–64; Reading Summaries, pp. 95–96; Activity Book Answer Key
Teacher Resource CD-ROM
Assessment Program: Unit 4, Chapter Quiz, pp. 61–62; Teacher and Student Resources, pp. 115–144
Assessment CD-ROM: Unit 4, Chapter 1
Transparencies
The Heinle Newbury House Dictionary/CD-ROM
Web site: http://visions.heinle.com

➤ **See the Teacher's Edition wrap-around for complete teaching suggestions for each section.**

Day 1

- **Unit Opener** (pp. 222–223) 20 MIN.
  Preview the unit reading selections. Complete the "View the Picture" activity.
- **Objectives** (p. 224) 5 MIN.
  Present the chapter objectives.
- **Use Prior Knowledge** (p. 224) 15 MIN.
  Activate prior knowledge about sources of information.
- **Build Background** (p. 225) 5 MIN.
  Provide the background information on public libraries.
- **Homework:** KWL (TRB, p. 42); Have students complete the first and second columns based on what they learned in class. Students will complete the third column at the end of the chapter.

Day 2

- **Check Homework** 5 MIN.
  OR
- **Warm Up** 5 MIN.
  Write on the board: List 2 things that you can borrow from a library.
- **Build Vocabulary** (p. 225) 15 MIN.
  Introduce using repetition to find meaning.
- **Text Structure** (p. 226) 10 MIN.
  Present the text features of fiction.
- **Reading Strategy** (p. 226) 10 MIN.
  Teach the strategy of comparing and contrasting.
- **Reading Selection Opener** (p. 227) 5 MIN.
  Preview the chapter reading selections.
- **Homework:** Activity Book (p. 121)

Day 3

- **Check Homework** 5 MIN.
  OR
- **Warm Up** 5 MIN.
  Write on the board: A plot has a ______, a ______, and an ______.
- **Reading Selections** (pp. 228–233) 25 MIN.
  Have students read the selections and use the reading strategy. Teach spelling, capitalization, and punctuation points on TE pp. 228–233.
- **Reading Comprehension** (p. 234) 10 MIN.
  Have students answer the questions.
- **Build Reading Fluency** (p. 234) 5 MIN.
  Teach how to build reading fluency by reading chunks of words silently.
- **Homework:** Activity Book (p. 122)

Day 4

- **Check Homework** 5 MIN.
  OR
- **Warm Up** 5 MIN.
  Write on the board: Do you think that Mongoose will go to the library much in the future? Why or why not?
- **Listen, Speak, Interact** (p. 235) 15 MIN.
  Have students take notes, organize, and summarize.
- **Elements of Literature** (p. 235) 15 MIN.
  Present writing style.
- **Word Study** (p. 236) 10 MIN.
  Present historical influences on English words.
- **Homework:** Activity Book (pp. 123–124)

Day 5

- **Check Homework** 5 MIN.
  OR
- **Warm Up** 5 MIN.
  Write on the board: In "The Library Card," the author begins several sentences in a row with <u>and</u> to show excitement. This is an example of the author's writing ______.
- **Grammar Focus** (p. 236) 15 MIN.
  Present sentences with relative clauses.
- **From Reading to Writing** (p. 237) 15 MIN.
  Teach how to write a story.
- **Across Content Areas** (p. 237) 10 MIN.
  Introduce related language arts content on using the library.
- **Homework:** Activity Book (pp. 125–128); Have students complete the third column of the KWL chart from Day 1. Have students study for the Unit 4, Chapter 1 Quiz.

Class ______________________ Date ______________________

UNIT 4 Discoveries

CHAPTER 2 • Discovering the Ice Maiden, by Johan Reinhard

Chapter Materials

Activity Book: pp. 129–136
Audio: Unit 4, Chapter 2
Student Handbook
Student CD-ROM: Unit 4, Chapter 2
Teacher Resource Book: Lesson Plan, p. 20; Teacher Resources, pp. 35–64; Reading Summaries, pp. 97–98; Activity Book Answer Key
Teacher Resource CD-ROM
Assessment Program: Unit 4, Chapter 2 Quiz, pp. 63–64; Teacher and Student Resources, pp. 115–144
Assessment CD-ROM: Unit 4, Chapter 2
Transparencies
The Heinle Newbury House Dictionary/CD-ROM
Web site: http://visions.heinle.com

➤ **See the Teacher's Edition wrap-around for complete teaching suggestions for each section.**

Day 1

- **Unit 4, Chapter 1 Quiz** (Assessment Program, pp. 61–62) 20 MIN.
- **Objectives** (p. 238) 5 MIN.
  Present the chapter objectives.
- **Use Prior Knowledge** (p. 238) 15 MIN.
  Activate prior knowledge about mountains.
- **Build Background** (p. 239) 5 MIN.
  Provide the background information on Inca culture.
- **Homework:** KWL (TRB, p. 42); Have students complete the first and second columns based on what they learned in class. Students will complete the third column at the end of the chapter.

Day 2

- **Check Homework** 5 MIN.
  OR
- **Warm Up** 5 MIN.
  Write on the board: List 3 things that you learned about the Inca people.
- **Build Vocabulary** (p. 239) 15 MIN.
  Introduce key terms and related terms.
- **Text Structure** (p. 240) 10 MIN.
  Present the text features of a nonfiction narrative.
- **Reading Strategy** (p. 240) 10 MIN.
  Teach the strategy of using graphic sources of information.
- **Reading Selection Opener** (p. 241) 5 MIN.
  Preview the chapter reading selection.
- **Homework:** Activity Book (p. 129)

Day 3

- **Check Homework** 5 MIN.
  OR
- **Warm Up** 5 MIN.
  Write on the board: A nonfiction narrative gives facts. It answers the questions Who, _____, _____, _____, _____, and _____?
- **Reading Selection** (pp. 242–247) 25 MIN.
  Have students read the selection and use the reading strategy. Teach spelling, capitalization, and punctuation points on TE pp. 242–247.
- **Reading Comprehension** (p. 248) 10 MIN.
  Have students answer the questions.
- **Build Reading Fluency** (p. 248) 5 MIN.
  Teach how to build reading fluency by reading to scan for information.
- **Homework:** Activity Book (p. 130)

Day 4

- **Check Homework** 5 MIN.
  OR
- **Warm Up** 5 MIN.
  Write on the board: The author thinks that finding the Inca Ice Maiden was important. Why?
- **Listen, Speak, Interact** (p. 249) 15 MIN.
  Have students describe personal accomplishments.
- **Elements of Literature** (p. 249) 15 MIN.
  Present first-person point of view.
- **Word Study** (p. 250) 10 MIN.
  Present the spelling of *-ed* forms.
- **Homework:** Activity Book (pp. 131–132)

Day 5

- **Check Homework** 5 MIN.
  OR
- **Warm Up** 5 MIN.
  If an author tells a story using the pronouns *I, me, we,* and *us,* this is called writing in _____-_____ point of view.
- **Grammar Focus** (p. 250) 15 MIN.
  Present *be* + adjective + infinitive.
- **From Reading to Writing** (p. 251) 15 MIN.
  Teach how to write a first-person nonfiction narrative.
- **Across Content Areas** (p. 251) 10 MIN.
  Introduce related social studies content on the atmosphere and altitude.
- **Homework:** Activity Book (pp. 133–136); Have students complete the third column of the KWL chart from Day 1. Have students study for the Unit 4, Chapter 2 Quiz.

Class ______________________ Date ______________

UNIT 4 Discoveries

CHAPTER 3 • The Art of Swordsmanship, by Rafe Martin

Chapter Materials

Activity Book: pp. 137–144
Audio: Unit 4, Chapter 3
Student Handbook
Student CD-ROM: Unit 4, Chapter 3
Teacher Resource Book: Lesson Plan, p. 21; Teacher Resources, pp. 35–64; Reading Summaries, pp. 99–100; Activity Book Answer Key
Teacher Resource CD-ROM
Assessment Program: Unit 4, Chapter 3 Quiz, pp. 65–66; Teacher and Student Resources, pp. 115–144
Assessment CD-ROM: Unit 4, Chapter 3
Transparencies
The Heinle Newbury House Dictionary/CD-ROM
Web site: http://visions.heinle.com

➤ **See the Teacher's Edition wrap-around for complete teaching suggestions for each section.**

Day 1

- **Unit 4, Chapter 2 Quiz** (Assessment Program, pp. 63–64) 20 MIN.
- **Objectives** (p. 252) 5 MIN.
  Present the chapter objectives.
- **Use Prior Knowledge** (p. 252) 15 MIN.
  Activate prior knowledge about learning experiences.
- **Build Background** (p. 253) 5 MIN.
  Provide the background information on swordfighting.
- **Homework:** KWL (TRB, p. 42); Have students complete the first and second columns based on what they learned in class. Students will complete the third column at the end of the chapter.

Day 2

- **Check Homework** 5 MIN.
  OR
- **Warm Up** 5 MIN.
  Write on the board: The different types of fighting arts from Asia are called _____ _____.
- **Build Vocabulary** (p. 253) 15 MIN.
  Introduce related words.
- **Text Structure** (p. 254) 10 MIN.
  Present the text features of a folktale.
- **Reading Strategy** (p. 254) 10 MIN.
  Teach the strategy of using dialogue to understand character.
- **Reading Selection Opener** (p. 255) 5 MIN.
  Preview the chapter reading selection.
- **Homework:** Activity Book (p. 137)

Day 3

- **Check Homework** 5 MIN.
  OR
- **Warm Up** 5 MIN.
  Write on the board: Rewrite these sentences to make them correct.
  a. Tales were originally in the written tradition.
  b. A tale is about events in the present.
  c. A tale is written to make us laugh.
- **Reading Selection** (pp. 256–259) 25 MIN.
  Have students read the selection and use the reading strategy. Teach spelling, capitalization, and punctuation points on TE pp. 256–259.
- **Reading Comprehension** (p. 260) 10 MIN.
  Have students answer the questions.
- **Build Reading Fluency** (p. 260) 5 MIN.
  Teach how to build reading fluency by doing repeated reading.
- **Homework:** Activity Book (p. 138)

Day 4

- **Check Homework** 5 MIN.
  OR
- **Warm Up** 5 MIN.
  Write on the board: Was Manjuro surprised at Banzo's behavior? Why?
- **Listen, Speak, Interact** (p. 261) 15 MIN.
  Have students participate in a dramatic read-aloud.
- **Elements of Literature** (p. 261) 10 MIN.
  Present character traits and changes.
- **Word Study** (p. 262) 15 MIN.
  Present word origins and prefixes.
- **Homework: Activity Book** (pp. 139–140)

Day 5

- **Check Homework** 5 MIN.
  OR
- **Warm Up** 5 MIN.
  Write on the board: At first, Manjuro was _____, but later he became patient.
- **Grammar Focus** (p. 262) 15 MIN.
  Present adverbs to show time.
- **From Reading to Writing** (p. 263) 15 MIN.
  Teach how to write a folktale.
- **Across Content Areas** (p. 263) 10 MIN.
  Introduce related arts content on art in everyday objects.
- **Homework:** Activity Book (pp. 141–144); Have students complete the third column of the KWL chart from Day 1. Have students study for the Unit 4, Chapter 3 Quiz.

Class ______________________ Date ______________

UNIT 4 Discoveries

CHAPTER 4 • Mae Jemison, Space Scientist, by Gail Sakurai

Chapter Materials

Activity Book: pp. 145–152
Audio: Unit 4, Chapter 4
Student Handbook
Student CD-ROM: Unit 4, Chapter 4
Teacher Resource Book: Lesson Plan, p. 22; Teacher Resources, pp. 35–64; Reading Summaries, pp. 101–102; Activity Book Answer Key
Teacher Resource CD-ROM
Assessment Program: Unit 4, Chapter 4 Quiz, pp. 67–68; Teacher and Student Resources, pp. 115–144
Assessment CD-ROM: Unit 4, Chapter 4
Transparencies
The Heinle Newbury House Dictionary/CD-ROM
Web site: http://visions.heinle.com

➤ **See the Teacher's Edition wrap-around for complete teaching suggestions for each section.**

Day 1

- **Unit 4, Chapter 3 Quiz** (Assessment Program, pp. 65–66) 20 MIN.
- **Objectives** (p. 264) 5 MIN.
  Present the chapter objectives.
- **Use Prior Knowledge** (p. 264) 15 MIN.
  Activate prior knowledge about astronauts.
- **Build Background** (p. 265) 5 MIN.
  Provide the background information on the United States Space Shuttle.
- **Homework:** KWL (TRB, p. 42); Have students complete the first and second columns based on what they learned in class. Students will complete the third column at the end of the chapter.

Day 2

- **Check Homework** 5 MIN.
  OR
- **Warm Up** 5 MIN.
  Write on the board: List 3 things that you remember about astronauts and the space shuttle.
- **Build Vocabulary** (p. 265) 15 MIN.
  Introduce adjusting your reading rate.
- **Text Structure** (p. 266) 10 MIN.
  Present the text features of inductive organization.
- **Reading Strategy** (p. 266) 10 MIN.
  Teach the strategy of finding main ideas and supporting details.
- **Reading Selection Opener** (p. 267) 5 MIN.
  Preview the chapter reading selection.
- **Homework:** Activity Book (p. 145)

Day 3

- **Check Homework** 5 MIN.
  OR
- **Warm Up** 5 MIN.
  Write on the board: If you give facts first and then give a conclusion, you are using _____ organization.
- **Reading Selection** (pp. 268–273) 25 MIN.
  Have students read the selection and use the reading strategy. Teach spelling, capitalization, and punctuation points on TE pp. 268–273.
- **Reading Comprehension** (p. 274) 10 MIN.
  Have students answer the questions.
- **Build Reading Fluency** (p. 274) 5 MIN.
  Teach how to build reading fluency by reading silently.
- **Homework:** Activity Book (p. 146)

Day 4

- **Check Homework** 5 MIN.
  OR
- **Warm Up** 5 MIN.
  Write on the board: What was Mae Jemison's job on the space shuttle? Did she fly it, do science experiments on it, or was she the doctor?
- **Listen, Speak, Interact** (p. 275) 15 MIN.
  Have students discuss their goals.
- **Elements of Literature** (p. 275) 10 MIN.
  Present flashbacks.
- **Word Study** (p. 276) 15 MIN.
  Present Greek and Latin word origins.
- **Homework:** Activity Book (pp. 147–148)

Day 5

- **Check Homework** 5 MIN.
  OR
- **Warm Up** 5 MIN.
  Write on the board: Choose the correct answer.
  The meaning of the word astrology relates to:
  a. water
  b. animals
  c. stars
- **Grammar Focus** (p. 276) 15 MIN.
  Present the use and punctuation of dependent clauses with *although* and *when.*
- **From Reading to Writing** (p. 277) 15 MIN.
  Teach how to write a short biography.
- **Across Content Areas** (p. 277) 10 MIN.
  Introduce related science content on gravity.
- **Homework:** Activity Book (pp. 149–152); Have students complete the third column of the KWL chart from Day 1. Have students study for the Unit 4, Chapter 4 Quiz.

Class ______________________ Date ______________

UNIT 4 Discoveries

APPLY AND EXPAND

End-of-Unit Materials

Student Handbook
CNN Video: Unit 4
Teacher Resource Book: Lesson Plan, p. 23; Teacher Resources, pp. 35–64; Home-School Connection, pp. 140–146; Video Script, pp. 167–168; Video Worksheet, p. 176
Teacher Resource CD-ROM
Assessment Program: Unit 4 Test, pp. 69–74; Teacher and Student Resources, pp. 115–144
Assessment CD-ROM: Unit 4 Test
Transparencies
The Heinle Newbury House Dictionary/CD-ROM
Heinle Reading Library
Web site: http://visions.heinle.com

➤ See the Teacher's Edition wrap-around for complete teaching suggestions for each section.

Day 1

- **Unit 4, Chapter 4 Quiz** (Assessment Program, pp. 67–68) 20 MIN.
- **Listening and Speaking Workshop** (pp. 278–279) 25 MIN.
  Introduce the assignment of presenting a biographical sketch about a person's hobby. Have students prepare questions and conduct their interviews (steps 1–3).
- **Homework:** Have students review and organize their notes (step 4, item 1).

Day 2

- **Listening and Speaking Workshop** (pp. 278–279) 45 MIN.
  Have students give their biographical sketches (step 4, items 2–5).
- **Homework:** Have students make their presentation to family members.

Day 3

- **Viewing Workshop** (p. 279) 45 MIN.
  Use maps of different kinds to help students understand how different maps give different ideas. Show the Visions CNN video for this unit. Have students do the Video Worksheet.
- **Homework:** In preparation for the Writer's Workshop, ask students to make a list of books that they have enjoyed.

Day 4

- **Writer's Workshop** (pp. 280–281) 45 MIN.
  Present the writing assignment of writing an e-mail message to inform. Have students do pre-writing and write a draft (steps 1–3).
- **Homework:** Have students review their writing in preparation for revising it on Day 5.

Day 5

- **Writer's Workshop** (pp. 280–281) 45 MIN.
  Have students revise, edit, and publish their writing (steps 4–6).
- **Homework:** Have students send their writing, as an e-mail message or as regular mail, to a friend or family member.

Day 6

- **Review and Reteach** 45 MIN.
  In small groups, have students list major points from the unit. Ask students to choose three points that they are least clear on and would like to review. Based on results of chapter quizzes and student feedback, choose points from the unit to reteach to the class.
- **Homework:** Have students study for the Unit 4 Test.

Day 7

- **Unit 4 Test** (Assessment Program, pp. 69–74) 45 MIN.
  After the Unit 4 Test, reassess student learning. Record strong and weak areas based on the unit test. Review weak areas before the End-of-Book Exam.

Class ______________________ Date ______________

UNIT 5 Communication

CHAPTER 1 • How Tía Lola Came to ~~Visit~~ Stay, by Julia Alvarez

Chapter Materials

Activity Book: pp. 153–160
Audio: Unit 5, Chapter 1
Student Handbook
Student CD-ROM: Unit 5, Chapter 1
Teacher Resource Book: Lesson Plan, p. 24; Teacher Resources, pp. 35–64; Reading Summaries, pp. 103–104; Activity Book Answer Key
Teacher Resource CD-ROM
Assessment Program: Unit 5, Chapter 1 Quiz, pp. 75–76; Teacher and Student Resources, pp. 115–144
Assessment CD-ROM: Unit 5, Chapter 1
Transparencies
The Heinle Newbury House Dictionary/CD-ROM
Web site: http://visions.heinle.com

➤ See the Teacher's Edition wrap-around for complete teaching suggestions for each section.

Day 1

- **Unit Opener** (pp. 284–285) 20 MIN.
  Preview the unit reading selections. Complete the "View the Picture" activity.
- **Objectives** (p. 286) 5 MIN.
  Present the chapter objectives.
- **Use Prior Knowledge** (p. 286) 15 MIN.
  Activate prior knowledge about different cultures and languages.
- **Build Background** (p. 287) 5 MIN.
  Provide the background information on the Dominican Republic.
- **Homework:** KWL (TRB, p. 42); Have students complete the first and second columns based on what they learned in class. Students will complete the third column at the end of the chapter.

Day 2

- **Check Homework** 5 MIN.
  OR
- **Warm Up** 5 MIN.
  Write on the board: List as many languages as you can think of.
- **Build Vocabulary** (p. 287) 15 MIN.
  Introduce using context clues.
- **Text Structure** (p. 288) 10 MIN.
  Present the text features of a narrative.
- **Reading Strategy** (p. 288) 10 MIN.
  Teach the strategy of predicting.
- **Reading Selection Opener** (p. 289) 5 MIN.
  Preview the chapter reading selection.
- **Homework:** Activity Book (p. 153)

Day 3

- **Check Homework** 5 MIN.
  OR
- **Warm Up** 5 MIN.
  Write on the board: A narrative is made up of a ______, a ______, and an ______.
- **Reading Selection** (pp. 290–297) 25 MIN.
  Have students read the selection and use the reading strategy. Teach spelling, capitalization, and punctuation points on TE pp. 290–297.
- **Reading Comprehension** (p. 298) 10 MIN.
  Have students answer the questions.
- **Build Reading Fluency** (p. 298) 5 MIN.
  Teach how to build reading fluency by reading silently.
- **Homework:** Activity Book (p. 154)

Day 4

- **Check Homework** 5 MIN.
  OR
- **Warm Up** 5 min.
  Write on the board: Miguel and Juanita have moved to ______. Their Tía Lola is coming for a ______. Miguel is ______ very happy about that.
- **Listen, Speak, Interact** (p. 299) 15 MIN.
  Have students role-play a dialogue.
- **Elements of Literature** (p. 299) 10 MIN.
  Present point of view.
- **Word Study** (p. 300) 15 MIN.
  Present the prefixes *un-* and *im-*.
- **Homework:** Activity Book (pp. 155–156)

Day 5

- **Check Homework** 5 MIN.
  OR
- **Warm Up** 5 MIN.
  Write on the board: Who tells the story in "Tía Lola Comes to ~~Visit~~ Stay?" What pronouns does the storyteller use?
- **Grammar Focus** (p. 300) 10 MIN.
  Present the present perfect tense.
- **From Reading to Writing** (p. 301) 20 MIN.
  Teach how to write a narrative with dialogue.
- **Across Content Areas** (p. 301) 10 MIN.
  Introduce related social studies content on reading a weather map.
- **Homework:** Activity Book (pp. 157–160); Have students complete the third column of the KWL chart from Day 1. Have students study for the Unit 5, Chapter 1 Quiz.

Class ______________________ Date ______________________

UNIT 5 Communication

CHAPTER 2 • Helen Keller, by George Sullivan, & The Miracle Worker, by William Gibson

Chapter Materials

Activity Book: pp. 161–168
Audio: Unit 5, Chapter 2
Student Handbook
Student CD-ROM: Unit 5, Chapter 2
Teacher Resource Book: Lesson Plan, p. 25; Teacher Resources, pp. 35–64; Reading Summaries, pp. 105–106; Activity Book Answer Key

Teacher Resource CD-ROM
Assessment Program: Unit 5, Chapter 2 Quiz, pp. 77–78; Teacher and Student Resources, pp. 115–144
Assessment CD-ROM: Unit 5, Chapter 2
Transparencies
The Heinle Newbury House Dictionary/CD-ROM
Web site: http://visions.heinle.com

➤ See the Teacher's Edition wrap-around for complete teaching suggestions for each section.

Day 1

- **Unit 5, Chapter 1 Quiz** (Assessment Program, pp. 75–76) 20 MIN.
- **Objectives** (p. 302) 5 MIN.
  Present the chapter objectives.
- **Use Prior Knowledge** (p. 302) 15 MIN.
  Activate prior knowledge about blindness and deafness.
- **Build Background** (p. 303) 5 MIN.
  Provide the background information on Helen Keller.
- **Homework:** KWL (TRB, p. 42); Have students complete the first and second columns based on what they learned in class. Students will complete the third column at the end of the chapter.

Day 2

- **Check Homework** 5 MIN.
  OR
- **Warm Up** 5 MIN.
  Write on the board: True or false: When Helen Keller was born, she was blind and deaf.
- **Build Vocabulary** (p. 303) 15 MIN.
  Introduce synonyms for action verbs.
- **Text Structure** (p. 304) 10 MIN.
  Present the text features of a biography and a drama.
- **Reading Strategy** (p. 304) 10 MIN.
  Teach the strategy of comparing and contrasting.
- **Reading Selection Opener** (p. 305) 5 MIN.
  Preview the chapter reading selections.
- **Homework:** Activity Book (p. 161)

Day 3

- **Check Homework** 5 MIN.
  OR
- **Warm Up** 5 MIN.
  Write on the board: List 1 thing about the structure of a biography and 1 thing about the structure of a drama.
- **Reading Selections** (pp. 306–311) 25 MIN.
  Have students read the selections and use the reading strategy. Teach spelling, capitalization, and punctuation points on TE pp. 306–311.
- **Reading Comprehension** (p. 312) 10 MIN.
  Have students answer the questions.
- **Build Reading Fluency** (p. 312) 5 MIN.
  Teach how to build reading fluency by adjusting your reading rate.
- **Homework:** Activity Book (p. 162)

Day 4

- **Check Homework** 5 MIN.
  OR
- **Warm Up** 5 MIN.
  Write on the board: Annie Sullivan communicated with Helen Keller by spelling words into Helen's ______. The first word that Helen understood was ______.
- **Listen, Speak, Interact** (p. 313) 15 MIN.
  Have students interpret lines from a play.
- **Elements of Literature** (p. 313) 10 MIN.
  Teach students to analyze stage directions.
- **Word Study** (p. 314) 15 MIN.
  Present the suffix *-ly*.
- **Homework:** Activity Book (pp. 163–164)

Day 5

- **Check Homework** 5 MIN.
  OR
- **Warm Up** 5 MIN.
  Write on the board: In a play, ______ ______ tell the actors what to do.
- **Grammar Focus** (p. 314) 15 MIN.
  Present past progressive verbs.
- **From Reading to Writing** (p. 315) 15 MIN.
  Teach how to write a scene from a play.
- **Across Content Areas** (p. 315) 10 MIN.
  Introduce related science content on causes of diseases.
- **Homework:** Activity Book (pp. 165–168); Have students complete the third column of the KWL chart from Day 1. Have students study for the Unit 5, Chapter 2 Quiz.

Class ______________________ Date ______________________

UNIT 5 Communication

CHAPTER 3 • Hearing: The Ear

Chapter Materials

Activity Book: pp. 169–176
Audio: Unit 5, Chapter 3
Student Handbook
Student CD-ROM: Unit 5, Chapter 3
Teacher Resource Book: Lesson Plan, p. 26; Teacher Resources, pp. 35–64; Reading Summaries, pp. 107–108; Activity Book Answer Key
Teacher Resource CD-ROM
Assessment Program: Unit 5, Chapter 3 Quiz, pp. 79–80; Teacher and Student Resources, pp. 115–144
Assessment CD-ROM: Unit 5, Chapter 3
Transparencies
The Heinle Newbury House Dictionary/CD-ROM
Web site: http://visions.heinle.com

➤ **See the Teacher's Edition wrap-around for complete teaching suggestions for each section.**

Day 1

- **Unit 5, Chapter 2 Quiz** (Assessment Program, pp. 77–78) 20 MIN.
- **Objectives** (p. 316) 5 MIN.
  Present the chapter objectives.
- **Use Prior Knowledge** (p. 316) 15 MIN.
  Activate prior knowledge about listening to learn.
- **Build Background** (p. 317) 5 MIN.
  Provide the background information on the ear.
- **Homework:** KWL (TRB, p. 42); Have students complete the first and second columns based on what they learned in class. Students will complete the third column at the end of the chapter.

Day 2

- **Check Homework** 5 MIN.
  OR
- **Warm Up** 5 MIN.
  Write on the board: The ear is made up of three main parts: the _____ ear, the _____ ear, and the _____ ear.
- **Build Vocabulary** (p. 317) 15 MIN.
  Introduce science vocabulary.
- **Text Structure** (p. 318) 10 MIN.
  Present the text features of a textbook.
- **Reading Strategy** (p. 318) 10 MIN.
  Teach the strategy of representing text information in an outline.
- **Reading Selection Opener** (p. 319) 5 MIN.
  Preview the chapter reading selection.
- **Homework:** Activity Book (p. 169)

Day 3

- **Check Homework** 5 MIN.
  OR
- **Warm Up** 5 MIN.
  Write on the board: _____ tell you what part of a text is about. _____ are ways of showing information with drawings, charts, and other features.
- **Reading Selection** (pp. 320–323) 25 MIN.
  Have students read the selection and use the reading strategy. Teach spelling, capitalization, and punctuation points on TE pp. 320–323.
- **Reading Comprehension** (p. 324) 10 MIN.
  Have students answer the questions.
- **Build Reading Fluency** (p. 324) 5 MIN.
  Teach how to build reading fluency by reading to scan for information.
- **Homework:** Activity Book (p. 170)

Day 4

- **Check Homework** 5 MIN.
  OR
- **Warm Up** 5 MIN.
  Write on the board: Write 3 things that you remember about hearing and the ear.
- **Listen, Speak, Interact** (p. 325) 15 MIN.
  Have students discuss how sound waves travel.
- **Elements of Literature** (p. 325) 15 MIN.
  Present descriptive language.
- **Word Study** (p. 326) 10 MIN.
  Present words with Greek origins.
- **Homework:** Activity Book (pp. 171–172)

Day 5

- **Check Homework** 5 MIN.
  OR
- **Warm Up** 5 MIN.
  Write on the board: *Tele-* is a Greek word root that means _____. Three words with this root are _____, _____, and _____.
- **Grammar Focus** (p. 326) 15 MIN.
  Present subject and verb agreement in the present tense.
- **From Reading to Writing** (p. 327) 15 MIN.
  Teach how to write to inform.
- **Across Content Areas** (p. 327) 10 MIN.
  Introduce related arts content on the voice.
- **Homework:** Activity Book (pp. 173–176); Have students complete the third column of the KWL chart from Day 1. Have students study for the Unit 5, Chapter 3 Quiz.

Class ______________________________ Date ______________________

UNIT 5 Communication

CHAPTER 4 • The Art of Making Comic Books, by Michael Morgan Pellowski

Chapter Materials

Activity Book: pp. 177–184
Audio: Unit 5, Chapter 4
Student Handbook
Student CD-ROM: Unit 5, Chapter 4
Teacher Resource Book: Lesson Plan, p. 27; Teacher Resources, pp. 35–64; Reading Summaries, pp. 109–110; Activity Book Answer Key

Teacher Resource CD-ROM
Assessment Program: Unit 5, Chapter 4 Quiz, pp. 81–82; Teacher and Student Resources, pp. 115–144
Assessment CD-ROM: Unit 5, Chapter 4
Transparencies
The Heinle Newbury House Dictionary/CD-ROM
Web site: http://visions.heinle.com

➤ **See the Teacher's Edition wrap-around for complete teaching suggestions for each section.**

Day 1

- **Unit 5, Chapter 3 Quiz** (Assessment Program, pp. 79–80) 20 MIN.
- **Objectives** (p. 328) 5 MIN.
  Present the chapter objectives.
- **Use Prior Knowledge** (p. 328) 15 MIN.
  Activate prior knowledge about comic books.
- **Build Background** (p. 329) 5 MIN.
  Provide the background knowledge about the history of comic books.
- **Homework:** KWL (TRB, p. 42); Have students complete the first and second columns based on what they learned in class. Students will complete the third column at the end of the chapter.

Day 2

- **Check Homework** 5 MIN.
  OR
- **Warm Up** 5 MIN.
  Write on the board: The first comic superhero was ______.
- **Build Vocabulary** (p. 329) 15 MIN.
  Introduce using a dictionary to learn words about art.
- **Text Structure** (p. 330) 10 MIN.
  Present the text features of an illustrated "how-to" article.
- **Reading Strategy** (p. 330) 10 MIN.
  Teach the strategy of making inferences using text evidence.
- **Reading Selection Opener** (p. 331) 5 MIN.
  Preview the chapter reading selection.
- **Homework:** Activity Book (p. 177)

Day 3

- **Check Homework** 5 MIN.
  OR
- **Warm Up** 5 MIN.
  Write on the board: List 2 features of an illustrated how-to article.
- **Reading Selection** (pp. 332–337) 25 MIN.
  Have students read the selection and use the reading strategy. Teach spelling, capitalization, and punctuation points on TE pp. 332–337.
- **Reading Comprehension** (p. 338) 10 MIN.
  Have students answer the questions.
- **Build Reading Fluency** (p. 338) 5 MIN.
  Teach how to build reading fluency by doing repeated reading.
- **Homework:** Activity Book (p. 178)

Day 4

- **Check Homework** 5 MIN.
  OR
- **Warm Up** 5 MIN.
  Write on the board: True or false?
  You don't need imagination to create a comic book character.
  Comic book heroes are usually like normal people.
- **Listen, Speak, Interact** (p. 339) 15 MIN.
  Have students explain a concept for a character.
- **Elements of Literature** (p. 339) 15 MIN.
  Present writing style.
- **Word Study** (p. 340) 10 MIN.
  Present the suffix *-ian*.
- **Homework:** Activity Book (pp. 179–180)

Day 5

- **Check Homework** 5 MIN.
  OR
- **Warm Up** 5 MIN.
  Write on the board: ______ is the way writers use language to express themselves.
- **Grammar Focus** (p. 340) 15 MIN.
  Present the present conditional.
- **From Reading to Writing** (p. 341) 15 MIN.
  Teach how to write an illustrated how-to article.
- **Across Content Areas** (p. 341) 10 MIN.
  Introduce related arts content on learning about art forms.
- **Homework:** Activity Book (pp. 181–184); Have students complete the third column of the KWL chart from Day 1. Have students study for the Unit 5, Chapter 4 Quiz.

Class ______________________ Date ______________________

UNIT 5 Communication

APPLY AND EXPAND

End-of-Unit Materials

Student Handbook
CNN Video: Unit 5
Teacher Resource Book: Lesson Plan, p. 28; Teacher Resources, pp. 35–64; Home-School Connection, pp. 147–153; Video Script, pp. 169–170; Video Worksheet, p. 177
Teacher Resource CD-ROM
Assessment Program: Unit 5 Test, pp. 83–88; Teacher and Student Resources, pp. 115–144
Assessment CD-ROM: Unit 5 Test
Transparencies
The Heinle Newbury House Dictionary/CD-ROM
Heinle Reading Library
Web site: http://visions.heinle.com

➤ **See the Teacher's Edition wrap-around for complete teaching suggestions for each section.**

Day 1

- **Unit 5, Chapter 4 Quiz** (Assessment Program, pp. 81–82) 20 MIN.
- **Listening and Speaking Workshop** (pp. 342–343) 25 MIN.
  Introduce the assignment of presenting an oral summary of a reading. Have students organize and plan their summaries (steps 1–2).
- **Homework:** Have students review their information so that they will be familiar with it for Day 2.

Day 2

- **Listening and Speaking Workshop** (pp. 342–343) 45 MIN.
  Have students practice and present their summaries (steps 3–4).
- **Homework:** Have students present their summaries to their families.

Day 3

- **Viewing Workshop** (p. 343) 45 MIN.
  Have students analyze various visual media. Show the Heinle CNN video for this unit. Have students do the Video Worksheet.
- **Homework:** Have students write a summary of what they found about the media they examined.

Day 4

- **Writer's Workshop** (pp. 344–345) 45 MIN.
  Present the writing assignment of writing a persuasive editorial. Have students do pre-writing and write a draft (steps 1–3).
- **Homework:** Have students review their drafts in preparation for revising and editing it on Day 5.

Day 5

- **Writer's Workshop** (pp. 344–345) 45 MIN.
  Have students revise, edit, and publish their writing (steps 4–5).
- **Homework:** Have students exchange their writing with another student. For homework, they should write one strength and one weakness of the other student's work.

Day 6

- **Review and Reteach** 45 MIN.
  In small groups, have students list major points from the unit. Ask students to choose three points that they are least clear on and would like to review. Based on results of chapter quizzes and student feedback, choose points from the unit to reteach to the class.
- **Homework:** Have students study for the Unit 5 Test.

Day 7

- **Unit 5 Test** (Assessment Program, pp. 83–88) 45 MIN.
  After the Unit 5 Test, reassess student learning. Record strong and weak areas based on the unit test. Review weak areas before the End-of-Book Exam.

Class ______________________ Date ______________________

UNIT 6 Frontiers

CHAPTER 1 • The Lewis and Clark Expedition

Chapter Materials

Activity Book: pp. 185–192
Audio: Unit 6, Chapter 1
Student Handbook
Student CD-ROM: Unit 6, Chapter 1
Teacher Resource Book: Lesson Plan, p. 29; Teacher Resources, pp. 35–64; Reading Summaries, pp. 111–112; Activity Book Answer Key

Teacher Resource CD-ROM
Assessment Program: Unit 6, Chapter 1 Quiz, pp. 89–90; Teacher and Student Resources, pp. 115–144
Assessment CD-ROM: Unit 6, Chapter 1
Transparencies
The Heinle Newbury House Dictionary/CD-ROM
Web site: http://visions.heinle.com

➤ **See the Teacher's Edition wrap-around for complete teaching suggestions for each section.**

Day 1

- **Unit Opener** (pp. 348–349) 20 MIN.
  Preview the unit reading selections. Complete the "View the Picture" activity.
- **Objectives** (p. 350) 5 MIN.
  Present the chapter objectives.
- **Use Prior Knowledge** (p. 350) 15 MIN.
  Activate prior knowledge about frontiers.
- **Build Background** (p. 351) 5 MIN.
  Provide the background information on the Louisiana Purchase.
- **Homework:** KWL (TRB, p. 42); Have students complete the first and second columns based on what they learned in class. Students will complete the third column at the end of the chapter.

Day 2

- **Check Homework** 5 MIN.
  OR
- **Warm Up** 5 MIN.
  Write on the board: The _____ _____ added 828,000 acres of land to the United States.
- **Build Vocabulary** (p. 351) 15 MIN.
  Introduce the use of a word wheel.
- **Text Structure** (p. 352) 10 MIN.
  Present the text features of an informational text.
- **Reading Strategy** (p. 352) 10 MIN.
  Teach the strategy of identifying chronology.
- **Reading Selection Opener** (p. 353) 5 MIN.
  Preview the reading selection.
- **Homework:** Activity Book (p. 185)

Day 3

- **Check Homework** 5 MIN.
  OR
- **Warm Up** 5 MIN.
  Write on the board: True or false: Nonfiction writing tells about real people and events.
- **Reading Selection** (pp. 354–357) 25 MIN.
  Have students read the selection and use the reading strategy. Teach spelling, capitalization, and punctuation points on TE pp. 354–357.
- **Reading Comprehension** (p. 358) 10 MIN.
  Have students answer the questions.
- **Build Reading Fluency** (p. 358) 5 MIN.
  Teach how to build reading fluency by reading silently.
- **Homework:** Activity Book (p. 186)

Day 4

- **Check Homework** 5 MIN.
  OR
- **Warm Up** 5 MIN.
  Write on the board: The Lewis and Clark expedition began in the year _____ and ended in the year _____.
- **Listen, Speak, Interact** (p. 359) 15 MIN.
  Have students use inference to act out a story.
- **Elements of Literature** (p. 359) 15 MIN.
  Teach how to analyze characters.
- **Word Study** (p. 360) 10 MIN.
  Present using a thesaurus and synonym finder to find synonyms.
- **Homework:** Activity Book (pp. 187–188)

Day 5

- **Check Homework** 5 MIN.
  OR
- **Warm Up** 5 MIN.
  Write on the board: List as many characters from "The Lewis and Clark Expedition" as you can.
- **Grammar Focus** (p. 360) 15 MIN.
  Present appositives.
- **From Reading to Writing** (p. 361) 15 MIN.
  Teach how to write an informational text.
- **Across Content Areas** (p. 361) 10 MIN.
  Introduce related social studies content on using headings.
- **Homework:** Activity Book (pp. 189–192); Have students complete the third column of the KWL chart from Day 1. Have students study for the Unit 6, Chapter 1 Quiz.

Class ______________________ Date ______________________

UNIT 6 Frontiers

CHAPTER 2 • A Wrinkle in Time, by Madeleine L'Engle

Chapter Materials

Activity Book: pp. 193–200
Audio: Unit 6, Chapter 2
Student Handbook
Student CD-ROM: Unit 6, Chapter 2
Teacher Resource Book: Lesson Plan, p. 30; Teacher Resources, pp. 35–64; Reading Summaries, pp. 113–114; Activity Book Answer Key
Teacher Resource CD-ROM
Assessment Program: Unit 6, Chapter 2 Quiz, pp. 91–92; Teacher and Student Resources, pp. 115–144
Assessment CD-ROM: Unit 6, Chapter 2
Transparencies
The Heinle Newbury House Dictionary/CD-ROM
Web site: http://visions.heinle.com

➤ **See the Teacher's Edition wrap-around for complete teaching suggestions for each section.**

Day 1

- **Unit 6, Chapter 1 Quiz** (Assessment Program, pp. 89–90) 20 MIN.
- **Objectives** (p. 362) 5 MIN.
  Present the chapter objectives.
- **Use Prior Knowledge** (p. 362) 15 MIN.
  Activate prior knowledge about space travel.
- **Build Background** (p. 363) 5 MIN.
  Provide the background information on travel in science fiction.
- **Homework:** KWL (TRB, p. 42); Have students complete the first and second columns based on what they learned in class. Students will complete the third column at the end of the chapter.

Day 2

- **Check Homework** 5 MIN.
  OR
- **Warm Up** 5 MIN.
  Write on the board: The three dimensions are length, _____, and _____.
- **Build Vocabulary** (p. 363) 15 MIN.
  Introduce using context clues.
- **Text Structure** (p. 364) 10 MIN.
  Present the text features of science fiction.
- **Reading Strategy** (p. 364) 10 MIN.
  Teach the strategy of describing mental images.
- **Reading Selection Opener** (p. 365) 5 MIN.
  Preview the chapter reading selection.
- **Homework:** Activity Book (p. 193)

Day 3

- **Check Homework** 5 MIN.
  OR
- **Warm Up** 5 MIN.
  Write on the board: True or false: Science fiction has imaginary characters and events.
- **Reading Selection** (pp. 366–375) 25 MIN.
  Have students read the selection and use the reading strategy. Teach spelling, capitalization, and punctuation points on TE pp. 366–375.
- **Reading Comprehension** (p. 376) 10 MIN.
  Have students answer the questions.
- **Build Reading Fluency** (p. 376) 5 MIN.
  Teach how to build reading fluency by doing echo read aloud.
- **Homework:** Activity Book (p. 194)

Day 4

- **Check Homework** 5 MIN.
  OR
- **Warm Up** 5 MIN.
  Write on the board: In "A Wrinkle in Time," which character seems to understand the tesseract the best, Meg, Charles Wallace, or Calvin?
- **Listen, Speak, Interact** (p. 377) 15 MIN.
  Have students present a story.
- **Elements of Literature** (p. 377) 15 MIN.
  Present mood.
- **Word Study** (p. 378) 10 MIN.
  Present the prefixes *un-*, *in-*, and *im-*.
- **Homework:** Activity Book (pp. 195–196)

Day 5

- **Check Homework** 5 MIN.
  OR
- **Warm Up** 5 MIN.
  Write on the board: Write a word that is the opposite of each of these words:
  a. practical **c.** impolite
  b. unexpected **d.** tolerable
- **Grammar Focus** (p. 378) 15 MIN.
  Present the past perfect tense.
- **From Reading to Writing** (p. 379) 15 MIN.
  Teach how to write a science fiction narrative.
- **Across Content Areas** (p. 379) 10 MIN.
  Introduce related science content on the speed of light.
- **Homework:** Activity Book (pp. 197–200); Have students complete the third column of the KWL chart from Day 1. Have students study for the Unit 6, Chapter 2 Quiz.

Class ______________________ Date ______________________

UNIT 6 Frontiers

CHAPTER 3 • I Have a Dream, by Martin Luther King Jr.

Chapter Materials

Activity Book: pp. 201–208
Audio: Unit 6, Chapter 3
Student Handbook
Student CD-ROM: Unit 6, Chapter 3
Teacher Resource Book: Lesson Plan, p. 31; Teacher Resources, pp. 35–64; Reading Summaries, pp. 115–116; Activity Book Answer Key
Teacher Resource CD-ROM
Assessment Program: Unit 6, Chapter 3 Quiz, pp. 93–94; Teacher and Student Resources, pp. 115–144
Assessment CD-ROM: Unit 6, Chapter 3
Transparencies
The Heinle Newbury House Dictionary/CD-ROM
Web site: http://visions.heinle.com

➤ **See the Teacher's Edition wrap-around for complete teaching suggestions for each section.**

Day 1

- **Unit 6, Chapter 2 Quiz** (Assessment Program, pp. 91–92) 20 MIN.
- **Objectives** (p. 380) 5 MIN.
  Present the chapter objectives.
- **Use Prior Knowledge** (p. 380) 15 MIN.
  Activate prior knowledge about freedom.
- **Build Background** (p. 381) 5 MIN.
  Provide the background information on segregation and Martin Luther King Jr.
- **Homework:** KWL (TRB, p. 42); Have students complete the first and second columns based on what they learned in class. Students will complete the third column at the end of the chapter.

Day 2

- **Check Homework** 5 MIN.
  OR
- **Warm Up** 5 MIN.
  Write on the board: What does segregated mean—together or separated?
- **Build Vocabulary** (p. 381) 15 MIN.
  Introduce distinguishing denotative and connotative meanings.
- **Text Structure** (p. 382) 10 MIN.
  Present the text features of a speech.
- **Reading Strategy** (p. 382) 10 MIN.
  Teach the strategy of drawing conclusions with text evidence.
- **Reading Selection Opener** (p. 383) 5 MIN.
  Preview the chapter reading selection.
- **Homework: Activity Book** (p. 201)

Day 3

- **Check Homework** 5 MIN.
  OR
- **Warm Up** 5 MIN.
  Write on the board: In a speech, the speaker often repeats key words to help the audience _____ and _____.
- **Reading Selection** (pp. 384–387) 25 MIN.
  Have students read the selection and use the reading strategy. Teach spelling, capitalization, and punctuation points on TE pp. 384–387.
- **Reading Comprehension** (p. 388) 10 MIN.
  Have students answer the questions.
- **Build Reading Fluency** (p. 388) 5 MIN.
  Teach how to build reading fluency by adjusting your reading rate.
- **Homework:** Activity Book (p. 202)

Day 4

- **Check Homework** 5 MIN.
  OR
- **Warm Up** 5 MIN.
  Write on the board: Give one example of repeated words in the "I Have a Dream" speech.
- **Listen, Speak, Interact** (p. 389) 15 MIN.
  Have students present a speech.
- **Elements of Literature** (p. 389) 15 MIN.
  Present audience and purpose.
- **Word Study** (p. 390) 10 MIN.
  Present figurative language.
- **Homework:** Activity Book (pp. 203–204)

Day 5

- **Check Homework** 5 MIN.
  OR
- **Warm Up** 5 MIN.
  Write on the board:
  a. A _____ meaning is what the word is usually about.
  b. A _____ meaning is about the images or feelings that a word gives.
- **Grammar Focus** (p. 390) 15 MIN.
  Present dependent clauses with *that.*
- **From Reading to Writing** (p. 391) 15 MIN.
  Teach how to write a persuasive speech.
- **Across Content Areas** (p. 391) 10 MIN.
  Introduce related social studies content on the United States Constitution.
- **Homework:** Activity Book (pp. 205–208); Have students complete the third column of the KWL chart from Day 1. Have students study for the Unit 6, Chapter 3 Quiz.

Class ______________________________ Date ______________________

UNIT 6 Frontiers

CHAPTER 4 • Lyndon Baines Johnson: Our Thirty-Sixth President, by Melissa Maupin, & Speech to the Nation: July 2, 1964, by Lyndon Baines Johnson

Chapter Materials

Activity Book: pp. 209–216
Audio: Unit 6, Chapter 4
Student Handbook
Student CD-ROM: Unit 6, Chapter 4
Teacher Resource Book: Lesson Plan, p. 32; Teacher Resources, pp. 35–64; Reading Summaries, pp. 117–118; Activity Book Answer Key
Teacher Resource CD-ROM
Assessment Program: Unit 6, Chapter 4 Quiz, pp. 95–96; Teacher and Student Resources, pp. 115–144
Assessment CD-ROM: Unit 6, Chapter 4
Transparencies
The Heinle Newbury House Dictionary/CD-ROM
Web site: http://visions.heinle.com

See the Teacher's Edition wrap-around for complete teaching suggestions for each section.

Day 1

- **Unit 6, Chapter 3 Quiz** (Assessment Program, pp. 93–94) 20 MIN.
- **Objectives** (p. 392) 5 MIN.
  Present the chapter objectives.
- **Use Prior Knowledge** (p. 392) 15 MIN.
  Activate prior knowledge about what United States presidents do.
- **Build Background** (p. 393) 5 MIN.
  Provide background on presidential elections.
- **Homework:** KWL (TRB, p. 42); Have students complete the first and second columns based on what they learned in class. Students will complete the third column at the end of the chapter.

Day 2

- **Check Homework** 5 MIN.
  OR
- **Warm Up** 5 MIN.
  Write on the board: Presidential elections are held every _____ years. If a president dies, the _____ president becomes president.
- **Build Vocabulary** (p. 393) 15 MIN.
  Introduce key words about government.
- **Text Structure** (p. 394) 10 MIN.
  Present the text features of a biography.
- **Reading Strategy** (p. 394) 10 MIN.
  Teach the strategy of distinguishing fact from opinion.
- **Reading Selection Opener** (p. 395) 5 MIN.
  Preview the chapter reading selections.
- **Homework:** Activity Book (p. 209)

Day 3

- **Check Homework** 5 MIN.
  OR
- **Warm Up** 5 min.
  Write on the board: True or false?
  a. A biography is about a place or a thing.
  b. A biography tells the important events in a person's life.
- **Reading Selections** (pp. 396–401) 25 MIN.
  Have students read the selections and use the reading strategy. Teach spelling, capitalization, and punctuation points on TE pp. 396–401.
- **Reading Comprehension** (p. 402) 10 MIN.
  Have students answer the questions.
- **Build Reading Fluency** (p. 402) 5 MIN.
  Build reading fluency by doing choral read aloud.
- **Homework:** Activity Book (p. 210)

Day 4

- **Check Homework** 5 MIN.
  OR
- **Warm Up** 5 MIN.
  Write on the board: After John F. Kennedy died, _____ _____ _____ became president of the U.S.
- **Listen, Speak, Interact** (p. 403) 15 MIN.
  Have students conduct an interview.
- **Elements of Literature** (p. 403) 15 MIN.
  Present repetition in a speech.
- **Word Study** (p. 404) 10 MIN.
  Present adjectives.
- **Homework:** Activity Book (pp. 211–212)

Day 5

- **Check Homework** 5 MIN.
  OR
- **Warm Up** 5 MIN.
  Write on the board: Copy this sentence and underline the adjectives: For my birthday, I got a blue sweater, some great sneakers, and a big dictionary.
- **Grammar Focus** (p. 404) 15 MIN.
  Present the conjunction *yet* to show contrast.
- **From Reading to Writing** (p. 405) 15 MIN.
  Teach how to write a biography.
- **Across Content Areas** (p. 405) 10 MIN.
  Introduce related social studies content about the branches of government.
- **Homework:** Activity Book (pp. 213–216); Have students complete the third column of the KWL chart from Day 1. Have students study for the Unit 6, Chapter 4 Quiz.

Class ______________________ Date ______________________

UNIT 6 Frontiers

APPLY AND EXPAND

End-of-Unit Materials

Student Handbook
CNN Video: Unit 6
Teacher Resource Book: Lesson Plan, p. 33; Teacher Resources, pp. 35–64; Home-School Connection, pp. 154–160; Video Script, pp. 171–172; Video Worksheet, p. 178
Teacher Resource CD-ROM
Assessment Program: Unit 6 Test, pp. 97–102; End-of-Book Exam, pp. 103–108; Teacher and Student Resources, pp. 115–144
Assessment CD-ROM: Unit 6 Test, End-of-Book Exam
Transparencies
The Heinle Newbury House Dictionary/CD-ROM
Heinle Reading Library
Web site: http://visions.heinle.com

➤ **See the Teacher's Edition wrap-around for complete teaching suggestions for each section.**

Day 1

- **Unit 6, Chapter 4 Quiz** (Assessment Program, pp. 95–96) 20 MIN.
- **Listening and Speaking Workshop** (pp. 406–407) 45 MIN.
  Introduce the assignment of giving a persuasive speech. Have students plan and write their speeches (steps 1–2).
- **Homework:** Have students review their speech at home and make revisions as necessary.

Day 2

- **Listening and Speaking Workshop** (pp. 406–407) 45 MIN.
  Have students practice and present their speeches (steps 3–4).
- **Homework:** Have students write a self-evaluation of their speech.

Day 3

- **Viewing Workshop** (p. 407) 45 MIN.
  Play videos of the two speeches from the unit. Have students compare and contrast them. Show the Visions CNN video for this unit. Have students do the Video Worksheet.
- **Homework:** Have students write a paragraph comparing and contrasting the video and text versions of one of the speeches.

Day 4

- **Writer's Workshop** (pp. 408–409) 45 MIN.
  Present the writing assignment of writing a research report. Have students do pre-writing preparation and write a draft (steps 1–5).
- **Homework:** Have students review their reports in preparation for revising them on Day 5.

Day 5

- **Writer's Workshop** (pp. 408–409) 45 MIN.
  Have students revise, edit, and publish their writing (steps 6–7).
- **Homework:** Have students take their writing home to share with their family.

Day 6

- **Review and Reteach** 45 MIN.
  In small groups, have students list major points from the unit. Ask students to choose three points that they are least clear on and would like to review. Based on results of chapter quizzes and student feedback, choose points from the unit to reteach to the class.
- **Homework:** Have students study for the Unit 6 Test.

Day 7

- **Unit 6 Test** (Assessment Program, pp. 97–102) 45 MIN.
  After the Unit 6 Test, reassess student learning. Record strong and weak areas based on the unit test. Review weak areas before the End-of-Book Exam.
- **Homework:** Have students study for the End-of-Book Exam.

Day 8

- **End-of-Book Exam** (Assessment Program, pp. 103–108) 45 MIN.

Name ______________________________ Date ______________________

Venn Diagram

Compare and Contrast

➤ Use a Venn Diagram for listening and speaking, writing, and viewing activities.

1. Write the two things you are comparing on the lines in the two circles.
2. List ways the two things are different under the lines.
3. List ways the two things are alike in the space where the circles overlap.

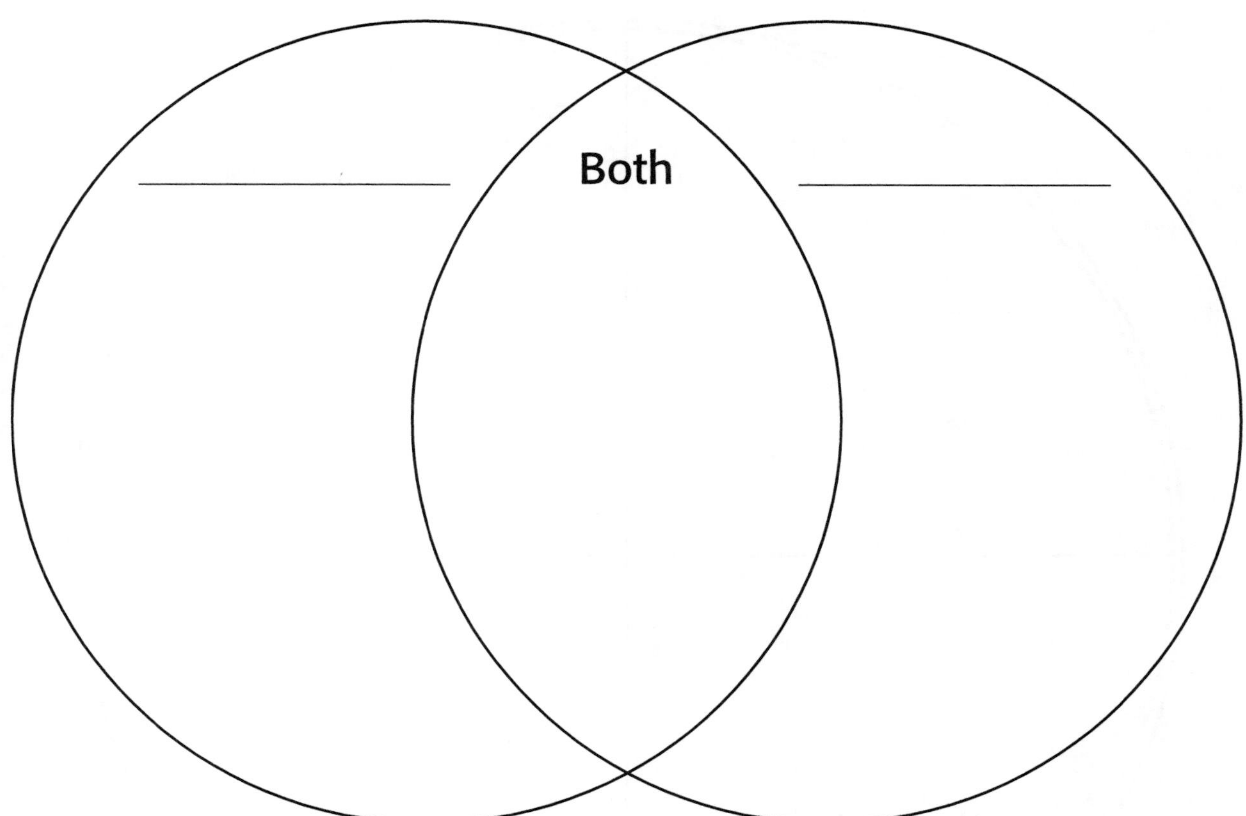

Name ______________________________ Date ______________________

Word or Concept Wheel

➤ Use a Word (Concept) Wheel to help build your vocabulary and better understand word meanings.

1. Write the key word or concept on the line in the wheel.
2. Write the dictionary definition of the key word or concept below the line.
3. Write related words in the other sections.

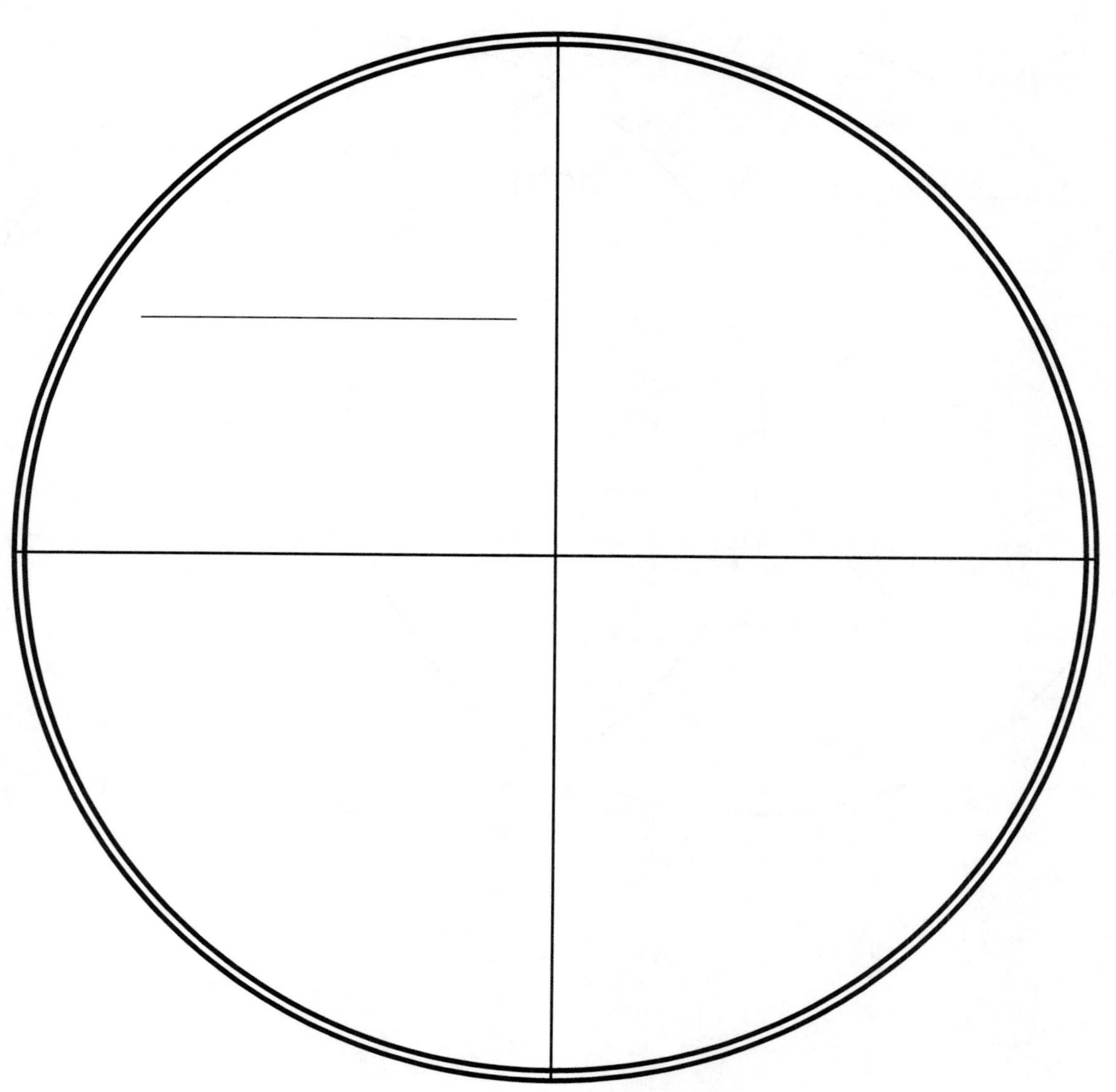

Name ______________________________ Date ____________________

Web

➤ A Web is useful for building vocabulary or for main idea and details.

1. Write the main vocabulary word or main idea in the large oval in the middle.
2. Write related vocabulary words or details in the smaller ovals.
3. Add or delete ovals as needed.

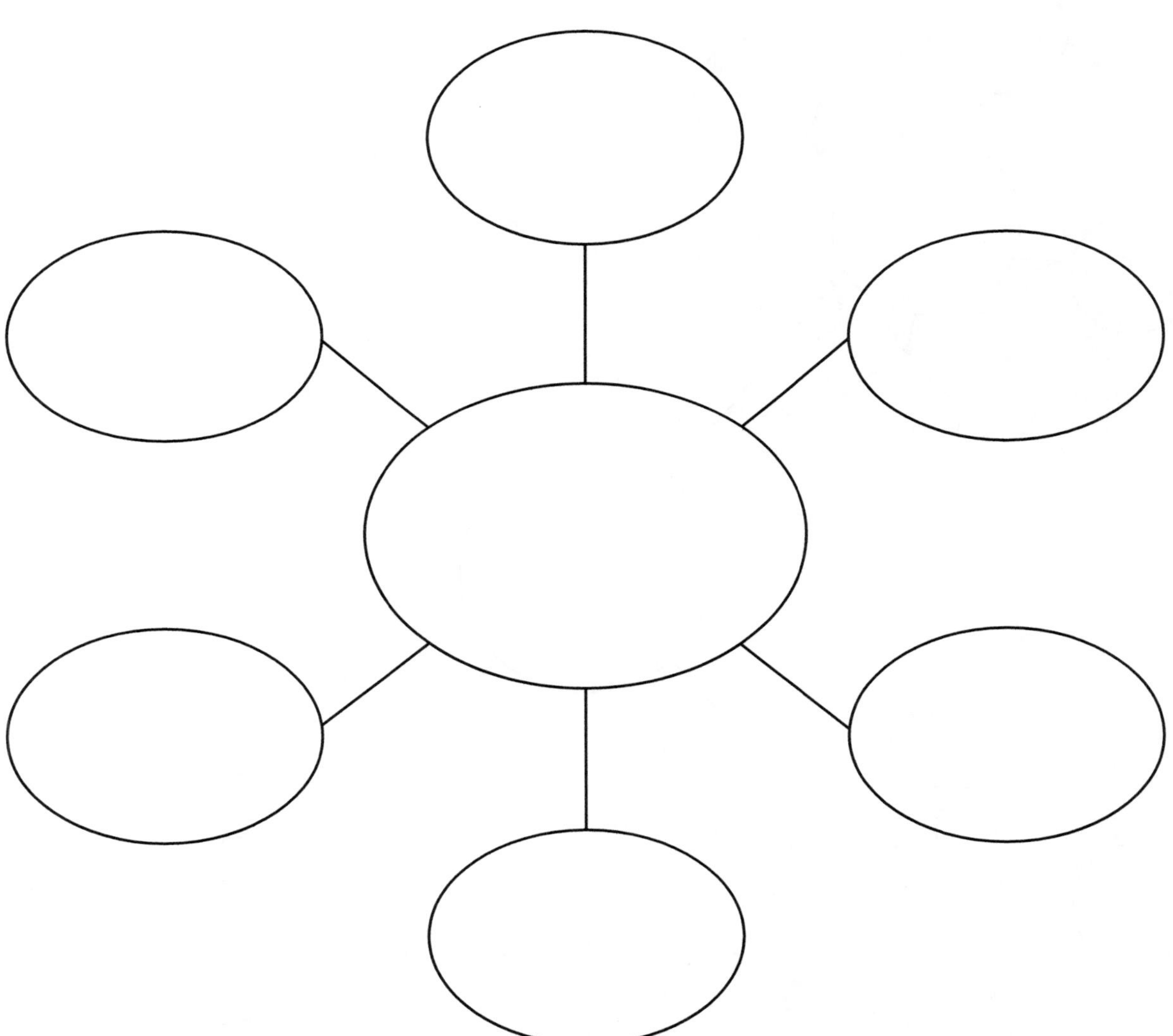

Name ______________________________ Date ______________________

Cluster Map

Compare and Contrast

➤ Use a Cluster Map to help you organize your ideas.

1. Write the topic in the largest circle.
2. Write the main ideas about the topic in the medium circles.
3. Write details about the main ideas in the smallest circles.

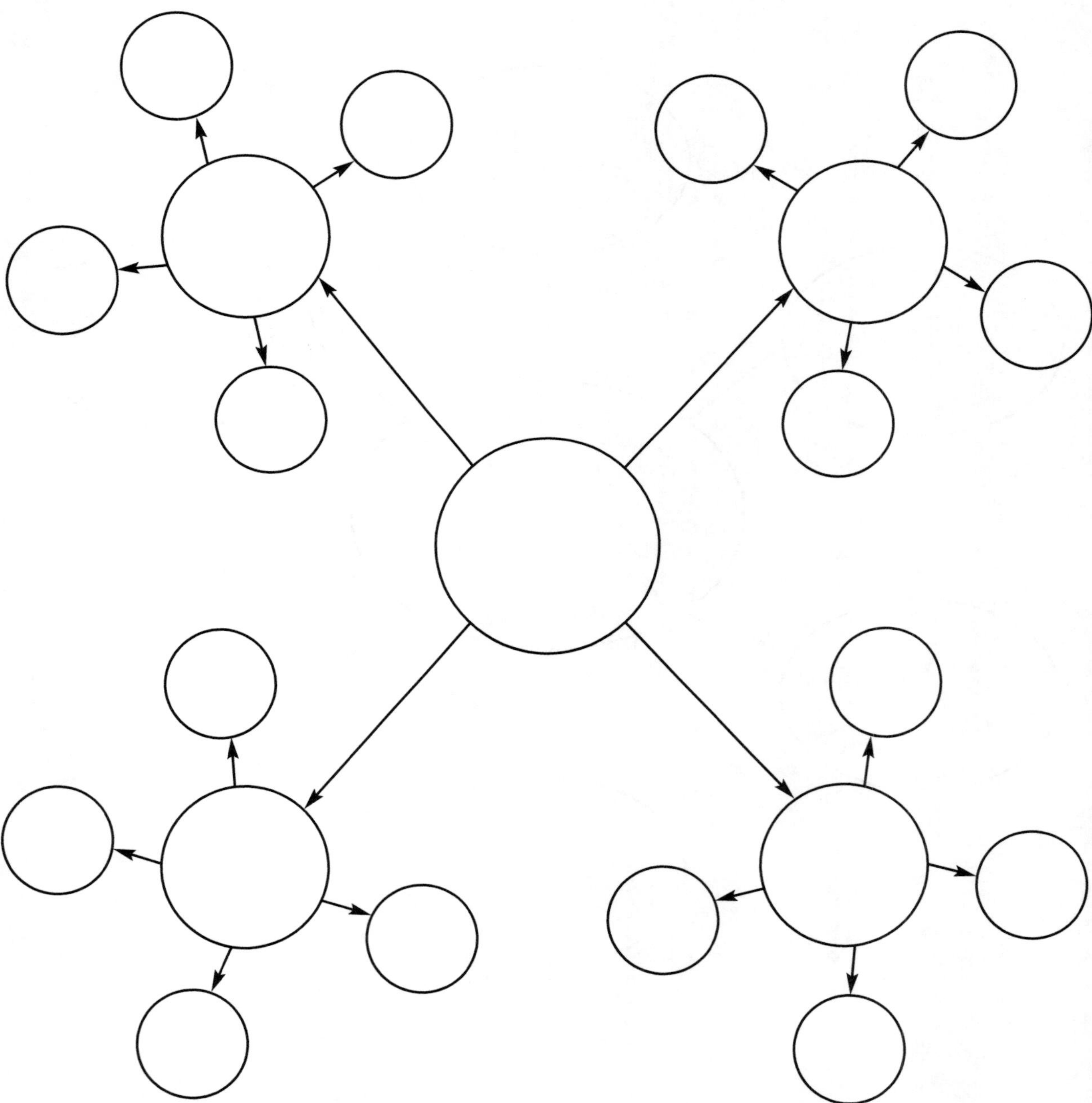

Name ______________________________ Date ____________________

Timelines

➤ Select one of the timelines to show order of events.

1. Write the events in the order they took place.
2. On the left, write the first event and the date.
3. On the right, put the latest event and the date.

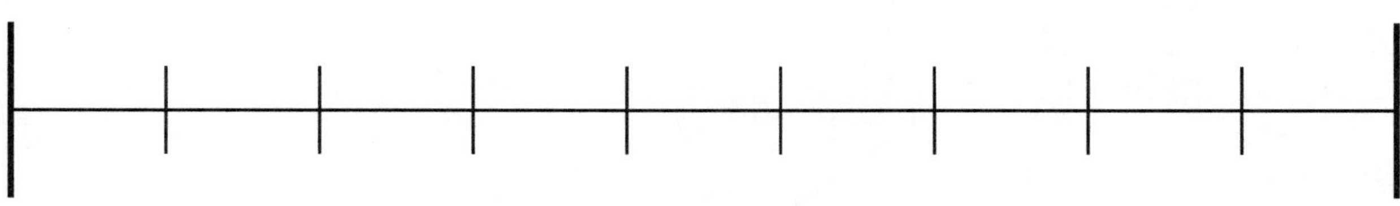

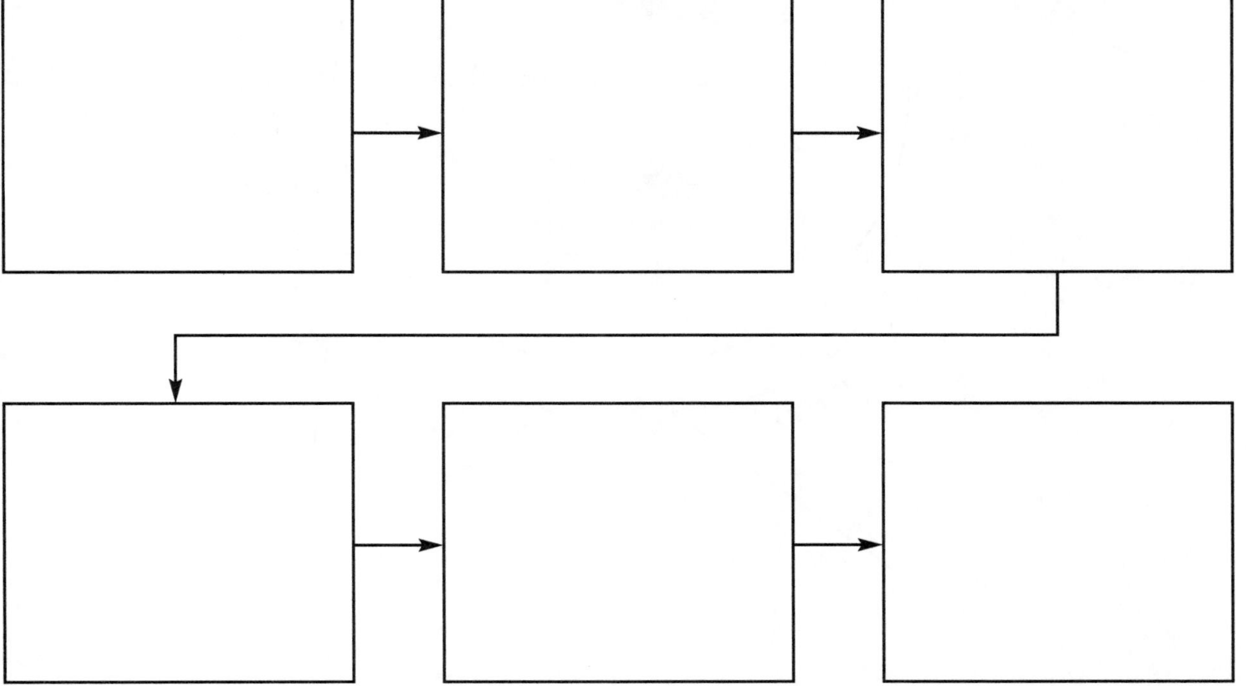

Name ______________________ Date ______________________

Sunshine Organizer

Reporting

➤ Use a Sunshine Organizer to help you answer questions about a story or to write a report.

1. Write the topic in the circle in the middle.
2. Write answers to the *wh-* questions next to the triangles.

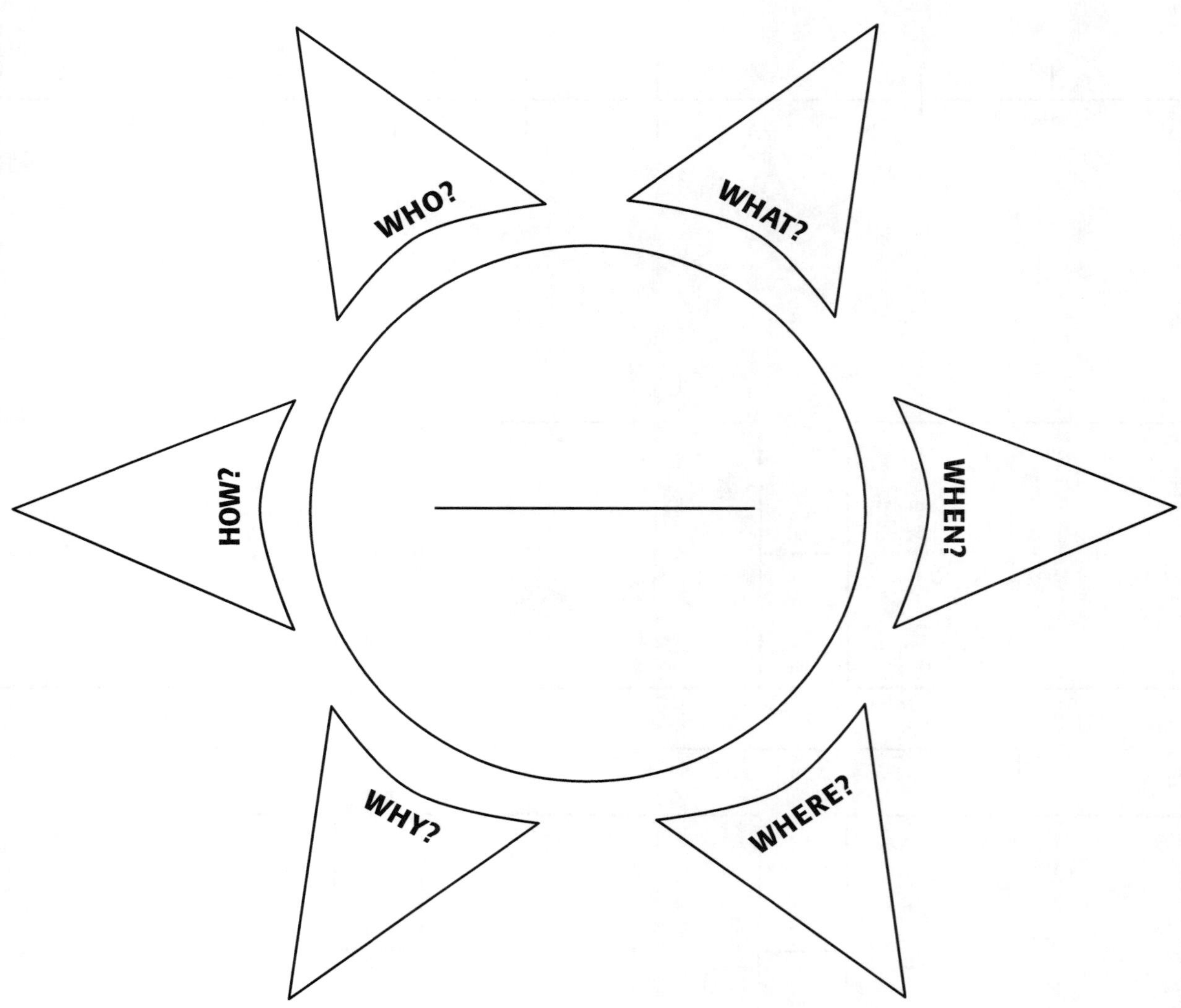

Name ________________________________ Date ______________________

Word Squares

Build Vocabulary

➤ Use Word Squares to help you remember the meanings of new words.

1. Write a new word you do not know in the **Word** box.
2. Use a dictionary or glossary. Write the meaning of the word in the **Meaning** box.
3. Draw a symbol to remember the word in the **Symbol** box.
4. Write a sentence with the word in the **Sentence** box.

Word	**Symbol**	**Word**	**Symbol**
Meaning	**Sentence**	**Meaning**	**Sentence**
Word	**Symbol**	**Word**	**Symbol**
Meaning	**Sentence**	**Meaning**	**Sentence**
Word	**Symbol**	**Word**	**Symbol**
Meaning	**Sentence**	**Meaning**	**Sentence**

Name ______________________ Date ______________________

Know/Want to Know/Learned Chart (KWL)

1. Write the topic in the top box.
2. Write things you **know** in the first column.
3. Write things you **want to know** in the second column.
4. Write things you **learned** in the third column.

Topic:		
Know What do I already know about the topic?	**Want to Know** What do I want to know about the topic?	**Learned** What did I learn about the topic?

Name ______________________ Date ______________________

Storyboard

➤ Use a Storyboard to summarize, outline, and show sequence with pictures and words.

1. Write a sequence of the most important events in a story.
2. Put the events in the order in which they happened.
3. Draw a simple picture above each sentence if you wish.

1. **First,** ______________________ ______________________ ______________________	**2.** **Second,** ______________________ ______________________ ______________________
3. **Third,** ______________________ ______________________ ______________________	**4.** **Fourth,** ______________________ ______________________ ______________________
5. **Fifth,** ______________________ ______________________ ______________________	**6.** **Finally,** ______________________ ______________________ ______________________

Name ______________________ Date ______________________

Two-Column Chart

Taking Notes

➤ Use this chart when you read and take notes on Main Idea/Details, Fact/Opinion, Cause/Effect, Problem/Resolution, Words/Synonyms (or Antonyms), and Advantage/Disadvantages.

1. Write the topic or title in the top box.
2. In the left column, write the first word; for example: Main Idea.
3. In the right column, write the second word; for example: Details.

Name ______________________ Date ______________________

Three-Column Chart

Categorize or Classify

➤ Use this chart for analyzing characters, style, mood and tone, or for vocabulary words and their connotative and denotative meanings.

1. Write the topic or title in the top box.
2. Write the names of the three categories in the next box.
3. List words in the three categories as appropriate.

Name ____________________ Date ____________________

Paragraph

1. Write in a notebook or on the computer.
2. Write a topic sentence, supporting details, and a closing sentence.
3. Use a dictionary or computer software for help with words and spelling.

Title

Indent

____

(Topic Sentence)

____

____

(Details, Supporting Facts, Examples)

____

____

____

____

____

(Closing Sentence: topic sentence with different words)

____

____

Name ______________________________ Date ____________________

Open Mind Diagram

Characterization

➤ Use an Open Mind Diagram to analyze characters. Choose from the **Topics** in the chart and write what the character is thinking.

Topics				
Describe the character's **traits.**	Write what the character is thinking. **(motivation)**	Write about the character's **conflicts.**	Describe a character's **point of view.**	Write about the character's **relationships.**

Name ______________________________ Date ______________________

Narrative

Brainstorming

➤ Use this graphic organizer for listening/speaking presentations and for writing.

Headings	Notes or drawings to help you plan your presentation/writing
Title	
Who? What? When? Where? Why? How?	
First Event	
Complication	
Resolution	
Summary or Conclusion	

Name ______________________ Date ______________________

Narrative

Draft

➤ Use this graphic organizer when you write your first draft. Use transition words.

Title Page

Title

Name

Date

Beginning

Indent **Introduction**

Indent **Body**

Middle

Indent

Indent

End

Indent **Conclusion or Resolution**

VISIONS **TEACHER RESOURCE**

Name ______________________ Date ______________________

Chronological Order

Narrative or Informational Text

➤ Use this graphic organizer when you write in chronological order.

Title

Beginning

Indent | **Setting**
Who? What? When? Where? Why? How?

Indent | **Events in Time Order**
Event 1

Indent | Event 2

Middle

Indent | Event 3

Indent | Event 4

End

Indent | **Conclusion/Ending**

Name ____________________ Date ____________________

Persuasive – Debate and Writing

For and Against

➤ Use this graphic organizer when preparing an oral or a written persuasive presentation.

ARGUMENTS FOR	SUPPORTING EVIDENCE
1.	
2.	
3.	
ARGUMENTS AGAINST	**SUPPORTING EVIDENCE**
1.	
2.	
3.	
CONCLUSION or SUMMARY	

Name ______________________ Date ______________________

Persuasive Essay

Three Paragraphs

➤ Use this graphic organizer for oral presentations or writing assignments.

1. Write in a notebook or on the computer.
2. Write a thesis stating your position.
3. Give reasons with examples and a conclusion.
4. Use words such as *first of all, next,* and *in conclusion.*
5. Use a dictionary or computer software to help with words and spelling.

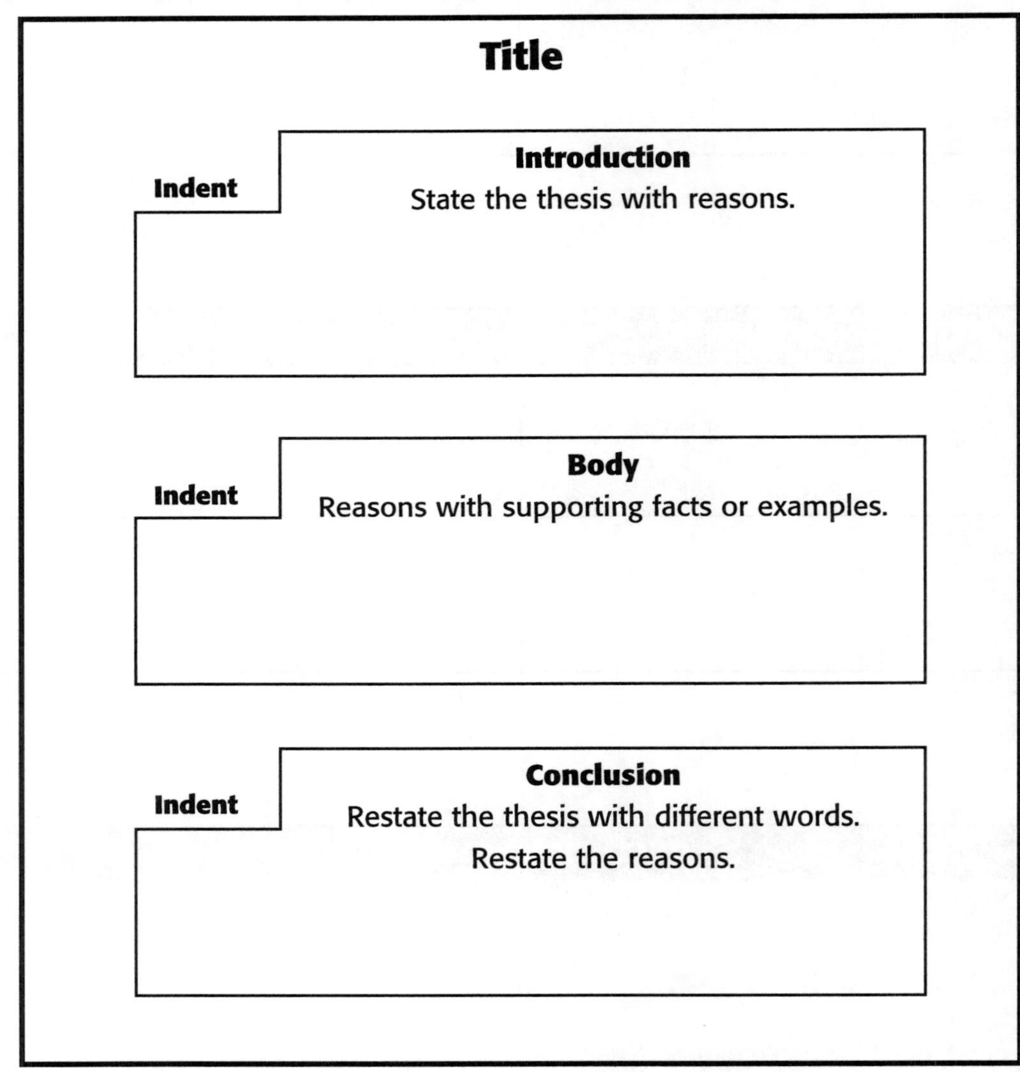

Name ______________________________ Date ____________________

Persuasive Essay

Five Paragraphs

➤ Use this graphic organizer for oral presentations or writing assignments.

1. Write in a notebook or on the computer.
2. Write a thesis stating your position.
3. Give three reasons with examples and a conclusion.
4. Use words such as *first of all, next, finally,* and *in conclusion.*
5. Use a dictionary or computer software to help with words and spelling.

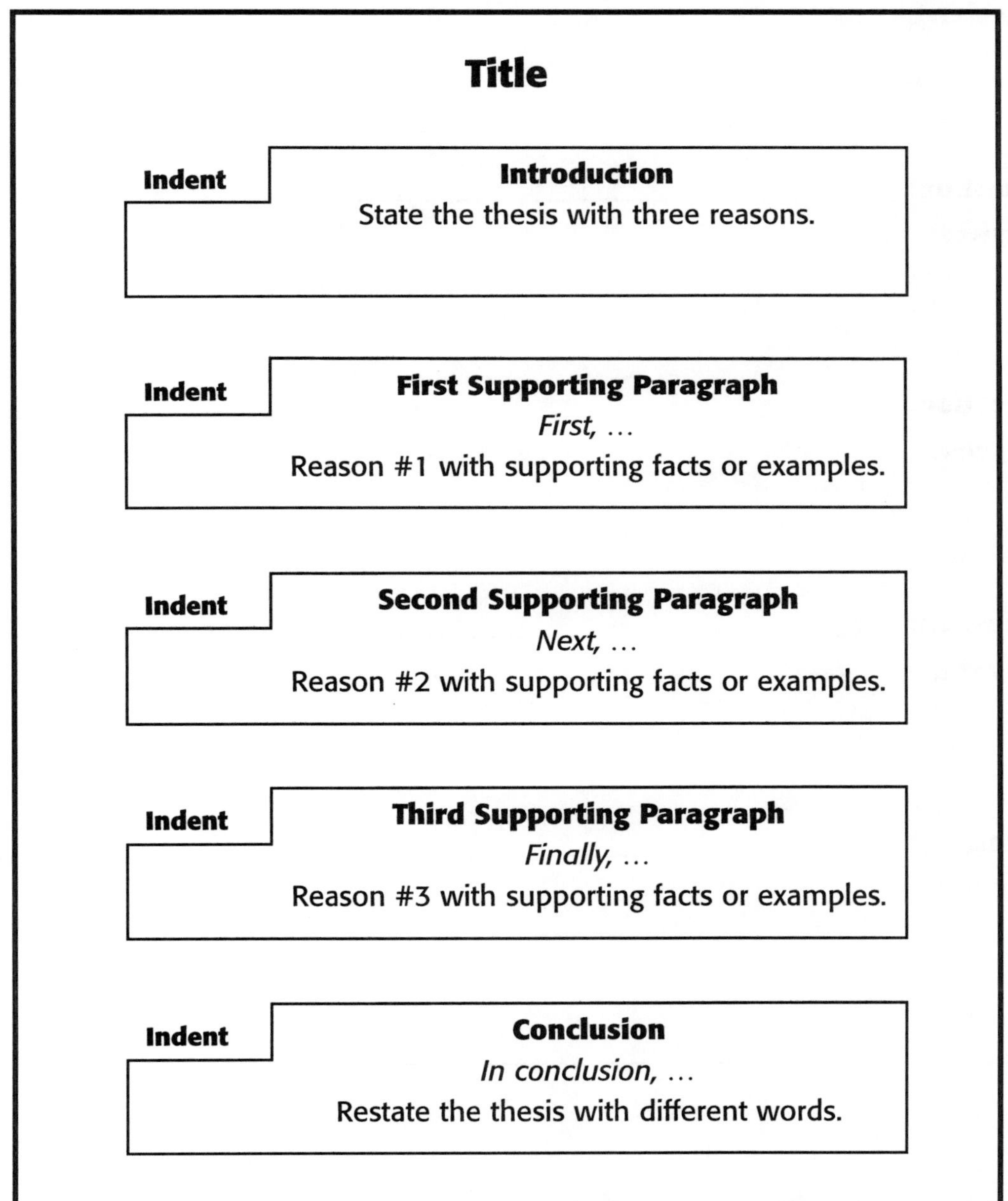

Name ______________________ Date ______________________

Interview

1. Write a list of questions.
2. Record the interviewee's answers.

Interview questions for ______________________
(Name of interviewee)

1. **Question:** ______________________?
   Answer:

2. **Question:** ______________________?
   Answer:

3. **Question:** ______________________?
   Answer:

4. **Question:** ______________________?
   Answer:

5. **Question:** ______________________?
   Answer:

Name ______________________________ Date ______________________

Step-by-Step Instructions

Procedural

➤ Use this graphic organizer for directions, recipes, and games.

1. Write information in each section.
2. Use this during your first draft of oral presentations or writing assignments.

INTRODUCTION Tell about the process. What is to be done?
REQUIREMENTS What is needed to complete the task? (tools, parts, materials, utensils)
INSTRUCTIONS What is to be done? **1.** **2.** **3.** **4.** **5.** **6.** **7.** **8.**
CONCLUSION Summarize the process.

Name ______________________ Date ______________________

Friendly Letter

➤ This format is used for writing a letter to a friend.

1. Write on an 8 1/2 by 11 inch piece of paper or on personal stationery.
2. Write using good penmanship.
3. Proofread your spelling and punctuation.

____
(Date)

Dear ______________ ,

Indent

Describe yourself and where you are.

Indent

Describe your daily life.

Indent

Talk about the person you are writing to.

Yours truly,

(Your name)

VISIONS **TEACHER RESOURCE**

Name ______________________________ Date ______________________

Business Letter/Letter to the Editor

➤ A business letter is different from a friendly letter. It is brief, direct, and limited to one or two points.

1. In the first paragraph, clearly state what you want or why you are writing.
2. Add supporting information in the second paragraph.
3. Write a polite closing.
4. If possible, use a computer for your final draft.
5. Proofread for spelling, grammar, capital letters, and proper business form.

Your Street
City, State/Country
Date

Company Name
Address

Dear ____________ :

Indent

Indent

Explain what you introduced in the first paragraph.

Indent

Closing (Conclusion)

Sincerely,

(signature)

Name ______________________ Date ______________________

Note-Taking

Research Report

1. Use 4 x 6 inch cards.
2. Use a variety of resources: encyclopedias, the Internet, books, magazines, software resources, experts, etc.
3. Think of three or four questions about the topic.
4. Write each question at the top of a different note card.
5. Paraphrase an idea or copy a "quotation" on each card.
6. In the bottom left-hand corner, identify the source and page number.
7. In the upper right-hand corner, write the general heading of the information.

Question: ______________________ **General Heading:** ______________________

(What do you want to know?)

Paraphrase your source.

or

Summarize from your source.

or

"Quote" your source.

Source, page

Name ______________________ Date ______________________

Outline

Informational Texts and Research Papers

1. Sort your note cards before you do your outline.
2. Organize topics and subtopics into logical order.
3. Keep it simple. Write a topic or a thesis—not complete sentences.
4. List major headings after a Roman numeral and a period.
5. List subtopics after a capital letter and a period.
6. List supporting details and examples after a number and a period.

Title

I. Topic 1 or Thesis
    A. Subtopic 1
        1. Detail/Example
        2. Detail/Example

    B. Subtopic 2
        1. Detail/Example
        2. Detail/Example

II. Topics or Thesis
    A. Subtopic 1
        1. Detail/Example
        2. Detail/Example

    B. Subtopic 2
        1. Detail/Example
        2. Detail/Example

III. Conclusion (Restate thesis)

Name ______________________ Date ______________________

Research Report

Final Draft

Title Page

Title **Name** **Date**

Thesis (an opening paragraph) A statement that clearly and briefly says why you chose this topic to research.
Topic (the two to three subtopics you researched) The information should be relevant to the topic.
Subtopic 1 Start a new page.
Subtopic 2 Start a new page.
Conclusion A paragraph that summarizes your report and tells how your research helped you achieve the purpose of your report.

1. **Visuals:** You may want to include pictures, graphs, tables, or photos.
2. **Bibliography:** Check with your teacher for a copy of the correct format required for a bibliography. Also see your Student Handbook.
3. **Format:** If you use a computer, use double space and use 12–14 point font with one inch margins around the paper. If you write by hand, use black or blue pen and cursive writing.
4. **Proofread:** Check for spelling and grammar mistakes. Remember that computer software spell-check only catches words that are spelled incorrectly. It does not catch words that are spelled correctly but used incorrectly.

Name ______________________ Date ______________________

Sense Chart

Description

1. Write the name of the object or thing in the first column.
2. Write down what you see, hear, smell, and touch.

Title:				
Name of Thing	**See**	**Hear**	**Smell**	**Touch**

Name ______________________ Date ______________________

Problem/Resolution Chart

➤ This chart can be used for listening/speaking presentations and for writing assignments.

1. Write a problem. List two possible resolutions and two results of those resolutions. Write an end result.
2. Use a dictionary or computer software for help with words and spelling.

Title:	
State Problem: (Include some of this information: Who? What? When? Where? Why? How?)	
Resolution 1:	**Result 1:**
Resolution 2:	**Result 2:**
End Result:	

Name ______________________ Date ______________________

Personal Dictionary

➤ Use a Personal Dictionary for building your vocabulary.

1. Organize your Personal Dictionary into two sections.
2. One section will have pages for taking notes or for vocabulary activities from the chapter.
3. The other section will have a page for each letter of the alphabet. As you learn new words, write them on the correct pages.

Unit and Chapter ***or*** **Letter of the Alphabet:** ______________________

Name ______________________ Date ______________________

Reading Log

➤ Use a Reading Log for recording information about your reading.

1. Organize your Reading Log by date.
2. Write the date you are making the entry. Then write the title of the reading.

Date: ______________________ **Title:** ______________________

Name ______________________ Date ______________

UNIT 1 • CHAPTER 1

The Race, by Jennifer Trujillo, & **The Camel Dances,** by Arnold Lobel

ENGLISH

In the poem "The Race," a young girl rides a horse named Fina. When she rides, the girl laughs and sings. It is a time when women do not ride horses. The girl's great-grandmother finds out about her riding and plans to stop her. One day, they hear about a horse race. The girl enters the race. She beats all the men and wins the race.

"The Camel Dances" is a fable. It is about a camel that wants to be a ballet dancer. She practices for months. Finally, the Camel dances for friends and critics. One person tells her that she cannot dance. The audience laughs and walks away. The Camel decides to dance only for herself.

SPANISH

En el poema "The Race", una niña monta un caballo llamado Fina. Cuando monta, la niña ríe y canta. El poema está escrito en una época en que las mujeres no montaban a caballo. Al enterarse de que la niña monta a caballo, su tatarabuela trata de hacer que la niña deje de montar. Un día, se enteran de una carrera de caballos. La niña compite en la carrera y les gana a todos los hombres.

"The Camel Dances" es una fábula acerca de un camello que quiere ser bailarina. El camello practíca por meses y finalmente llega a bailar en frente de amigos y críticos. Alguien le dice que ella no sabe bailar. Los espectadores que la ven bailar se ríen de ella y se van. De ahí en adelante, la bailarina decide bailar sólo para sí misma.

HMONG

Hauv zaj lus paivyi "The Race," no yog hais txog ib tug me ntxhais caij ib tug nees hu ua Fina. Thaum tus me ntxhais no caij nws hu nkauj thiab luag ua ke. Nws yog ntu uas tseem tsi tau muaj poj niam caij nees li. Thaum nws pog koob paub tias nws tau caij nees, nws tau npaj cheem tsi pub rau tus me ntxhais ntawd caij ntxiv. Muaj ib hnub lawv nov txog tias yuav muaj caij nees sib xeem. Tus me ntxhais ntawd txawm mus sau npe nrog lawv xeem. Nws txeeb tau cov txiv neej ntej tagnrho thiab tau yeej qhov kev sib xeem ntawd.

"The Camel Dances" yog ib zaj lus uas tsi muaj tseeb tiam si piav li nws tau muaj tiag. Nws hais txog tus ntxhuav xav los ua ib tug seev cev ntawm ntsis taw los sis hu hais tias ballet dancer. Nws xyaum tau ob peb lub hlis lawm. Ces tus Ntxhuav txawm mus seev cev rau nws tej phooj ywg thiab rau lwm cov neeg saib es qhia rau nws saib nws puas ua tau zoo. Muaj ib tug neeg tau hais rau nws hais tias nws tsi txawj seev cev. Tagnrho cov tibneeg saib ntawd lawv txawm luag nws thiab khiav mus tag lawm. Ces tus Ntxhuav txawm txiav txim siab tias cia nws seev cev rau nws saib xwb.

Name ______________________ Date ______________________

VIETNAMESE

Trong bài thơ “The Race”, một cô bé cưỡi một con ngựa tên Fina. Khi cưỡi ngựa, cô bé cười vui và ca hát. Vào thời điểm này phụ nữ thường không được cưỡi ngựa. Bà cố của cô bé khám phá ra rằng cô cưỡi ngựa và bà dự định ngăn cản. Một ngày nọ, hai bà cháu nghe nói về một cuộc đua ngựa. Cô bé ghi danh tranh tài. Cô bé qua mặt tất cả những người đàn ông và thắng cuộc.

“The Camel Dances” là một truyện ngụ ngôn. Câu chuyện nói về một chị lạc đà muốn trở thành diễn viên múa balê. Chị luyện tập trong mấy tháng trời và cuối cùng cũng biểu diễn múa cho bạn bè và những nhà phê bình văn nghệ xem. Có một người nói với chị là chị không biết múa. Khán giả cười rộ rồi quay lưng đi. Thế là Chị Lạc Đà quyết định chỉ múa cho riêng mình mà thôi.

CHINESE

The Race 這首詩是講一個小女孩，她有一匹馬叫做菲納，她騎著菲納時，就會一邊唱一邊笑。在當時，女子是不騎馬的，所以她的太婆發現她騎馬後，便設法阻止。有一日，他們聽說有場賽馬會，那女孩便報名參加。結果她擊敗所有參賽的男子，並且贏得冠軍。

The Camel Dances 是個寓言，講的是一隻想成為芭蕾舞蹈家的駱駝。它練習了好幾個月，終於有一日可以表演給朋友和批評家看，但是其中有個人對駱駝講它不能跳舞，於是觀眾哄堂大笑後離開。駱駝便決定從此只為自己跳舞了。

CAMBODIAN

នៅក្នុងកំណាព្យ “The Race,” ក្មេងស្រីម្នាក់ជិះសេះឈ្មោះ ហ្វីណា។ ពេលនាងជិះ នាងសើចនិងច្រៀង។ វាជាជំនាន់ដែលស្ត្រីមិនជិះសេះទេ។ ជីដូនរបស់ក្មេងស្រីនោះ ដឹងអំពីរឿងដែលនាងជិះសេះ ហើយគំរោងនឹងបញ្ឈប់នាង។ ថ្ងៃមួយ គេឮអំពីការប្រណាំងសេះមួយ។ នាងចូលក្នុងការប្រណាំង។ នាងប្រណាំងឈ្នះប្រុសៗទាំងអស់ ហើយទទួលជោគជ័យក្នុងការប្រណាំង។

“The Camel Dances” ជារឿងល្បើក។ វាជារឿងនៃសត្វអូដ្ឋមួយ ដែលចង់ក្លាយជាអ្នករបាំបាឡេ។ សត្វអូដ្ឋហាត់ ហ្វឹកហ្វឺនរាប់ខែ។ ទីបំផុត សត្វអូដ្ឋរាំឲ្យមិត្តភក្តិនិងអ្នកវិនិច្ឆ័យមើល។ មនុស្សម្នាក់ប្រាប់វាថា វាមិនអាចរាំបានទេ។ ទស្សនិកជនសើច ហើយដើរចេញ។ សត្វអូដ្ឋសំរេចចិត្តថា រាំសំរាប់តែខ្លួនឯង។

HAITIAN CREOLE

Nan powèm “The Race” lan, yon jèn tifi monte yon cheval yo rele Fina. Pandan li monte cheval lan, tifi an ap ri epi l ap chante. Se yon epòk kote fi pa monte cheval. Gran grann tifi an vin aprann l ap monte cheval epi li gen entansyon pou li fè l sispann fè sa. Yon jou, yo tande nouvèl gen yon kous cheval ki pral fèt. Tifi an rantre nan kous lan. Li bat tout gason yo epi li genyen kous lan.

“The Camel Dances” se yon fab. Se istwa yon chamo ki vle vin tounen yon dansè balè. Li egzèse pou dè mwa. Finalman, Chamo an danse pou zanmi l yo ak kritik yo. Yon moun di l li pakab danse. Oditè yo ri epi vire do yo ale. Chamo an deside pou l danse pou tèt li sèlman.

Name ______________________________ Date ______________________

UNIT 1 • CHAPTER 2

Hatchet, by Gary Paulsen

ENGLISH

In this novel, 13-year-old Brian is on an airplane to visit his father. The pilot becomes ill. So Brian lands the plane. Now, he is alone in the woods. He must start a fire. Brian can make sparks, but the sparks will not turn into fire. First he uses his hatchet and a stone to make sparks in grass and twigs. Nothing happens. Brian finds bark from a tree and tries to light it. It does not catch fire. Brian spends two hours cutting the bark into thin pieces. Again he tries to light the bark, but it still will not catch fire. Then, Brian remembers that fire needs oxygen. So he gently blows on the glowing bark. The bark bursts into flames.

SPANISH

En esta novela, un niño de 13 años llamado Brian vuela en avión a visitar a su padre. El piloto del avión se enferma y Brian tiene que hacer aterrizar el avión. Al aterrizar, se encuentra solo en un bosque y trata de encender una hoguera. Aunque Brian puede sacar chispas, las chispas no se convierten en fuego. Al principio, Brian usa un hacha y una piedra para sacar chispas con pasto y ramitas, pero no ocurre nada. Luego, Brian trata de encender pedacitos de ramas de un árbol, pero no se encienden. Brian pasa dos horas cortando las ramitas en pedacitos. Vuelve a tratar de encender los pedacitos de madera, pero no se encienden. Entonces, Brian recuerda que para hacer fuego se necesita oxígeno, y decide soplar suavemente las ramitas que están a punto de prender y así finalmente encienden.

HMONG

Nyob rau hauv zaj lus no, Brian uas yog muaj 13 xyoos tab tom caij nyoob hoom mus xyuas nws txiv. Thaum nkawv tseem ya saum ntsuab ntug, tus tsav txawm cia li mob lawm. Ces Brian los muab lub nyoob hoom tsav los tsaws. Tam sim no tshuav nws ib leeg nyob tom hav zoo lawm xwb. Nws yuav tsum rauv kom tau hluav taws cig. Brian ua tau rau kom tawg cig pes plaws tiam si nws ua tsi tau kom hluav taws cig li. Thaum nws pib ua ces yog nws siv nws tsab tau thiab ib lub pob zeb sib txhuam rau cov nyom thiab tej ntsis khaub. Tiam si nws tsi ua li cas li. Brian nrhiav tau ib daim tawv ntoo ces nws txawm sim kis saib puas cig. Tiam sis nws tsi txais hluav taws li. Brian siv ob xoob moos los phua daim tawv ntoo kom nws ua tej tug me me. Nws rov qab muab sim kis rau tiam sis nws kuj tsi txais hluav taws li thiab. Brian txawm nco dheev txog tias yuav tsum muaj cua hluav taws thiaj cig taus. Ces nws mam li mab mam tshuab rau qhov liab pliv hauv daim tawv ntoo. Daim tawv ntoo txawm cig plaws ua nplaim taws.

VISIONS **READING SUMMARIES Unit 1**

Name ______________________ Date ______________________

VIETNAMESE

Trong cuốn tiểu thuyết này, cậu bé Brian 13 tuổi đi máy bay tới thăm cha mình. Người phi công tự nhiên mắc bệnh, vì thế Brian phải hạ cánh máy bay. Giờ đây, cậu ta ở một mình trong rừng. Cậu cần phải nhóm lửa. Brian có thể tạo ra những tia lửa, nhưng không thể làm cho tia lửa bùng cháy lên được. Trước tiên cậu dùng chiếc rìu nhỏ của mình và một hòn đá để đánh lửa đốt cỏ và các nhánh cây con. Lửa không lên. Brian tìm một miếng vỏ cây rồi cố gắng đốt lửa. Lửa không bắt. Brian bỏ ra cả hai tiếng đồng hồ để cắt vỏ cây thành nhiều dải mỏng. Một lần nữa cậu cố đốt lửa vỏ cây, nhưng vỏ cây vẫn không bắt lửa. Lúc đó, Brian mới nhớ ra là lửa cần có oxy. Thế là cậu thổi nhẹ vào vỏ cây đang cháy âm ỉ. Vỏ cây bùng lên thành ngọn lửa lớn.

CHINESE

這部小說講一個名叫伯萊恩的十三歲男孩，他坐飛機去探望他的父親。機上的飛機師忽然生病，於是伯萊恩將飛機降落。這時他獨自在樹林，所以必須生火。伯萊恩可以擦出火花，但火花不會變成火，於是他先用一塊石頭和他的短柄斧，在草和樹枝中生出火花。但是，火仍未點着。伯萊恩從樹上找來樹皮，想將樹皮點着，但卻點不着。伯萊恩費了兩小時將樹皮切成薄片，再嘗試將樹皮點着，仍然點不着。他想起火需要氧氣，於是便輕輕地往樹皮上吹氣，火焰就立即從樹皮中冒出來。

CAMBODIAN

នៅក្នុងរឿងប្រលោមលោកនេះ ប្រាយ៉ែន អាយុ ១៣ ឆ្នាំ ជិះយន្តហោះទៅលេងឪពុករបស់វា។ អ្នកបើកយន្តហោះចាប់ផ្ដើមឈឺ។ ដូច្នេះ ប្រាយ៉ែនបើកយន្តហោះចុះចត។ ឥឡូវនេះ វានៅក្នុងព្រៃឈើម្នាក់ឯង។ វាត្រូវបង្កាត់ភ្លើង។ ប្រាយ៉ែនអាចធ្វើឲ្យមានផ្កាភ្លើង តែផ្កាភ្លើងមិនក្លាយទៅជាភ្លើងសោះ។ ដំបូង វាប្រើពូថៅដែររបស់វាហើយនិងថ្មមួយដុំ ដើម្បីធ្វើឲ្យមានផ្កាភ្លើងនៅក្នុងស្មៅនិងមែកឈើតូចៗ។ គ្មានអ្វីកើតឡើងសោះ។ ប្រាយ៉ែនរកសំបកឈើ ហើយសាកល្បងបង្កាត់វា។ វាមិនឆេះសោះ។ ប្រាយ៉ែនចំណាយពេលពីរម៉ោង កាត់សំបកឈើឲ្យទៅជាបន្ទះស្ដើងៗ។ វាសាកល្បងបង្កាត់សំបកឈើម្ដងទៀត តែវានៅតែមិនឆេះដដែល។ បន្ទាប់មក ប្រាយ៉ែននឹកឃើញថាភ្លើងត្រូវការខ្យល់។ ដូច្នេះវាផ្លុំថ្នមៗទៅលើសំបកឈើដែលមានរងើកក្រហម។ សំបកឈើបញ្ចេញអណ្ដាតភ្លើងឡើង។

HAITIAN CREOLE

Nan woman sa a, Brian ki gen 13 an monte nan yon avyon pou l ale vizite papa l. Pilòt avyon an vin tonbe malad. Kidonk se Brian ki ateri avyon an. Kounye a, li poukont li nan rak bwa yo. Fòk li limen yon dife. Brian ka fè kèk ti entensèl, men entesèl yo paka fè dife an pran. Dabò li itilize ti rach li an ak yon wòch pou l fè kèk entesèl nan zèb lan ak kèk ti moso bwa sèk. Anyen pa rive. Brian jwenn moso ekòs yon pye bwa epi li limen l. Li pa pran dife. Brian pase de zè ap koupe moso ekòs lan an ti moso fen. Li eseye limen moso ekòs lan ankò, men li toujou pa pran dife. Epi, Brian vin sonje pou yon dife ka pran li bezwen oksijèn. Kidonk li soufle dousman sou moso ekòs lan ki briye. Moso ekòs lan fè yon gwo flanm dife.

Name ______________________ Date ______________

UNIT 1 • CHAPTER 3

Antarctic Adventure, by Meredith Hooper

ENGLISH

This historical narrative is about Ernest Shackleton and a group of men. In 1914, they were exploring Antarctica in a ship called the *Endurance.* The ship gets stuck in ice for 278 days. Water begins to flood the ship. This forces the men to camp on the ice. The men try to walk 312 miles to land. After three days, they travel only two miles. Shackleton thinks the ice might carry them to land. Five months later, the men are still on the ice. When the ice starts to break, they sail in lifeboats to an island. Then Shackleton and five men sail across the water to get help. It takes three months, but Shackleton comes back and rescues everyone.

SPANISH

Esta narrativa histórica es acerca de Ernest Shackleton y un grupo de hombres, que en el año 1914 exploraron la Antártica en un barco llamado *Endurance.* Durante el viaje, el barco queda encallado por 278 días y empieza a inundarse. Eso obliga a los hombres a acampar en el hielo. Los náufragos tratan de caminar las 312 millas a tierra firme, pero en tres días sólo avanzan dos millas. Shackleton piensa que el hielo mismo podría llevarles a tierra firme, pero después de cinco meses, aún están sobre el hielo. Cuando comienza el deshielo, ellos se embarcan en botes salvavidas y bogan hasta una isla. Luego Shackleton y cinco de los tripulantes viajan a buscar ayuda. La travesía les toma tres meses, pero Shackleton regresa y rescata al resto de la tripulación.

HMONG

Zaj lus cimmeej tsab los yog dab neeg no yog hais txog Ernest Shackleton thiab ib pab txiv neej. Nyob rau xyoo 1914, lawv tau caij ib lub nkoj hu ua Endurance mus nrhiav saib Antarctica puas muaj abtsi. Lawv lub nkoj txawm mus daig dej nab kuab tau 278 hnub nkaus. Dej txawm pib phwj los rau hauv lub nkoj zuj zug. Thaum zoo li no lawm ces cov txiv neej thiaj yuav tsum tau kho chaw so rau saum cov dej nab kuab. Cov txiv neej ntawm tau mus ko taw li 312 mais mam li mus txog rau cov av. Tau peb hnub tom qab, lawv nim qhuav mus tau kev deb li ob mile xwb. Shackleton tau xav hais tias tej zaum cov dej nab kuab ntawd yuav thauj tau lawv mus txog rau cov av. Twb tau ntev li tsib lub hlis lawm los cov txiv neej ntawd lawv tseem nyob lawv saum cov nab kuab li. Ces cov nab kuaj txawm pib tawg nyias mus nyias, lawv mam li caij ib lub nkoj me uas yog lawv coj pab cawm rau thaum tsi muaj lwm txoj kev lawm mus rau ib thaj me nyuam ab hauv plaws dej. Thaum lawv mus txog ntawm cov av ntawd lawm, Shackleton thiab tsib tug txiv neej mam li caij lub nkoj me ntawd mus nrhiav neeg pab lawv. Nws siv ntev li peb lub hlis tiam sis Shackleton tau rov qab mus pab cawm tau lawv txhua txhia tus tagnrho huv tibsi lawm thiab.

Name ______________________ Date ______________________

VIETNAMESE

Chuyện kể mang tính chất lịch sử này nói về Ernest Shackleton và một nhóm chàng trai. Vào năm 1914, họ đến thám hiểm vùng Nam Cực trên một chiếc thuyền có tên *Endurance* (Nhẫn Nại). Chiếc thuyền mắc kẹt trong băng đá trong vòng 278 ngày. Nước bắt đầu chảy tràn vào chiếc thuyền, khiến cho họ phải cắm trại trên băng đá. Các chàng trai này cố gắng đi bộ 312 dặm đến đất liền. Sau ba ngày, họ chỉ đi được hai dặm đường. Shackleton nghĩ rằng băng đá có thể chở họ đến đất liền. Năm tháng sau, họ vẫn còn ở trên băng đá. Khi băng đá bắt đầu vỡ, họ chèo thuyền cứu đắm đến một hòn đảo. Sau đó Shackleton và năm chàng trai chèo thuyền xuyên qua đại dương để nhờ giúp đỡ. Phải đến ba tháng mới xong việc, nhưng cuối cùng Shackleton cũng quay trở lại và cứu được mọi người.

CHINESE

這段歷史是關於安尼士•石寇頓和一群男士，他們坐一艘名叫 *Endurance* 的船到南極探險，船陷在冰中 278 日。水開始浸船，這些人逼不得已，只好在冰上露營。他們想步行到陸地，但需要步行 312 英哩。他們行走了三日，才走了兩英哩。石寇頓猜想那些冰或者會把他們帶到陸地，但過了五個月，他們還是在冰上。後來，冰開始破裂，他們就坐救生船到一個海島。石寇頓和五個人再坐船出去求救，費時三個月，但石寇頓還是回去將所有的人救出。

CAMBODIAN

ការអធិប្បាយប្រវត្តិសាស្ត្រនេះ អំពី អើនែស ហ្សាកល់ថុន និង ប្រុសៗមួយក្រុម។ នៅឆ្នាំ ១៩១៤ ពួកគេបានទៅរុករកទ្វីប អង់តាក់តិកា ដោយជិះសំពៅមួយឈ្មោះ អែនឌួរែន្ស។ សំពៅជាប់នៅលើទឹកកកអស់ ២៧៨ ថ្ងៃ។ ទឹកក៏ចាប់ផ្តើមជន់ចូលក្នុងសំពៅ។ បញ្ហានេះជំរុញឲ្យប្រុសទាំងនោះបោះជំរុំនៅលើទឹកកក។ ប្រុសៗទាំងនោះសាកដើរ ៣២១ ម៉ាយ ទៅរកដីគោក។ បីថ្ងៃក្រោយមក ពួកគេដើរបានចម្ងាយតែពីរម៉ាយតែប៉ុណ្ណោះ។ ហ្សាកល់ថុន គិតថា ទឹកកកអាចនាំពួកគេឲ្យទៅដល់ដីគោក។ ប្រាំខែក្រោយមក ពួកគេនៅតែនៅលើទឹកកកដដែល។ ពេលដែលទឹកកកចាប់ផ្តើមបែកចេញពីគ្នា ពួកគេជិះទូកសំរាប់សង្គ្រោះជីវិតទៅកាន់កោះមួយ។ បន្ទាប់មក ហ្សាកល់ថុន និង បុរសប្រាំនាក់ទៀត ជិះទូកកាត់ទឹកទៅរកជំនួយ។ ចំណាយពេលអស់បីខែ តែ ហ្សាកល់ថុន វិលត្រឡប់មកវិញ ហើយសង្គ្រោះអ្នកទាំងអស់បាន។

HAITIAN CREOLE

Narasyon istorik sa a pale konsènan Ernest Shackleton ak yon gwoup mesye. An 1914, yo t ap eksplore Antatik lan nan yon bato yo te rele Endurance. Bato an kole nan glas pandan 278 jou. Dlo kòmanse ap rantre nan bato an. Sa vin oblije fè mesye yo al fè kanpin sou glas lan. Mesye yo eseye mache yon distans 312 mil pou rive jwen tè fèm. Aprè twa jou, se sèlman sou yon distans de (2) mil yo vwayaje. Shackleton panse glas lan ka mennen yo rive sou tè fèm. Senk mwa pase, mesye yo toujou sou glas lan. Lè glas lan kòmanse kase, yo monte sou yon ti bato sovtaj pou ale sou yon zile. Aprè sa Shackleton ak senk mesye yo fè vwal sou dlo an pou ale chèche èd. Sa te pran yo twa mwa, men Shackleton retounen epi li sove tout moun.

Name ______________________ Date ______________________

UNIT 1 • CHAPTER 4

Yang the Youngest, by Lensey Namioka

ENGLISH

In this novel, Yang and his family have moved from China to the United States. Yang is having a hard time making friends because he does not speak English very well. He also thinks American kids are rough and loud. They scare him. Sometimes, the kids laugh at Yang because he acts differently. He is very lonely. As time passes, Yang learns to act more like the other kids. His parents tell him that he is becoming loud like an American kid. Finally, Yang meets a boy named Matthew. Now that Yang has a friend, he is not so lonely.

SPANISH

En esta novela, Yang y su familia han emigrado de la China a los Estados Unidos. A Yang se le hace difícil hacer amigos, porque no habla bien el inglés. También piensa que los niños de este país son ruidosos y poco corteses. En verdad, les teme. A veces, los niños se ríen de Yang, porque él es diferente de ellos. Yang se siente muy solo, pero con el tiempo, Yang aprende a ser más como los otros niños. Ahora sus padres le dicen que se está volviendo ruidoso, como los niños con que juega. Entonces, Yang conoce a un niño llamado Matthew. Ahora que Yang tiene un amigo, ya no se siente tan solo.

HMONG

Nyob hauv zaj lus no, Yang thiab nws tsev neeg tau khiav teb chaws Suav tuaj rau teb chaws United States. Yang ntau phooj ywg nyuaj heev vim hais tias nws hais tsi tau lus Askiv zoo. Thiab nws kuj xav hais tias cov menyuam Asmesliskas yog ib co neeg nyiam ua si sib zog tsi ntshai ua rau tej phooj ywg raug mob thiab hais lus los kuj nrov heev. Lawv tau ua rau nws ntshai. Tej lub sibhawm cov menyuam ntawd kuj luag Yang thiab vim nws tus yam ntxwv txawv lawv. Nws tsi muaj phooj ywg li ces kho siab heev. Ntev tom qab no, Yang mam xyaum coj tus yam ntxwv zoo li lwm cov menyuam zuj zug. Nws niam thiab nws txiv hais rau nws tias nws hais lus nrov zuj zug li ib tug menyuam Asmesliskas lawm. Thaum kawg, Yang kuj tau ntsib ib tug menyuam tub hu ua Matthew no. Tam sim no Yang muaj ib tug phooj ywg lawm, nws yuav tsi nyob kho siab khuav ib leeg lawm.

Name ______________________________ Date ____________________

VIETNAMESE

Trong cuốn tiểu thuyết này, Yang và gia đình rời Trung Quốc đến định cư ở Hoa Kỳ. Yang khó kết bạn vì cậu ta không biết nói tiếng Anh giỏi. Cậu nghĩ rằng những đứa trẻ người Mỹ thô lỗ và ầm ĩ quá. Chúng nó làm cho cậu sợ. Đôi khi, bọn trẻ cười trêu Yang bởi vì cậu xử sự khác với chúng. Cậu bé rất cô đơn. Thời gian trôi qua, Yang học hỏi cách xử sự cho giống hơn với các đứa trẻ khác. Ba mẹ Yang nói với cậu là cậu cũng trở nên ầm ĩ giống một đứa trẻ Mỹ. Cuối cùng, Yang gặp một cậu bé có tên Matthew. Giờ đây Yang có một người bạn, và cậu không cô đơn như trước nữa.

CHINESE

這部小説是講楊兒和他的家人從中國搬到美國後的經歷。由於楊兒英文講得不好，很難交到朋友。同時他亦認爲美國孩子既粗魯又大聲，所以怕了他們。有時候，這些孩子還取笑楊兒，因爲楊兒的作風和他們不同，楊兒因此感到很寂寞。時間慢慢過去，楊兒學會了比較類似其他孩子的動作。他的父母告訴他，他越來越似美國孩子那樣吵鬧。楊兒後來認識了一個叫做馬蕭的男孩，所以楊兒現在有個朋友，不再那麼寂寞了。

CAMBODIAN

នៅក្នុងប្រលោមលោកនេះ យ៉ែង និង គ្រួសារវាបានផ្លាស់ពីប្រទេសចិនទៅនៅប្រទេសអាមេរិក។ យ៉ែង មានការលំបាកក្នុងការរកមិត្ត ពីព្រោះវានិយាយភាសាអង់គ្លេសមិនបានល្អ។ វាគិតថា ក្មេងអាមេរិករឹងរូស និង ឡូឡា។ គេធ្វើឲ្យវាខ្លាច។ ពេលខ្លះ ក្មេងៗសើចចំអកឲ្យយ៉ែង ពីព្រោះវាមានកាយវិកាខុសគេ។ វាកំសត់តែម្នាក់ឯង។ ពេលវេលាចេះតែកន្លងទៅ យ៉ែងរៀនសំដែងកាយវិកាឲ្យដូចក្មេងឯទៀត។ ឪពុកម្ដាយវាប្រាប់វាថា វាចាប់ផ្ដើមឡូឡាដូចក្មេងអាមេរិកដែរ។ ទីបំផុត យ៉ែង ជួបក្មេងប្រុសមួយឈ្មោះ ម៉ែតធ្យូ។ ឥឡូវ យ៉ែង នោះមានមិត្តម្នាក់ហើយ វាមិនកំសត់ម្នាក់ឯងទេ។

HAITIAN CREOLE

Nan woman sa a, Yang ak fanmi li kite Lachin pou vin abite Ozetazini. Yang gen pwoblèm pou l fè zanmi paske li pa pale anglè twò byen. Epitou li panse ti ameriken yo yon jan di epi yo renmen fè bri. Yo fè l pè. Kèkfwa, timoun yo pase Yang nan rizib paske li konpòte l yon jan diferan. Li santi l trè izole. Amezi tan ap pase, Yang vin aprann kòman pou l konpòte l tankou lòt timoun yo. Paran l di l li kòmanse ap fè bri menm jan ak yon ti ameriken. Finalman, Yang rankontre ak yon tigason yo rele Matthew. Kounye a Yang gen yon zanmi, li pa santi l izole ankò.

Name ______________________ Date ______________________

UNIT 1 • CHAPTER 5

The Scholarship Jacket, by Marta Salinas

ENGLISH

In this short story, Martha attends a school that gives a jacket to the best student. Martha expects to win the jacket because she has the best grades in her class. A teacher thinks that another girl, Joann, should receive the jacket. Joann's father is an important person. In a meeting, the principal tells Martha that the rules have changed. She has to pay for the jacket. Martha asks her grandfather for the money. He will not give it to her. He says if she pays for the jacket, the award will not be an award. She will be buying it. Martha tells the principal she will not pay for the jacket. The principal changes his mind and gives Martha the jacket. Martha is so happy. She runs home to tell her grandfather the good news.

SPANISH

En esta historieta, Martha va a una escuela que premia al mejor estudiante con una chamarra. Ella espera ganar el premio, porque tiene las mejores calificaciones de su clase, pero un profesor cree que una estudiante llamada Joann debería recibirla. El papá de Joann es una persona importante. En una reunión, el director de la escuela le dice a Martha que las reglas han cambiado y que tiene que pagar por la chamarra. Martha le pide a su abuelo el dinero para pagarla, pero él no se lo da, diciendo que la chamarra deja de ser premio si se tiene que pagar por ella. Martha le dice al director de la escuela que no pagará por la chamarra. El director cambia de parecer y le da la chamarra a Martha. Ella se pone muy contenta y corre a casa a darle las buenas noticias al abuelo.

HMONG

Nyob rau hauv zaj cim meej tsab los sis dab neeg no, Martha mus kawm ntawv nyob hauv ib lub tsev kawm ntawv uas yuav muab ib tsho tiv no rau tub me nyuam kawm ntawv zoo tshaj plaws tag nrho sawv daws huv tib si. Martha tau npaj tias nws yuav tsum yeej lub tsho tiv no ntawd los ua nws li xwb vim tias nyob hauv nws hoob nws yog tus tau cov qhab nia zoo tshaj sawv daws. Muaj ib tug xib hwb qhia ntawv xav hais tias tus me nyuam ntxhais ua yog Joann yuav tsum yog tus uas yeej lub tsho tiv no ntawd. Joann txiv kuj yog ib tus neeg tseem ceeb. Thaum lawv tuaj sib tham, ces tus thawj saib lub tsev kawm ntawv uas yog tus principal txawm hais rau Martha tias lawv tau hloov txojcai lawm. Nws yuav tsum tau them nyiaj rau lub tsho tiv no. Ces Martha mus thov nyiaj ntawm nws yawg. Nws yawg tsi kam muab nyiaj rau nws. Nws yawg qhia rau nws tias yog nws muab nyiaj them rau lub tsho ces tsi yog lawv muab ua kev zoo siab uas yog award rau nws. Qhov ntawd yog nws yuav xwb. Martha thiaj mus hais rau tus thawj saib lub tsev kawm ntawv tias nws tsi kam them nyiaj rau lub tsho tiv no. Tus thawj saib lub tsev kawm ntawv txawm hloov siab ces muab lub tsho tiv no rau Martha lawm. Martha zoo siab heev. Nws cia li khiav tiaj liag mus tsev coj qhov xov zoo no mus qhia rau nws yawg paub.

Name ______________________________ Date ______________________

VIETNAMESE

Trong truyện ngắn này, Martha theo học ở một trường có thông lệ tặng một chiếc áo khoác cho học sinh giỏi nhất. Martha nghĩ mình sẽ đoạt chiếc áo khoác đó vì cô có điểm cao nhất lớp. Một giáo viên muốn tặng chiếc áo khoác cho một học sinh khác tên là Joann. Cha của Joann là một người có địa vị quan trọng. Trong một cuộc họp, hiệu trưởng cho Martha biết nội quy đã thay đổi, rằng cô phải trả tiền cho chiếc áo khoác. Martha xin ông ngoại cho tiền, nhưng ông không chịu. Ông nói rằng nếu cô trả tiền cho chiếc áo khoác thì đó không phải là phần thưởng nữa, mà đó chỉ là mua chiếc áo khoác. Martha nói với hiệu trưởng là cô sẽ không trả tiền cho chiếc áo khoác. Hiệu trưởng đổi ý và tặng cho Martha chiếc áo khoác. Martha rất sung sướng. Cô bé chạy về nhà và báo cho ông ngoại tin vui.

CHINESE

這個短篇故事是講馬莎和外套。馬莎的學校會送一件外套給最優秀的學生。馬莎因為成績是班上最好的，於是認為自己能夠贏得這件外套。但有位老師卻覺得另一個學生喬安才應該贏得外套，而且喬安的父親是位重要人物。於是校長在一次會議中告訴馬莎，學校的規定改了，她必須付錢購買外套。馬莎問祖父要錢，但是祖父不肯給她，他說如果外套是要用錢買的話，就不是獎品而是購買品了。馬莎告訴校長她不會付錢買這件外套，校長就改變主意把外套送給馬莎。馬莎高興得跑回家，告訴祖父這個好消息。

CAMBODIAN

នៅក្នុងរឿងខ្លីនេះ ម៉ាថា ចូលរៀនសាលាមួយដែលផ្តល់អាវចាកែតទៅដល់សិស្សណាដែលរៀនពូកែ។ ម៉ាថា សង្ឃឹមថានឹងឈ្នះបានអាវចាកែត ព្រោះនាងបានពិន្ទុល្អនៅក្នុងថ្នាក់នាង។ គ្រូគិតថា ក្មេងស្រីម្នាក់ទៀតឈ្មោះ ចូអាន គួរបានទទួលចាកែតវិញ។ ឪពុករបស់ចូអាន ជាមនុស្សសំខាន់ម្នាក់។ នៅក្នុងកិច្ចប្រជុំមួយ នាយកសាលាប្រាប់ ម៉ាថា ថាច្បាប់ត្រូវផ្លាស់ប្តូរ។ នាងត្រូវបង់ថ្លៃសំរាប់អាវចាកែត។ ម៉ាថា សុំលុយពីជីតានាង។ គាត់មិនឲ្យលុយនាងទេ។ គាត់និយាយថា រង្វាន់នោះមិនមែនជារង្វាន់ទេ បើសិននាងបង់លុយសំរាប់អាវចាកែត។ នាងនឹងទៅជាទិញវាទៅវិញ។ ម៉ាថា និយាយប្រាប់នាយកសាលាថា នាងមិនបង់ថ្លៃសំរាប់អាវចាកែតទេ។ នាយកដូរគំនិត ហើយប្រគល់អាវចាកែតឲ្យទៅម៉ាថា។ ម៉ាថា រីករាយណាស់។ នាងរត់សំដៅទៅផ្ទះ ប្រាប់ជីតានាងអំពីដំណឹងល្អនេះ។

HAITIAN CREOLE

Nan ti istwa kout sa a, Martha nan yon lekòl kote yo bay meyè elèv lan yon djakèt. Martha espere genyen djakèt lan paske li gen meyè nòt nan klas li an. Gen yon pwofesè ki panse se yon lòt tifi, Joann, ki ta dwe resevwa djakèt lan. Papa Joann se moun enpòtan li ye. Nan yon reyinyon, direktè an di Martha règ yo te chanje. L ap gen pou peye pou djakèt lan. Martha mande granpè l lajan an. Li pa vle bali l. Li fè l konnen si l peye pou djakèt lan, prim lan pap yon prim vre. Se achte li pral achte l. Martha di direktè an li pap peye pou djakèt lan. Direktè an chanje lide l epi li bay Martha djakèt lan. Martha kontan anpil. Li kouri ale lakay li pou l rakonte granpè bòn nouvèl lan.

Name ______________________ Date ______________________

UNIT 2 • CHAPTER 1

Why Do Leaves Change Color in the Fall?

ENGLISH

This science article explains why leaves change color in the fall. Photosynthesis is the process that plants use to make food. Chlorophyll is a chemical that helps photosynthesis happen. Chlorophyll gives leaves their green color. In the winter, there is not enough light for photosynthesis to happen. This causes the chlorophyll to disappear. As a result, leaves lose their green color. They turn orange and yellow. These colors are already in the leaves. The green chlorophyll covers these colors. Leaves also turn red, purple, or brown in the fall. This also happens because chlorophyll disappears.

SPANISH

Este artículo científico explica por qué las hojas cambian de color en el otoño. La fotosíntesis es el proceso que usan las plantas para producir alimento. La clorofila es la sustancia química que permite que ocurra la fotosíntesis. La clorofila le da a las plantas el color verde. En el invierno, no hay suficiente luz para que ocurra la fotosíntesis y la falta de luz hace que desaparezca la clorofila. Cuando desaparece la clorofila, las hojas dejan de ser verdes y se vuelven anaranjadas y amarillas. Esos son colores que las hojas tienen naturalmente, pero que son cubiertos por la clorofila verde. En el otoño, la clorofila también desaparece y las hojas se vuelven rojas, púrpuras o marrones.

HMONG

Tsab ntawv tshawb nrhiav los sis tsab ntawv science no piav qhia tias yog vim li cas nplooj ntoos hloov xim rau lub caij ntuj tsaug (fall) los yog nqes pis lias mus rau lub caij ntuj no. Photosynthesis yog ib lub sib hawm uas tej nroj tsuag xyoob ntoo siv coj los ua lawv tej zaub mov. Chlorophyll yog ib yam khoom chemical uas pab photosynthesis peemtsheej taus. Chlorophyll ua rau cov nplooj ntsuab. Nyob rau lub caij ntuj no, nws pom kev tsi txaus rau photosynthesis peemtsheej taus. Qhov tsi pom kev txaus no ua rau chlorophyll ploj lawm. Twb yog li no ntag, lub caij ntuj no nplooj thiaj tsi ntsuab. Cov nplooj hloov ua xim txiv maj kiab thiab thiaj daj lawm. Cov xim no nws yeej muaj nyob hauv cov nplooj ua ntej lawm. Cov xim ntsuab chlorophyll no thaiv cov xim ntawd lawm xwb. Nplooj kuj hloov mus ua xim liab, xim pab yeeb, los yog hloov ua xim av (brown) lub caij ntuj tsaug ntawd thiab. Qhov nws hloov xim zoo li no los vim yog tsim muaj chlorophyll lawm thiab xwb.

Name ______________________________ Date ____________________

VIETNAMESE

Bài viết khoa học này giải thích tại sao lá đổi màu vào mùa thu. Sự quang hợp là tiến trình cây xanh sử dụng để tạo ra chất dinh dưỡng cho cây. Chất diệp lục là một hóa chất giúp quá trình quang hợp xảy ra. Chất diệp lục là nguyên nhân khiến cho lá có màu xanh lá cây. Vào mùa đông, không có đủ ánh sáng cho quá trình quang hợp xảy ra, nên chất diệp lục dần dần mất đi. Kết quả là lá mất màu xanh lá cây và ngả sang màu cam và màu vàng. Những màu này đã có sẵn trong lá cây. Chất diệp lục màu xanh che phủ các màu này. Lá cũng ngả sang màu đỏ, tím, hay nâu vào mùa thu. Điều này cũng do chất diệp lục biến mất.

CHINESE

這是一篇與科學有關的文章，解釋樹葉為何在秋天變色。光合作用是植物製造食物的過程，葉綠素則是幫助光合作用進行的化合物。樹葉因為有葉綠素而呈綠色。冬天時，陽光不足，不能進行光合作用，葉綠素便消失，樹葉因而失去綠色，變成橙色和黃色。樹葉裏面本來就有橙色和黃色，但被葉綠素蓋住了。秋天時，樹葉也會變成紅色、紫色或咖啡色，這也是因為葉綠素消失的緣故。

CAMBODIAN

អត្ថបទវិទ្យាសាស្ត្រនេះពន្យល់អំពីហេតុដែលស្លឹកឈើដូរពណ៌នៅរដូវឈើជ្រុះស្លឹក។ ហ្វូតូសែនទីស៊ិស គឺជាដំណើរការដែលរុក្ខជាតិបង្កើតចំណីអាហារ។ ក្លរ៉ូហ្វីល គឺជាជាតិគីមីដែលជួយឲ្យកើតមាន ហ្វូតូសែនទីស៊ិស។ ក្លរ៉ូហ្វីល ផ្តល់ស្លឹកឈើឲ្យមានពណ៌បៃតង។ នៅរដូវធ្លាក់ទឹកកក មិនមានពន្លឺថ្ងៃគ្រប់គ្រាន់សំរាប់ បង្កើតឲ្យមាន ហ្វូតូសែនទីស៊ិស ទេ។ បញ្ហានេះបណ្តាលឲ្យ ក្លរ៉ូហ្វីល បាត់បង់ទៅ។

ដូច្នេះលិតផលគឺស្លឹកឈើត្រូវបាត់ពណ៌ បៃតងរបស់វា។ វាក្លាយទៅជាពណ៌ស្វាទុំនិងពណ៌លឿងទៅវិញ។

ពណ៌ទាំងនេះ វាមាននៅក្នុងស្លឹករួចទៅហើយ។ ពណ៌បៃតងនៃក្លរ៉ូហ្វីល គ្របពីលើពណ៌ទាំងនេះ។

ស្លឹកឈើក៏ដូរទៅជាពណ៌ ក្រហម, ស្វាយ, ឬត្នោត នៅរដូវ ឈើជ្រុះស្លឹកដែរ។ បញ្ហានេះកើតឡើងក៏ព្រោះតែ ក្លរ៉ូហ្វីល រលាយបាត់ទៅដែរ។

HAITIAN CREOLE

Atik sou syans sa a eksplike pouki rezon fèy yo chanje koulè an otòn. Fotosentèz se yon pwosesis plant yo itilize pou pwodui manje. Klowofil se pwodui chimik ki rann fotosentèz lan posib. Se klowofil lan ki fè fèy yo gen koulè vèt. Nan sezon ivè, pa gen ase limyè pou rann pwosesis fotosentèz lan posib. Sa fè klowofil lan disparèt. Sa vin lakòz fèy yo pèdi koulè vèt yo a. Yo vin gen koulè jòn abriko oswa jòn. Koulè sa yo deja nan fèy yo. Klowofil vèt lan kouvri koulè sa yo. Epitou fèy yo konn tounen koulè wouj, mov, oswa mawon nan sezon otòn lan. Sa rive tou paske klowofil lan disparèt.

Name ________________________________ Date ____________________

UNIT 2 • CHAPTER 2

Elizabeth's Diary, by Patricia Hermes

ENGLISH

In this historical fiction diary, Elizabeth writes about moving from England to Jamestown, Virginia, in 1609. Her family is on one of nine ships. There is a storm. Five of the ships sink, including the one that holds all their food. Finally, they reach Jamestown. Elizabeth thinks Jamestown is hot and full of bugs that bite. She says that the bug bites cause her neck to swell. Elizabeth's father tells her that their new house will have no bugs. They will begin to build it the next day. Elizabeth then writes about a man who lived in Jamestown before. He says that there are always bugs. Elizabeth thinks he is a mean man.

SPANISH

En este diario histórico ficticio, Elizabeth escribe acerca de su trasteo de Inglaterra a Jamestown, Virginia en 1609. Su familia viaja en uno de nueve barcos. Cuando hay una tormenta, cinco de los barcos naufragan, incluyendo el barco en el que está toda la comida. Eventualmente, llegan a Jamestown. La primera impresión de Elizabeth de Jamestown es que es demasiado cálido y que hay muchos insectos que pican. Ella dice que las picadas de los insectos hacen que se le hinche la nuca. Así que su padre le dice que en la casa que van a comenzar a construir al día siguiente no habrá insectos. Elizabeth escribe acerca de un hombre que vivió antes en ese pueblo, quien decía que allí siempre hubo insectos. Elizabeth dice que piensa que ese hombre era desagradable por decir eso.

HMONG

Zaj lus piv txwv no, Elizabeth sau txog kev khiav tawm tebchaws Askiv tuaj mus rau Jamestown, Virginia nyob rau xyoo 1609. Nws tsev neeg caij ib lub nkoj ntawm cuaj lub uas tuaj mus ntawd. Nws muaj ib plua nag xob nag cua. Muaj tsib lub nkoj txawm tog rau hauv dej lawm, muaj ib lub yog lub thauj tagnrho lawv cov zaub mov ntag. Dhau ntaw los mus nws tsev neeg mam los txog rau Jamestown. Elizabeth xav hais tias Jamestown yog ib lub zos uas kub heev thiab tseem muaj kab muaj yoov tom thiab. Nws hais tias cov kab thiab yoov ntawd tom ua rau nws lub caj dab cia li o li lawm. Elizabeth txiv tau hais rau nws tias lawv lub tsev tshiab yuav tsi muaj kab thiab yoov lawm. Lawv mam li pib ua lawv lub tsev tshiab hnub yuav los ntawd. Ces Elizabeth txawm sau txog ib tug txiv neej uas tau nyob Jamestown dhau los lawm. Tus txiv neej ntawd tau hais tias yeej muaj kab thiab yoov txhua lub sib hawm li. Qhov tus txiv neej tau hais no ua rau Elizabeth xav hais tias nws yog ib tug txiv neej phem heev.

Name ______________________________ Date ______________________

VIETNAMESE

Trong cuốn nhật ký lịch sử hư cấu này, Elizabeth viết về việc dời nhà từ Anh Quốc sang Jamestown, Virginia, vào năm 1609. Gia đình cô đi trên một trong chín con thuyền. Một cơn bão xảy đến. Năm thuyền bị chìm, bao gồm chiếc thuyền chở thức ăn. Cuối cùng, họ cập bến ở Jamestown. Elizabeth cho rằng thời tiết ở Jamestown nóng, và có nhiều loại côn trùng cắn người. Cô nói rằng các vết cắn của côn trùng làm cho cổ cô bị sưng lên. Cha của Elizabeth nói với cô rằng căn nhà mới của họ sẽ không có côn trùng. Họ sẽ bắt đầu xây nhà vào ngày hôm sau. Elizabeth sau đó viết về một người đàn ông trước đây đã từng sống ở Jamestown. Ông ta nói rằng ở đây lúc nào cũng có côn trùng. Elizabeth nghĩ rằng ông ta là một người đàn ông xấu tính.

CHINESE

這是以歷史做背景的幻想日記。伊麗莎白在日記裏寫她和家人在 1609 年，搭乘九隻船中之一隻，從英格蘭搬到維珍尼亞州的詹姆士鎮。途中遇到暴風，共沉了五隻船，其中有一隻裝載了他們所有的食物。他們終於抵達目的地後，伊麗莎白發覺詹姆士鎮好熱，而且到處都是會咬人的蟲，那些蟲咬到她頸都腫。父親告訴她，他們次日就會開始蓋新屋，新屋不會有蟲。伊麗莎白又寫及一個曾經在詹姆士鎮住過的男人，那個人講那個地方總是有蟲的，伊麗莎白覺得他很可惡。

CAMBODIAN

នៅក្នុងកំណត់ប្រចាំថ្ងៃនៃរឿងប្រឌិតជាប្រវត្តិសាស្ត្រនេះ អេលីសាបែត សរសេរអំពីការផ្លូវលំនៅពីប្រទេសអង់គ្លេស មកនៅទីក្រុង ចេមថោន, វើជីនីញ៉ា, ក្នុងឆ្នាំ ១៦០៩។ គ្រួសារនាងជិះនៅក្នុងសំពៅមួយ ចំណោមសំពៅប្រាំបួន។ មានព្យុះមួយ។ សំពៅប្រាំលិច រួមទាំងសំពៅមួយដែលផ្ទុកម្ហូបអាហាររបស់ពួកគេ។ ទីបំផុតពួកគេមកដល់ក្រុង ចេមថោន។ អេលីសាបែត គិតថាក្រុងចេមថោន ក្តៅ ហើយពោរពេញទៅដោយសត្វល្អិតដែលខាំ។ នាងនិយាយថា សត្វល្អិតខាំ បណ្តាលឲ្យកនាងហើម។ ឪពុករបស់អេលីសាបែត ប្រាប់នាងថា ផ្ទះថ្មីរបស់ពួកគេនឹងមិនមានសត្វល្អិតទេ។ ពួកគេនឹងចាប់ផ្តើមសង់នៅថ្ងៃបន្ទាប់។ បន្ទាប់មក អេលីសាបែត សរសេរអំពីមនុស្សប្រុសម្នាក់ដែលរស់នៅក្នុងក្រុងចេមថោននេះពីមុន។ គាត់និយាយថា សត្វល្អិតមានជានិច្ច។ អេលីសាបែត គិតថាគាត់ជាមនុស្សម្នាក់ដែលកាច។

HAITIAN CREOLE

Nan jounal istorik fiktif sa a, Elizabeth ekri osijè lè li t ap kite Angletè pou l ale Jamestown, Virginia, nan lane 1609. Fanmi li ap vwayaje nan youn nan nèf bato ki t ap fè vwayaj lan. Vin gen yon tanpèt. Senk nan bato yo koule, ikonpri bato ki te gen manje yo ladan l. Finalman, yo rive Jamestown. Elizabeth panse li fè cho nan Jamestown epi kote an plen ensèk k ap mòde moun. Li fè konnen kou l te anfle akòz ensèk yo ki te mòde l. Papa Elizabeth di li nouvo kay kote yo pral rete a pa gen ensèk. Yo pral kòmanse bati l nan demen. Aprè sa Elizabeth ekri osijè yon mesye ki te rete Jamestown anvan sa. Mesye an fè konnen toujou gen ensèk nan zòn lan. Elizabeth panse mesye an mechan.

VISIONS **READING SUMMARIES Unit 2**

Name ______________________________ Date ____________________

UNIT 2 • CHAPTER 3

And Now Miguel, by Joseph Krumgold

ENGLISH

This play is about a boy named Miguel. Miguel's only wish is to become a shepherd. In the opening scene, his brother tells him he must be patient. His grandfather tells him that the real work of a shepherd is to keep the flock together. One morning, several sheep are missing. Against his father's wishes, Miguel leaves school to look for the sheep. Finally, Miguel returns home with the sheep. His father is disappointed that Miguel left school. When it is time to take the sheep to the mountains, Miguel hopes that he can go. Finally, his wish comes true. Miguel's father tells him that he will go with the men to the mountains. In the final scene, Miguel stands high up in the mountains.

SPANISH

Esta obra de teatro es acerca de un joven llamado Miguel. El único deseo de Miguel es el de volverse pastor de ovejas. En la primera escena, su hermano le dice que debe tener paciencia. Su abuelo le dice que el verdadero trabajo de un pastor es el de mantener a las ovejas juntas. Una mañana se desaparecen algunas ovejas. En contra de los deseos de su padre, Miguel se sale de la escuela para buscar a las ovejas perdidas. Miguel encuentra las ovejas y regresa a casa, pero su padre está decepcionado de que Miguel haya dejado la escuela. Cuando es hora de llevar las ovejas al campo, Miguel espera que él pueda ir también. Eventualmente su deseo se cumple cuando su padre le dice que él podrá ir con los hombres al campo. En la última escena, Migue llega al alto de las montañas.

HMONG

Qhov kev piv txwv los sis yeeb yam no yog hais txog ib tug me nyuam tub npe hu ua Miguel. Qhov Miguel ntshaw txog ces yog tau ua tus tub yug yaj. Thaum lawv pib ua kiag qhov yeebyam no nws tus tijlaug hais rau kom nws yuav tsum ua siab ntev. Nws yawg hais rau nws hais tias teg num tiag ntawm tug tub yug yaj yog puav kom nws pab tsiaj nyob ua ib ke. Muaj ib tag kis, muaj ob peb tug yaj txawm ploj lawm. Nws txiv twb tsi kam los Miguel tseem cia li tawm ntawv mus nrhiav cov yaj lawm. Ces Miguel txawm nrhiav tau cov yaj los tsev nrog nws. Nws txiv tau chim rau nws vim nws tau tawm hauv tsev kawm ntawv mus lawm. Thaum yog lub caij coj cov yam mus noj zaub pem roob, Miguel cia siab tias nws yuav tau mus thiab. Ces thaum kawg nws txawm cia li tau mus lawm tiag. Miguel txiv hais rau nws tias nws txiv yuav nrog cov txiv neej mus pem tej roob. Nyob rau hauv qhov yeebyam no, Miguel sawv siab ntshuas puag saum cov roob.

Name ____________________ Date ____________________

VIETNAMESE

Vở kịch này nói về một cậu bé có tên Miguel. Điều ước duy nhất của Miguel là trở thành một người chăn cừu. Lúc khai màn, anh của Miguel nói với cậu là phải kiên nhẫn. Ông ngoại nói với cậu rằng công việc thực sự của một người chăn cừu là phải giữ cho bầy cừu ở tụm lại một chỗ. Một buổi sáng nọ, một vài con cừu bị mất. Miguel làm ngược lại ý của cha mình, rời trường để đi tìm các con cừu. Cuối cùng, Miguel cùng với các con cừu trở về nhà. Cha cậu thất vọng vì cậu đã trốn học. Khi đến lúc dẫn đàn cừu lên núi, Miguel hy vọng rằng cậu có thể đi theo. Cuối cùng, mong ước của cậu trở thành hiện thực. Cha của Miguel nói với cậu rằng cậu có thể lên núi cùng với những người đàn ông. Trong màn cuối của vở kịch, Miguel đứng sững trên ngọn núi cao.

CHINESE

這齣戲劇是關於一個名叫敏哥的男孩，他唯一的願望是成為一個牧羊人。開幕時，他的哥哥告訴他一定要有耐心，而他的祖父告訴他一個好牧羊人是要能保持羊群聚在一齊。有一日晨早，有幾隻羊失蹤，敏哥不顧爸爸反對，逃課去尋隻。雖然最後敏哥帶著走失的羊回家，但他爸爸卻因為他逃學而感到失望。當大家要帶羊群上山時，敏哥希望他也能一齊去，他的願望終於實現了！他爸爸說他可以跟著成年男人一齊上山。在最後一幕中，可以看到敏哥高高地站在山上。

CAMBODIAN

ល្ខោននេះលេងអំពីរឿងក្មេងប្រុសម្នាក់ឈ្មោះ មីគែល។ បំណងតែមួយរបស់មីគែល គឺឲ្យក្លាយទៅជាអ្នកគង្វាលចៀមម្នាក់។ នៅក្នុងឆាកចាប់ផ្តើម បងប្រុសវាប្រាប់ឲ្យវាមានអំណត់។ ជីតាវាប្រាប់វាថា កិច្ចការពិតរបស់គង្វាល គឺរក្សាហ្វូងចៀមឲ្យនៅជុំគ្នា។ ព្រឹកមួយ ចៀមពីរបីត្រូវបាត់។ មីគែលចេញពីសាលាទៅរកចៀមដែលជាការប្រឆាំងនឹងបំណងរបស់ឪពុកវា។ ឪពុកវាអាក់អន់ចិត្ត ដែលមីគែលចេញពីសាលា។ ដល់ពេលត្រូវនាំចៀមឡើងភ្នំ មីគែលសង្ឃឹមថាវាអាចទៅ។ ទីបំផុត បំណងរបស់វាក្លាយជាការពិត។ ឪពុករបស់មីគែលប្រាប់ថាវានឹងទៅភ្នំជាមួយពួកប្រុសៗ។ នៅក្នុងឆាកបញ្ចប់ មីគែលឈរខ្ពស់នៅលើកំពូលភ្នំ។

HAITIAN CREOLE

Pyès teyat sa se konsènan yon tigason yo te rele Miguel. Sèl souwè Miguel se pou l te devni yon bèje. Nan premye sèn lan, frè li di l li dwe gen pasyans. Granpè li di l vrè travay yon bèje se pou l kenbe twoupo an ansanm. Yon maten, yo pa wè plizyè mouton. Malgre papa l pat vle, Miguel kite lekòl li pou l ale chèche mouton yo. Finalman, Miguel retounen lakay li ak mouton yo. Papa l pat kontan wè Miguel kite lekòl lan. Lè moman an rive pou mennen mouton yo sou mòn yo, Miguel espere l ap kapab ale tou. Finalman, rèv li an reyalize. Papa Miguel di li l ap kapab ale ak mesye yo nan mòn yo. Nan dènye sèn lan, Miguel kanpe byen wo nan mòn yo.

Name ______________________ Date ______________________

UNIT 2 • CHAPTER 4

Tuck Triumphant, by Theodore Taylor

ENGLISH

This novel is about a boy named Chok-Do and his new family. Chok-Do is from Korea. When he was very young, his parents died in a war. A new family, the Ogdens, adopts Chok-Do. The Ogden family waits at the airport in Los Angeles to meet Chok-Do. They see a flight attendant. She is holding a Korean boy's hand. The boy has only a small bag and a stuffed koala bear. His new mother hugs and kisses him. The family is surprised to learn that Chok-Do is deaf. They think there must be a mistake. The flight attendant says there is no mistake. She says good luck and leaves the family..

SPANISH

Esta novela es acerca de un niño llamado Chok-Do y su nueva familia. Chok-Do es de Corea. Cuando Chok-Do era muy joven, sus padres murieron en una guerra. Una nueva familia de apellido Ogden adoptó a Chok-Do. Mientras la familia Ogden espera en el aeropuerto de Los Angeles para la llegada de Chok-Do, ven a una azafata caminando con un niño. El niño sólo tiene una bolsa pequeña y un oso koala de peluche. Su nueva madre abraza al niño y lo besa. La familia se sorprende de aprender que Chok-Do es sordo. Piensan que debe ser un error, pero la azafata les asegura que no lo es. La azafata entonces les desea suerte y se despide de ellos.

HMONG

Zaj lus ntawm no yog hais txog ib tug me nyuam tub npe hu ua Chok-Do thiab nws tsev neeg tshiab. Chok-Do yog ib tug neeg tuaj Kauslim tuaj. Thaum nws tseem me me, nws niam thiab nws txiv tau tag sim neej thaum ua tsov rog lawm. Nws tsev neeg tshiab uas yog Ogdens, tau txais yuav Chok-Do. Ogden tsev neeg tau tuaj mus tos Chok-Do nyob rau tom tshav dav hlau hauv Los Angeles. Lawv pom ib tug ntxhais ua hauj lwm taw kev rau dav hlau ya thiab raws. Nws tuav rawv ib tug me nyuam tub Kauslim txhais tes. Tus me nyuam tub ntawd ruas muaj ib lub hnab me thiab ib tug dais koala uas yog muab ntaub xaws xwb. Nws niam tshiab khawm kiag nws thiab nwj nws ob peb zaug. Thaum tsev neeg no pom tias tus me nyuam tub Chok-Do no lag ntseg, lawv cia li xav tsi thoob li. Lawv xav hais tias yuav tsum yog yuam kev lawm. Tus ntxhais taw kev rau dav hlau ya thiab raws hais tias yeej tsi tau yuam kev li. Nws txawm foom hmoov zoo rau tsev neeg ntawd ces nws txawm ncaim lawv mus lawm.

Name ______________________________ Date ______________________

VIETNAMESE

Cuốn tiểu thuyết này nói về một cậu bé có tên Chok-Do và gia đình mới của cậu. Chok-Do là người Hàn Quốc. Khi cậu còn bé, cha mẹ cậu đã chết trong một trận chiến. Một gia đình mới, mang họ Ogden, nhận nuôi Chok-Do. Gia đình Ogden chờ ở sân bay Los Angeles để đón Chok-Do. Họ thấy một cô tiếp viên hàng không. Cô ta đang nắm tay một cậu bé Hàn Quốc. Cậu bé chỉ mang theo một chiếc túi nhỏ và một con gấu túi nhồi bông. Người mẹ mới ôm cậu vào lòng và hôn cậu. Gia đình này ngạc nhiên khi biết rằng cậu bé Chok-Do bị điếc. Họ nghĩ rằng chắc hẳn có điều gì lầm lẫn. Cô tiếp viên hàng không nói rằng không có lầm lẫn gì cả. Cô chúc họ may mắn và quay lưng đi.

CHINESE

這本小說是關於一個名叫初渡的男孩和他的新家庭。初渡來自韓國，年幼時，雙親便在戰禍中喪生。奧格登一家收養了他，成為他的新家人。奧格登一家在洛杉磯的機場等著見初渡，他們看到一位空姐拖著一個韓國男孩的手，那男孩只帶著一個細袋和一隻玩具無尾熊。他的新媽媽一面擁抱他一面親他。奧格登一家知道初渡耳聾後，認爲一定搞錯了，但空姐卻說沒有錯，並且在祝他們好運之後便離開了。

CAMBODIAN

ប្រលោមលោកនេះ ជារឿងអំពីក្មេងប្រុសម្នាក់ឈ្មោះ ចូក-ដូ និងគ្រួសារថ្មីរបស់វា។ ចូក-ដូ មកពីប្រទេស កូរ៉េ។ កាលពីវានៅពីតូច ឪពុកម្ដាយវាស្លាប់នៅក្នុងសង្គ្រាម។ គ្រួសារថ្មីមួយ, អ័កឌីន, យក ចូក-ដូ មកចិញ្ចឹម។ គ្រួសារអ័កឌីន រងចាំនៅវាលយន្តហោះ ឡូស អែនជីឡែស ដើម្បីជួប ចូក-ដូ។ ពួកគេឃើញអ្នកបំរើការក្នុងយន្តហោះ។ នាងកាន់ដៃក្មេងប្រុសកូរ៉េម្នាក់។ ក្មេងនេះមានតែថង់តូចមួយ ហើយនឹងតុក្កតាខ្លាឃ្មុំកូឡាដែលប៉ោងមួយ។ ម្ដាយថ្មីរបស់វា អោបនិងថើបវា។ គ្រួសារត្រូវភ្ញាក់ផ្អើល ដោយដឹងថាក្មេង, ចូក-ដូ, ជាមនុស្សគរ។ ពួកគេគិតថា ពិតជាមានការភាន់ច្រឡំហើយ។ អ្នកបំរើការយន្តហោះនិយាយថា មិនមានការច្រឡំទេ។ នាងនិយាយថា សូមឲ្យមានសំណាងល្អ ហើយនាងក៏ចាកចេញពីគ្រួសារនេះទៅ។

HAITIAN CREOLE

Woman an pale konsènan yon tigason yo te rele Chok-Do ansanm ak nouvo fanmi li. Chok-Do te soti an Kore. Lè li te piti, paran l te mouri nan yon lagè ki te genyen. Yon nouvo fanmi, fanmi Ogdens, te adopte Chok-Do. Fanmi Ogden ap tann pou yo rankontre Chok-Do nan ayewopò Los Angeles lan. Yo wè yon otès de lè. Li kenbe men yon tigason Koreyen. Ti gason an gen sèlman yon ti valiz ak yon ti ous Kowala an jwèt. Nouvo manman l anbrase l epi bo li. Fanmi an sezi aprann tigason an, Chok-Do, soud. Yo panse gen yon erè ki fèt la a. Otès de lè fè konnen pa gen okenn erè ki te fèt. Li swete fanmi an bòn chans epi li vire kite yo.

VISIONS **READING SUMMARIES** Unit 2

Name ______________________________ Date ____________________

UNIT 2 • CHAPTER 5

The Journal of Jesse Smoke, by Joseph Bruchac, & **Ancient Ways,** by Elvania Toledo

ENGLISH

In "The Journal of Jesse Smoke," a Cherokee Indian named Jesse Smoke writes about his tribe. He is upset because the U.S. government is forcing his people to leave their land. It is 1838. A Cherokee leader named John Ross asks the government to let the Cherokee stay on their land. Some of the Cherokee leave. Some have no plans to leave. Jesse writes that many of his people do not understand what is happening.

"Ancient Ways" is a poem about changes in the way of life of the Navajo. They now live in trailers and neighborhoods instead of villages. They shop at grocery stores instead of raising sheep. A Navajo man tells his daughter that things are changing for their people.

SPANISH

En "The Journal of Jesse Smoke", un indígena cheroquí llamado Jesse Smoke escribe acerca de su tribu. Es el año 1838. Él está enojado porque el gobierno de los Estados Unidos está forzando a su gente a que abandone sus tierras. Un líder de los cheroquí llamado John Ross pide al gobierno que deje que los cheroquí permanezcan en sus tierras. Algunos cheroquí se van de sus tierras, pero otros no tienen planes para abandonarlas. Jesse escribe que muchos cheroquí no entienden lo que está ocurriendo.

"Ancient Ways" es un poema acerca de los cambios en la manera de vivir de los navajo. Ellos ahora viven en campamentos de casas-remolque en vez de vivir en sus propias aldeas. Ahora compran sus comestibles en tiendas, en vez de vivir del pastoreo. Un hombre navajo explica a su hija que las cosas están cambiando para su gente.

HMONG

Nyob rau hauv "Jesse Smoke Cov Lus Sau Tseg," nws qhia txog ib tug Khab Cherokee npe hu ua Jesse Smoke piav txog txog nws hais neeg. Nws tsi txaus siab vim tias tsoom hwv Asmeliskas tau yuam nws cov neeg khiav tawm hauv lawv daim av. Nws yog xyoo 1838. Cherokee ib tug thawj uas lub npe hu ua John Ross tau thov kom tsoom hwv tso lawv nyob lawv daim av. Cov Cherokee ib txhia khiav tawm lawm. Ib txhia lawv yeej tsi npaj khiav tawm li. Jesse sau hais tias nws cov neeg coob kawg li yeej tsi nkag siab thiab tsi paub hais tias yog vim li cas ho kom lawv khiav.

"Tej Kev Uas Ib Txwm Coj" yog ib zaj lus poem txog kev hloov lub neej nyob rau pab neeg Navajo. Niaj hnub tam sim no lawv nyob rau cov tsev cab los sis trailers thiab nyob sib ze xwb tsi ua zos lawm. Lawv mus yuav khoom noj tom tej kiab khw lawm xwb tsi yug yaj lawm. Muaj ib tug txiv neej Navajo hais rau nws tus ntxhais hais tias ntau yam ntawm nws cov neeg tau hloov zuj zus lawm.

Name ______________________________ Date ______________________

VIETNAMESE

Trong chuyện "The Journal of Jesse Smoke," một thanh niên người Da Đỏ thuộc bộ lạc Cherokee, có tên Jesse Smoke viết về bộ lạc của mình. Anh ta khổ sở vì chính quyền Mỹ ép buộc dân làng phải rời đất đai nhà cửa. Năm đó là năm 1838. Một người lãnh đạo bộ lạc Cherokee có tên John Ross yêu cầu chính quyền để cho dân Cherokee sống yên trên phần đất của mình. Một số người Cherokee bỏ đi. Một số không có ý định rời nơi ở. Jesse viết rằng nhiều người trong bộ lạc không hiểu điều gì xảy ra.

"Ancient Ways" là một bài thơ nói về những thay đổi về lối sống của người Navajo. Giờ đây họ sống trong những nhà lưu động và khu xóm thay vì làng mạc. Họ mua thực phẩm tại các cửa hàng tạp hóa thay vì tự nuôi cừu để ăn. Một người đàn ông Navajo nói với con gái của mình rằng giờ đây cuộc sống mỗi ngày một thay đổi đối với dân tộc của họ.

CHINESE

在 The Journal of Jesse Smoke 中，一個名叫傑西•史莫克的切羅基印地安人記錄了有關他族人的事蹟。他因為美國政府強迫他的族人遷離居地而生氣。1838年，一位名叫約翰•羅斯的切羅基首領要求美國政府讓切羅基族人留在自己的土地上。有些族人搬走了，有些卻沒有計劃離去。傑西寫道，有許多他的族人根本不明白發生了什麼事。

Ancient Ways 是一首關於那哇豪族印地安人改變生活方式的詩。他們現在住在拖車裏而不是住在村莊裏；他們在雜貨店裏購物而不再養羊。一位那哇豪族印地安爸爸告訴他女兒，他們族人週圍的事物正在發生變化。

CAMBODIAN

នៅក្នុង " The Journal of Jesse Smoke " ជនជាតិឥណ្ឌា ជារ៉ូគី ម្នាក់ឈ្មោះ ជេស៊ី ស្មូក សរសេរ អំពីកុលសម្ព័ន្ធរបស់គាត់។ គាត់មិនសប្បាយចិត្តចំពោះរដ្ឋាភិបាលអាមេរិក ដែលកំពុងបង្ខំប្រជាជនគាត់ឲ្យចាកចេញ ពីទឹកដីរបស់ពួកគេ។ គឺនៅឆ្នាំ ១៨៣៨។ មេរបស់ជារ៉ូគីម្នាក់ឈ្មោះ ចន រ៉ូស សុំរដ្ឋាភិបាលអនុញ្ញាតឲ្យពួកជារ៉ូគី រស់នៅលើទឹកដីរបស់គេ។ ពួកជារ៉ូគីខ្លះចាកចេញ។ ខ្លះគ្មានគំរោងចេញឡើយ។ ជេស៊ី សរសេរថា ប្រជាជនរបស់គាត់ជាច្រើនមិនយល់អំពីអ្វីដែលកំពុងកើតឡើងនេះទេ។

" Ancient Ways " ជាកំណាព្យមួយអំពីការផ្លាស់ប្តូររបៀបរស់នៅនៃកុលសម្ព័ន្ធ ណាវ៉ាហ្វូ។ ពួកគេសព្វថ្ងៃរស់ នៅក្នុងផ្ទះដូចឡាន (trailers) និងនៅក្បែរផ្ទះជិតខាងគ្នា ជំនួសភូមិទៅវិញ។ ពួកគេទិញអីវ៉ាន់នៅហាងលក់ម្ហូប ជំនួសការចិញ្ចឹមចៀមទៅវិញ។ បុរស ណាវ៉ាហ្វូម្នាក់ប្រាប់កូនស្រីគាត់ថា អ្វីៗកំពុងតែផ្លាស់ប្តូរសំរាប់ជនជាតិរបស់ ពួកគេ។

HAITIAN CREOLE

Nan "The Journal of Jesse Smoke," yon endyen Cherokee yo rele Jesse Smoke ap ekri osijè tribi an. Li fache paske gouvènman Etazini an ap fòse pèp pa l lan pou yo kite tè yo. Nou nan lane 1838. Yon lidè Cherokee yo rele John Ross mande gouvènman an pou li kite pèp Cherokee an rete sou tè yo. Kèk nan pèp Cherokee an pati. Gen kèk ki pa gen okenn entansyon pou yo pati. Jesse ekri pou fè konnen anpil moun nan pèp li an pa konprann sa k ap rive a.

"Ancient Ways" se yo powèm osijè chanjman nan estil lavi pèp Navajo an. Kounye an se nan karavàn ak kèk vwazinaj yo rete olye se nan yon vilaj. Yo achte nan boutik yo olye pou yo elve mouton. Yon mesye Navajo di pitit fi li bagay yo ap chanje pou pèp yo a.

Name ______________________ Date ______________________

UNIT 3 • CHAPTER 1

Life Doesn't Frighten Me, by Maya Angelou

ENGLISH

This poem is about facing fears. Noises and shadows do not frighten the speaker. Barking dogs and dragons also do not frighten her. She scares them away and makes fun of them. Sometimes, the speaker just smiles at them because these things do not frighten her. The boys and girls in the speaker's new classroom do not frighten her either. She is not afraid of lions, panthers, frogs, or snakes. The speaker does not scream or run away from them. The only time she is afraid is while she is dreaming.

SPANISH

Este poema es acerca de cómo confronta la narradora los temores. Los ruidos y las sombras no atemorizan a la narradora. Ni los ladridos de los perros ni los dragones le dan miedo. En vez de asustarse, ella los asusta y se burla de ellos. A veces, la narradora simplemente les sonríe, porque no la atemorizan. Los niños y las niñas del nuevo salón de clases de la narradora tampoco le dan miedo. Ella no le teme a los leones, a las panteras, a las ranas ni a las víboras. La narradora no les grita ni les hulle. Ella sólo tiene temores cuando sueña.

HMONG

Zaj lus paivyi no yog hais txog ntsib kev ntshai. Tej suab nrov thiab duab ntxoov ntxoo ua tsi tau rau tus xib hwb uas tab tom hais lus ntshai li. Txawm yog dev pheej tom thiab muaj zaj los nws twb tseem tsi ntshai. Nws ua rau lawv ntshai thiab khiav lawm. Thiab tseem muab lawv ua lus hais tso dag ua si huv tib si. Tej thaum tus xib hwb hais lus ntawd cia li luag ntxhi rau lawv xwb vim tias tej yam zoo li ntawd tsi ua rau nws ntshai. Cov me nyuam tub thiab me nyuam ntxhais ua nyob hauv nws hoob qhia ntawv tshiab ntawd los nws twb tsi ntshai li thiab. Nws kuj tsi ntshai tsov ntxhuav, tsov panther, qav, los yog nab tej ntawd tag nrho. Tus xib hwb hais lus ntawd nws tsi qw los yog khiav tsiv ntawm tej ntawd mus li. Tib zaug uas nws ntshai ces yog thaum nws ua npau suav xwb.

Name ______________________________ Date ____________________

VIETNAMESE

Bài thơ này nói về việc đương đầu với nỗi sợ hãi. Các tiếng động và bóng tối không làm cho tác giả khiếp sợ. Chó sủa và rồng cũng không làm cho bà kinh hãi. Bà còn xua đuổi và trêu chọc chúng nữa. Đôi khi, tác giả chỉ cười nhẹ vì những thứ này không dọa được bà. Những cô cậu học sinh trong lớp học mới của tác giả cũng không làm cho bà rung. Bà không sợ sư tử, báo đen, ếch, hay rắn. Tác giả không la hoảng hay chạy trốn những con vật này. Lần duy nhất bà sợ là lúc bà đang nằm mơ.

CHINESE

這首詩說的是如何面對恐懼。喧囂及陰影沒有嚇倒講話者。吠叫的狗與龍也沒有嚇倒她，反而在被她嘲弄後嚇跑了。有時候，講話者只是對它們笑笑，因為這些東西嚇不了她。講話者的新教室裡面的男孩與女孩也嚇不了她。她不怕獅子、豹子，也不怕青蛙或蛇，她不會驚叫，也不會逃走。只有在睡夢中，她才會感到害怕。

CAMBODIAN

កំណាព្យនេះនិយាយអំពីការប្រឈមមុខនឹងសេចក្ដីខ្លាច។ សំលេងនិងស្រមោលមិនធ្វើឲ្យអ្នកនិយាយភ័យទេ។ ការប្រួសរបស់ឆ្កែនិងនាគក៏មិនធ្វើឲ្យនាងភ័យដែរ។ នាងបំភ័យពួកវាឲ្យទៅឆ្ងាយ ហើយសើចចំអកដាក់ពួកវា។ ពេលខ្លះអ្នកនិយាយគ្រាន់តែសើចដាក់ពួកវា ពីព្រោះអ្វីទាំងអស់នេះមិនធ្វើឲ្យនាងភ័យបានឡើយ។ ក្មេងប្រុសស្រីនៅក្នុងថ្នាក់ថ្មីរបស់នាង ក៏មិនធ្វើឲ្យនាងភ័យដែរ។ នាងមិនខ្លាចសត្វតោ, ខ្លា, កង្កែប, ឬពស់ទេ។ អ្នកនិយាយមិនស្រែកឬរត់ចេញឆ្ងាយពីពួកវាទេ។ ម្ដងគត់ដែលនាងភ័យខ្លាច គឺពេលដែលនាងកំពុងយល់សប្ដិ៍។

HAITIAN CREOLE

Powèm sa a pale osijè lè moun ap fè fas ak laperèz. Bri ak lombraj pa fè oratè an pè. Chyen k ap jape ak dragon pa fè l pè nonplis. Se li ki fè yo pè epi li pase yo nan rizib. Kèlkefwa, oratè an sèlman souri ba yo paske bagay sa yo pa fè l pè. Tigason ak tifi ki nan nouvo sal de klas oratè an pa fè li pè nonplis. Li pa pè lyon, pantè, krapo, oswa koulèv. Oratè an pa konn rele pou yo oswa kouri pou yo. Sèl lè li konn pè se lè l ap reve.

Name ______________________________ Date ______________________

UNIT 3 • CHAPTER 2

Matthew A. Henson, by Wade Hudson

ENGLISH

This biography is about Matthew Henson. Henson was an African-American explorer. In 1909, Matthew Henson and other explorers traveled to the North Pole. They traveled on dog sleds. One day, Matthew Henson fell through the ice. One of the men quickly pulled him from the water. The group kept going and made it to the North Pole. Henson was happy about their victory. However, many people ignored Henson's achievement because he was African-American. They praised the other explorers but not Henson. Finally, in 1944, the United States government honored Henson.

SPANISH

Esta biografía es acerca de Matthew Henson. Henson fue un explorador afroamericano. En 1909, Henson y otros exploradores viajaron al Polo Norte en trineos de perros. Un día Henson se cayó en el hielo y uno de sus compañeros lo sacó rápidamente. El grupo siguió avanzando y eventualmente llegaron al Polo Norte. A Henson lo complació mucho su logro. Sin embargo, muchos ignoraron lo que Henson logró, porque él era afroamericano. Ellos reconocieron a los otros exploradores, pero no a Henson. No fue sino hasta 1944, cuando el gobierno de los Estados Unidos reconoció el logro de Henson.

HMONG

Zaj lus no yog sau hais txog Matthew Henson lub neej. Henson yog ib tug Asflikas-Asmeslikas uas ncig mus tshawb nrhiav tej lub teb chaws los yog chaw uas tsi tau muaj leejtwg mus dua li. Nyob rau xyoo 1909, Matthew Henson thiab coob tug cov ncig tebchaws li nws tau mus rau pem North Pole. Lawv caij cov xam laub uas dev cab mus. Muaj ib hnub, Matthew Henson tau hlauv poob rau hauv cov nab kuab-dej nkoog. Lawv cov txiv neej ntawd muaj ib tug tau rub nws tawm hauv cov dej los. Lawv pab ntawd tseem pheej mus tas zog ces thiaj tau mus txog rau pem North Pole. Henson nws zoo siab heev rau qhov txoj kev mus nyuaj kawg tiam si lawv tseem kov yeej thiab tau mus txog lawm. Tab si, coob tus neeg twb tsi xav paub txog qhov Henson tau muaj tsab peev xwm mus txog rau ped rov los li vim nws yog ib tug neeg Asflikas-Amesliskas. Lawv tau qhuas cov nrog nws mus tiam si tsi qhuas Henson. Ntev tom qab no uas yog xyoo 1944 lawm, tsoom fwv Amesliskas mam li ua kev zoo siab qhuas Henson.

Name ______________________________ Date ______________________

VIETNAMESE

Cuốn tiểu sử này nói về Matthew Henson. Henson là một nhà thám hiểm người Mỹ gốc Châu Phi. Vào năm 1909, Matthew Henson và một số nhà thám hiểm khác đi tới Bắc Cực. Họ đi bằng xe trượt tuyết do chó kéo. Một ngày nọ, mặt băng đá vỡ làm cho Matthew Henson té xuống nước. Một trong những người đi cùng nhanh chóng kéo ông ta lên khỏi mặt nước. Nhóm thám hiểm tiếp tục cuộc hành trình và cuối cùng đến được Bắc Cực. Henson rất sung sướng với sự thành công của nhóm mình. Tuy nhiên, nhiều người tảng lờ đi công trạng của Henson chỉ vì ông là người Mỹ gốc Châu Phi. Họ khen ngợi những nhà thám hiểm khác ngoại trừ Henson. Rốt cục vào năm 1944, chính quyền Hoa Kỳ ca ngợi công lao của Henson.

CHINESE

這是關於馬修˙亨生的傳記。亨生是位非洲裔美國探險家。1909 年，馬修˙亨生與其他探險家去北極探險。他們是坐狗拉雪橇去的。一天，馬修˙亨生掉進了冰窟。同行者中有人快速地將他從水中拉起。他們一行繼續向前，最後達到了北極。亨生對於成功十分喜悅。但是，因為他是非洲裔美國人，很多人對他的成就視而不見。他們贊揚其他的探險家，卻不提及亨生。最後，直到 1944 年，美國政府才給予亨生應有的榮譽。

CAMBODIAN

ប្រវត្តិរូបនេះអំពី ម៉ាធ្យូ ហែនសុន។ ហែនសុន ជាអ្នករុករក ជាតិអាហ្វ្រិកកែន-អាមេរិកកែន។ ក្នុងឆ្នាំ ១៩០៩ ម៉ាធ្យូ ហែនសុន និង ពួកអ្នករុករកផ្សេងទៀត ធ្វើដំណើរទៅប៉ូលខាងជើង។ គេជិះរទេះអូសដោយឆ្កែ។ ថ្ងៃមួយ ម៉ាធ្យូ ហែនសុន ធ្លាក់ចូលទៅក្នុងទឹកកក។ បុរសម្នាក់ទាយគាត់ចេញពីទឹកយ៉ាងប្រញាប់។ ក្រុមនេះនៅតែធ្វើដំណើរទៅទៀត ហើយបានក៏បានទៅដល់ប៉ូលខាងជើង។ ហែនសុនមានការរីករាយពីជោគជ័យរបស់ពួកគេ។ តែមនុស្សជាច្រើនធ្វើមិនដឹងមិនឮពីជោគជ័យរបស់ហែនសុន ពីព្រោះគាត់ជាជនជាតិអាហ្វ្រិកកែន-អាមេរិកកែន។ គេសរសើរអ្នករុករកឯទៀត តែមិនសរសើរហែនសុនឡើយ។ ទីបំផុត នៅឆ្នាំ១៩៤៤ រដ្ឋាភិបាលអាមេរិកផ្តល់កិត្តិយសដល់ហែនសុន។

HAITIAN CREOLE

Byografi sa a pale konsènan Matthew Henson. Henson se te yon eksploratè Afriken-Ameriken. An1909, Matthew Henson ak kèk lòt eksploratè te vwayaje nan Pol Nò a. Yo te vwayaje sou treno chyen t ap rale. Yon jou, Matthew Henson tonbe nan glas lan. Youn nan mesye yo rale l rapidman sot nan dlo an. Gwoup lan kontinye ale jiskaske yo rive nan Pol Nò an. Henson te kontan de viktwa yo a. Sepandan, anpil moun iyore tout sa Henson te akonpli yo paske se yon Afriken-Ameriken li te ye. Yo te fè lwanj pou lòt eksploratè yo men pa pou Henson. Finalman, an 1944, gouvènman Etazini an te vin bay Henson onè respè.

Name ______________________ Date ______________

UNIT 3 • CHAPTER 3

Anne Frank: The Diary of a Young Girl, by Anne Frank

ENGLISH

In her diary, Anne Frank describes why her family is hiding from the Nazis during World War II. In this diary entry, Anne writes that the Nazis want to send her sister, Margot, to a concentration camp. A concentration camp was a prison where the Nazis killed Jews. Anne writes that she cannot believe that the Nazis would send a young woman to a concentration camp. Anne then finds out that her parents are planning to hide. They quickly pack what is most important to them. Anne says that her only wish is to get away safely.

SPANISH

En su diario, Anne Frank describe por qué su familia se esconde de los nazis durante la Segunda Guerra Mundial. En esta anotación en su diario, Anne escribe que los nazis quieren enviar a su hermana Margot a un campo de concentración. Un campo de concentración era una prisión en donde los nazis mataban a los judíos. Anne escribe que ella no puede creer que los nazis fueran a enviar a una joven a un campo de concentración. Luego, Anne se entera de que sus padres planean esconderse. Ellos rápidamente empacan lo que es más importante para ellos. Anne expresa que su único deseo es el de huir para poder estar sanos y salvos.

HMONG

Nyob rau hauv nws phau ntawv uas sau txog yam tau tshwm rau hauv nws lub neej los yog yam nws tau raug, Anne Frank piav txog tias vim li cas nws tsev neeg khiav nkaum ntawm cov Nazis nyob rau tso rog ntiaj teb zaum ob-World War II. Nyob rau hauv phau ntawv no, Anne sau tias cov Nazis xav muab nws tus viv ncaus, Margot, xa mus rau hauv lub chaw txuvsiav-concentration camp. Qhov chaw txuvsiav no yog ib lub chaw lojcuj rau cov Nazis kaw Jews tua pov tseg. Anne sau tias nws tsi ntseeg txog ntawm cov Nazis muaj lub siab xa ib tug ntxhais coj mus rau hauv lub chaw txuvsiav ntawd li. Ces Anne mam li paub tias nws niam thiab txiv tab tom npaj yuav khiav nkaum. Lawv rua sau tsawg tsuag tej yam khoom uas tseem ceeb tshaj plaws rau lawv xwb. Anne hais tias qhov nws xav tau ces yog khiav tau tawm mus es tsi txhob muaj abtsi raug rau lawv xwb.

Name ______________________________ Date ______________________

VIETNAMESE

Trong cuốn nhật ký, Anne Frank mô tả lý do gia đình cô phải trốn bọn Đảng Quốc Xã Đức vào Thế Chiến Thứ II. Trong mục nhật ký này, Anne viết rằng bọn Đảng Quốc Xã Đức muốn đưa người chị của cô, là Margot, vào một trại tập trung. Trại tập trung là nhà tù nơi bọn Đảng Quốc Xã tiêu diệt người Do Thái. Anne viết rằng cô không thể tin nổi là bọn Đảng Quốc Xã lại muốn đưa một phụ nữ trẻ vào trại tập trung. Sau đó Anne phát hiện là cha mẹ cô đang dự tính trốn chạy. Họ nhanh chóng thu xếp những đồ đạc quan trọng nhất. Anne nói rằng điều ước duy nhất của cô là trốn chạy an toàn.

CHINESE

安妮˙法蘭克在日記中描述了她的家人在二次世界大戰中為何躲避納粹黨人。在日記中，安妮寫到納粹要把她姐姐瑪格送去集中營。集中營是納粹殺害猶太人的監獄。安妮寫道，她無法相信納粹會把一名年輕女子送進集中營。安妮後來發現她父母計劃躲藏起來，他們迅速收拾好最重要的物品。安妮說，她唯一的願望就是能安全逃離。

CAMBODIAN

នៅក្នុងកំណត់ប្រចាំថ្ងៃរបស់នាង អាននី ហ្វ្រែង រៀបរាប់អំពីហេតុដែលគ្រួសារនាងលាក់ខ្លួនពីពួកណាស៊ីស នៅពេលសង្គ្រាមលោកលើកទី២។ នៅក្នុងការចុះក្នុងកំណត់នេះ អាននីសរសេរថា ពួកណាស៊ីសចង់បញ្ជូនបងស្រីនាង, ម៉ារកត, ទៅកាត់ជំរុំប្រមូលផ្តុំ។ ជំរុំប្រមូលផ្តុំ ជាគុកដែលពួកណាស៊ីសសម្លាប់ពួកជ្វីស។ អាននីសរសេរថា នាងមិនអាចជឿថាពួកណាស៊ីសនឹងបញ្ជូនក្មេងស្រីម្នាក់ទៅកាន់ជំរុំប្រមូលផ្តុំទេ។ បន្ទាប់មក អាននីបានដឹងថា ឪពុកម្តាយនាងគំរោងនឹងទៅលាក់ខ្លួន។ គេនាំគ្នាវេចរបស់អ្វីដែលសំខាន់សំរាប់ពួកគេ។ អាននីនិយាយថា ការបន់ស្រន់របស់នាងតែមួយគត់ គឺគេចខ្លួនឲ្យបានយ៉ាងសុខសាន្ត។

HAITIAN CREOLE

Nan jounal li an, Anne Frank dekri pou ki rezon fanmi li ap kache pou Nazi yo pandan Dezyèm Gè Mondyal lan. Nan pati sa nan jounal lan, Anne ekri Nazi yo vle voye sè l, Margot, nan yon kan konsantrasyon. Yon kan konsantrasyon se kote Nazi yo te konn touye Jwif yo. Anne ekri li paka kwè Nazi yo ta ka voye yon jèn tifi nan yon kan konsantrasyon . Anne vin aprann paran l yo gen entansyon al kache. Yo ranmase rapidman tou zafè yo ki pi enpòtan. Anne di sèl souwè li se pou l rive chape poul li san danje.

Name ______________________ Date ______________________

UNIT 3 • CHAPTER 4

Lance Armstrong: Champion Cyclist, by President George W. Bush

ENGLISH

In this speech, President George W. Bush honors a brave athlete. Lance Armstrong has just won a famous bicycle race called the *Tour de France*. Bush describes Armstrong's great race and the challenges of winning. One challenge of the race is that the weather changes from very hot to very cold. Another challenge is the long ride through the mountains. The president praises Armstrong's great race and victory. The president also praises Armstrong for facing a different kind of challenge. A few years before the race, Armstrong had cancer. Cancer is a serious illness. Armstrong was very sick and weak, but he fought the cancer. Armstrong is a winner in two ways. The president says that Armstrong inspires many people to do great things in their lives.

SPANISH

En este discurso, el Presidente George W. Bush elogia al gran atleta Lance Armstrong, quien acababa de ganar una famosa carrera en bicicleta llamada el *Tour de France*. Bush describe la gran carrera de Armstrong y los retos que hay que sobrellevar para poder ganar. Uno de los grandes retos es que el clima cambia de muy cálido a muy frío, y otro reto es el largo tramo por las montañas. El presidente felicita a Armstrong por su carrera y su victoria. También lo felicita por sobrellevar otro tipo de reto. Unos años antes de esa carrera, a Armstrong le dio cancer. El cancer es una enfermedad muy seria. Armstrong estuvo muy enfermo y muy débil, pero batalló contra la enfermedad. Así que Armstrong es un ganador de dos maneras. El presidente dice que Armstrong inspira a mucha gente a hacer grandes cosas en sus vidas.

HMONG

Nyob rau hauv cov lus no, tus nom George W. Bush ua kev zoo siab nco thiab qhuas ib tug neeg kislas uas muaj tsab peev xwm. Lance Armstrong nim qhuav tau yeej qhov kev xeem caij luv thij nto moo lug uas yog hu ua Tour de France. Bush piav tias Armstrong yog ib tug xeem tau zoo thiab qhov nws tau xeem yeej. Ib qho ntawm txoj kev xeem no nws tau ntsib fuab cuaj kub heev thiab ho no heev. Ib qho uas nws tau ntsib thiab mas yog qhov caij hlas roob hav mud deb kawg li. Tus nom qhuas txog Armstrong txoj kev yeej thiab qhov nws xeem tau zoo. Tus nom kuj qhuas Armstrong rau qhov uas nws ntsib ntau yam uas yuav tau sib zog heev thiaj kov yeej. Ob peb xyoos ua ntev nws mus xeem ntawd, Armstrong tau mob khiabxawm-cancer. Cancer yog ib yam mob uas mob phem heev. Armstrong tau mob heev thiab tsi muaj zog li, tiam si nws sib zog tawm tsam tus cancer ntawd. Nws muaj ob txoj kev uas Armstrong yeej. Tus nom hais tias qhov Armstrong ua ntawd txhawb tau coob leej tib neeg lub zog uas yuav ua ntau yam zoo rau lawv lub neej.

Name ______________________ Date ______________

VIETNAMESE

Trong bài diễn văn này, Tổng Thống George W. Bush khen ngợi một vận động viên can đảm. Lance Armstrong vừa mới thắng cuộc đua xe đạp nổi tiếng có tên *Tour de France*. Bush mô tả cuộc đua tuyệt vời của Armstrong và những thử thách phải vượt qua để thắng cuộc. Một thử thách trong cuộc đua là thời tiết thay đổi từ rất nóng sang rất lạnh. Một thử thách khác là phải đạp xe một đoạn đường dài xuyên qua các dãy núi. Tổng thống ca ngợi cuộc đua tuyệt vời và chiến thắng của Armstrong. Tổng thống cũng ca ngợi Armstrong đã đương đầu với một loại thử thách khác. Trước cuộc đua một vài năm, Armstrong bị ung thư. Ung thư là một căn bệnh nghiêm trọng. Armstrong bệnh rất nặng và sức khỏe rất yếu, thế nhưng ông ta cố kháng cự lại căn bệnh ung thư. Armstrong là người đã thắng cuộc về hai mặt. Tổng thống nói rằng Armstrong là nguồn cảm hứng giúp nhiều người làm nhiều điều đáng quý trong cuộc sống.

CHINESE

在這篇講話中，喬治・W・布什總統表彰了一位勇敢的運動員。蘭思・阿姆斯壯剛贏得一次名為環法大賽（*Tour de France*）的著名自行車比賽。布什描述了阿姆斯壯的精彩比賽以及奪冠路上遇到的各種挑戰。比賽中的一項挑戰是氣溫的變化，從極為炎熱變到極為寒冷。另一項挑戰是在山區中的長途穿越。總統贊揚了阿姆斯壯在比賽中的精彩表現及取得的勝利。總統還贊揚了阿姆斯壯能夠勇敢面對另一種挑戰。在這次比賽的前幾年，阿姆斯壯患上了癌症。癌症是很嚴重的疾病。阿姆斯壯病得不輕，非常虛弱，但他與癌症抗爭。阿姆斯壯贏得了兩種比賽。總統說，阿姆斯壯鼓舞著許多人在生命中奮發有為。

CAMBODIAN

នៅក្នុងសន្ទរកថានេះ ប្រធានាធិបតេយ្យ ចូច ដែបែលយូ. បូស ផ្តល់កិត្តិយលឲ្យដល់អ្នកកីឡាអង់អាចម្នាក់។ ឡេន អាមស្រ្តង ទើបតែឈ្នះការប្រណាំងកង់ដ៏ល្បីមួយ ដែលហៅថា ថួរដឺហ្វ្រង់។ បូល រៀបរាប់ពីការប្រណាំងដ៏ធំរបស់អាមស្រ្តង និងការប្រជែងយកជ័យជំនះ។ ការប្រជែងនៃការប្រណាំងមួយគឺ ធេតុអាកាសជួរពីក្តៅខ្លាំង ទៅត្រជាក់ខ្លាំង។ ការប្រជែងមួយទៀតគឺ ការជិះយ៉ាងយូរកាត់តាមភ្នំ។ លោកប្រធានាធិបតេយ្យសរសើរការប្រណាំងនិងជោគជ័យរបស់អាមស្រ្តង។ លោកប្រធានាធិបតេយ្យក៏សរសើរអាមស្រ្តងដែរ ដែលបានប្រឈមមុខនឹងការប្រជែងមួយផ្សេងទៀត។ ពីរបីឆ្នាំមុនការប្រណាំង អាមស្រ្តងមានជម្ងឺមហារីក។ មហារីកជាជម្ងឺដ៏ធ្ងន់ធ្ងរ។ អាមស្រ្តងឈឺជាទម្ងន់ ហើយខ្សោយ តែគាត់ប្រឹងទប់ទល់នឹងជម្ងឺមហារីក។ អាមស្រ្តងជាអ្នកឈ្នះពីរបែប។ លោកប្រធានាធិបតេយ្យនិយាយថា អាមស្រ្តងមានឥទ្ធិពលទៅលើមនុស្សជាច្រើន គឺឲ្យធ្វើនូវអ្វីដែលធំសំរាប់ជីវិតរបស់គេ។

HAITIAN CREOLE

Nan diskou l lan, Prezidan George W. Bush bay onè respè a yon atlèt brav. Lance Armstrong fèk ranpote viktwa nan yon kous bisiklèt selèb yo rele Tour de France. Bush dekri gwo kous Armstrong lan ak tout difikilte li te genyen pou l te ka rive ranpòte laviktwa. Youn nan pwoblèm ki te gen nan kous lan sèke tanperati an te konn chanje soti nan cho anpil pou rive nan frèt anpil. Yon lòt pwoblèm se te chemen long nan mòn yo. Prezidan an fè lwanj Armstrong pou gwo kous sa a ak viktwa li. Prezidan an te fè lwanj Armstrong tou poutèt li te gen pou l fè fas a yon lòt kalite pwoblèm. Kèk ane de sa anvan kous lan, Armstrong te gen yon kansè. Kansè se maladi grav. Armstrong te malad anpil, li te fèb, men li te goumen ak kansè a. Armstrong pote laviktwa nan de fason. Prezidan fè konnen Armstrong enspire anpil moun pou fè de gran bagay nan lavi yo.

Name ______________________________ Date ______________________

UNIT 3 • CHAPTER 5

Earthquake, by Huynh Quang Nhuong

ENGLISH

This memoir takes place in a Vietnamese village. One day, the animals in the village sense that something is wrong. The buffaloes stamp their feet and howl. Some of the other animals run and hide. The villagers open the doors of the shed so the buffaloes can escape. The author's family runs to a shelter. An earthquake shakes the village. The family hears trees and buildings fall. The earthquake destroys the village. The author's home is ruined. He and his family must sleep in the garden. In the garden, the author sits with one of the buffaloes. Its warm body makes the author feel safe. He soon falls asleep.

SPANISH

Estas memorias se llevan a cabo en una aldea de Vietnám. Un día, los animales de la aldea presienten que algo está mal. Los búfalos se muestran inquietos y aullan. Otros animales corren y se esconden. Los habitantes de la aldea abren las puertas de los potreros para que los búfalos puedan escapar. La familia del autor corre hacia un refugio. Un terremoto hace temblar la aldea y la familia oye caer árboles y edificios. El terremoto destruye la aldea y la casa del autor es destruída. Él y su familia tienen que dormir en el jardín. En el jardín, el autor se sienta con uno de los búfalos. El cuerpo cálido del búfalo lo hace sentir seguro y pronto se duerme.

HMONG

Zaj lus nco tau tseg no yog nws muaj nyob rau hauv ib lub zos Nyablaj. Muaj ib hnub, cov tsiaj txawm nov nxhiab li muaj abtsi tsi zoo lawm. Tej twm los kuj xuas lawv cov tej taw ntaus av thiab pheej nyo hauv rau hauv pegteb. Ib txhia tsiaj kuj khiav thiab mus nkaum. Cov neeg zej zos qhib tej rooj vag rau cov tsev twm sub cov twm thiaj khiav tawm mus tau. Tus sau phau ntawv no tsev tibneeg khiav mus rau ib qhov chaw nraim. Ib qho av qeeg tshee ua lub zos ua zog kais. Nws tsev neeg nov tej ntoo thiab tej tsev vau. Qhov av qeeg ua rau lub zos puas tas nrho. Tus sau phauv ntawv no lub tsev piam tagnrho li lawm. Tus txiv neej ntawd thiab nws tsev neeg yuav tsum tau pw rau tom lub vaj zaub. Thaum nyob hauv lub vaj, tus sau phau ntawv no zaum ua ke nrog rau ib tug twm. Tus twm lub cev sov ces ua rau tus sau phau ntawv no cia li tsi ntshai. Ces tsi ntev nws txawm raug zog lawm.

Name ______________________________ Date ______________________

VIETNAMESE

Tập ký sự này kể về chuyện xảy ra ở một ngôi làng Việt Nam. Một ngày nọ, các con vật trong làng linh cảm có điều chẳng lành sắp xảy ra. Các con trâu dẫm chân và rú lên. Một số con vật khác chạy trốn. Dân làng mở cửa chuồng cho trâu thoát chạy. Gia đình tác giả chạy tới một nơi ẩn nấp. Một trận động đất làm chấn động cả ngôi làng. Gia đình này nghe thấy cây cối và tòa nhà đổ sập. Trận động đất tàn phá ngôi làng. Căn nhà của tác giả bị đổ nát. Ông ta và gia đình phải ngủ ngoài vườn. Trong vườn, tác giả ngồi chung với một trong những con trâu. Cơ thể ấm áp của trâu trấn an tác giả. Ông nhanh chóng rơi vào giấc ngủ.

CHINESE

這段回憶發生在越南的一個村莊裡。一天，村裡的動物感覺事情不妙。水牛跺著腳，發出吼叫；其他動物也紛紛逃避躲藏。村民們打開牛棚，讓水牛逃命。作者及家人逃進了一處庇護所。一場地震震撼了村莊。作者一家聽到樹木及房屋的倒塌聲。地震摧毀了村莊。作者家的房子倒了，他和家人們只能睡在園子裏。作者坐在園子中的一頭水牛旁。水牛溫暖的身體令作者有了安全感，不久他就睡著了。

CAMBODIAN

អានុស្សាវរីយ៍នេះកើតឡើងនៅក្នុងភូមិមួយនៃប្រទេសវៀតណាម។ ថ្ងៃមួយ សត្វនៅក្នុងភូមិមានអារម្មណ៍ដឹងថាមានអ្វីមួយដែលខុសប្លែក។ ក្របីទន្រ្ទាំជើង ហើយស្រែក។ សត្វខ្លះរត់និងពួន។ អ្នកភូមិបើកទ្វារក្រោលឲ្យក្របីអាចភៀសខ្លួនបាន។ គ្រួសារអ្នកនិពន្ធរត់ទៅរកទីជំរកមួយ។ ការរំជួយផែនដីមួយអង្រួនភូមិ។ គ្រួសារឮសូរដើមឈើនិងអាគាររលំ។ ការរំជួយផែនដីបំផ្លាញភូមិ។ ផ្ទះរបស់អ្នកនិពន្ធត្រូវខូចខាត។ គាត់និងគ្រួសារគាត់ត្រូវគេងនៅក្នុងសួនច្បារដំណាំ។ អ្នកនិពន្ធអង្គុយជាមួយក្របីមួយនៅក្នុងសួនច្បារ។ ខ្លួនក្តៅឧណ្ហៗរបស់ក្របីធ្វើឲ្យអ្នកនិពន្ធមានអារម្មណ៍ថាបានសេចក្តីសុខ។ គាត់ក៏ងុយគេងលក់ភ្លាម។

HAITIAN CREOLE

Memwa sa a ap dewoule nan yon vilaj vyetnamyen. Yon jou, bèt yo nan vilaj lan santi gen yon bagay ki pa mache byen. Bizon yo frape pye yo atè epi y ap rele. Gen kèk nan lòt bèt yo ki kouri epi y al kache. Moun nan vilaj yo louvri pòt anga a pou bizon yo ka sove. Fanmi otè an kouri ale nan yon refij. Yon tranbleman de tè souke vilaj lan. Fanmi an tande pye bwa ak kay k ap tonbe. Tranbleman de tè an kraze vilaj lan. Kay otè an kraze nèt. Limenm ak fanmi l oblije dòmi nan jaden an. Nan jaden an, otè an chita ak youn nan bizon yo. Kò cho bizon an fè otè santi li ansekirite. Li pa pèdi tan anvan dòmi pran l.

Name ______________________________ Date ____________________

UNIT 4 • CHAPTER 1

The Library Card, by Jerry Spinelli & **At the Library,** by Nikki Grimes

ENGLISH

"The Library Card" is a novel about a boy named Mongoose who finds a shell from a strange bug. He also finds a library card. Although he has never been there before, he goes to the library. There, he asks a lady about the shell. She brings him a book to help him learn about it. Mongoose runs home to read the book. He learns that the shell is from a bug called a cicada. Mongoose spends the rest of the night reading about interesting creatures.

"At the Library" is a poem about the joy of reading books. The speaker of the poem says books allow her to see seas and pirates. When reading, she visits lands where birds talk, children fly, and trees walk. Sometimes, the speaker even meets a strong, wise girl who looks like her.

SPANISH

"The Library Card" es una novela acerca de un niño llamado Mongoose, quien descubre la concha de un insecto raro y una tarjeta para la biblioteca. Aunque nunca antes había ido a una biblioteca, Mongoose decide ir. Allí le pregunta a una señora acerca de la concha y ella le muestra un libro que trata del insecto y su concha. Mongoose corre a casa para leer el libro y aprende que la concha es de un insecto llamado cigarra. Mongoose lee toda la noche acerca de criaturas interesantes.

"At the Library" es un poema acerca de la alegría de leer libros. La narradora dice que los libros le permiten ver mares y piratas. Cuando lee, visita lugares donde los pájaros hablan, los niños vuelan y los árboles caminan. A veces, descubre a una niña fuerte y sabia que se parece a ella misma.

HMONG

"The Library Card" yog ib zaj piav txog ib tug me nyuam tub npe hu ua Mongoose uas nrhiav tau ib lub khaujkhaum kab txawv heev. Nws kuj nrhiav tau ib daim khaj los sis npav rau chaw qiv ntawv. Txawm tias nws yeej tsi tau mus ntawd dua li los tam sim no nws mus tom chaw qiv ntawv lawm. Nyob rau to, nws nug tus pojniam txog ntawm lub khaujkhaum. Tus pojniam ntawd pab mus nqa tau ib phau ntawv los rau nws kawm txog lub khaujkhaum. Mongoose txawm khiav thiab coj phau ntawv mus nyeem tom tsev. Nws kawm tau tias lub khaujkhaum ntawd yog los ntawm ib tug kab hu ua cicada. Mongoose siv sib hawm mo ntawd nyeem txog ntau yam kab ua rau nws txaus siab kawg li.

"At the Library" yog ib zaj lus paivyi hais txog nyiam saib ntawv rau qhov nws ua rau yus zoo siab. Tus sau zaj lus no hais tias saib ntawv ua rau nws pom tej dej hiavtxwv thiab cov tub sab hav dej-pirates. Thaum nws nyeem ntawv, nws pom muaj tej chaw uas noog hais lus, me nyuam yaus ya, thiab tej ntoo los paub mus kev huvsi. Tej thaum tus coj uas tau piav zaj no kuj ntsib ib tug ntxhais uas muaj zog heev thiab tus txhais ntawd kuj nyiam nws.

Name ______________________ Date ______________________

VIETNAMESE

"The Library Card" là một tiểu thuyết kể về một cậu thiếu niên có tên Mongoose tìm thấy vỏ mai của một côn trùng lạ. Cậu cũng tìm thấy một thẻ thư viện. Cậu đi đến thư viện mặc dù cậu chưa tới đó bao giờ. Tại thư viện, cậu hỏi một cô ở đó về cái vỏ mai. Cô ta đưa cho cậu một quyển sách để giúp cậu tìm hiểu. Mongoose chạy nhanh về nhà để đọc sách. Cậu học được rằng cái vỏ mai đó là từ một con côn trùng có tên gọi là con ve sầu. Mongoose đọc về các sinh vật lý thú cho đến cuối buổi tối hôm ấy.

"At the Library" là một bài thơ nói về thú vui của việc đọc sách. Tác giả của bài thơ nói rằng bà ta có thể thấy biển cả và những tên hải tặc thông qua các cuốn sách. Khi đọc, bà có thể đến thăm những vùng đất nơi có chim biết nói tiếng người, con nít biết bay, và cây cối biết đi bộ. Đôi khi, thậm chí tác giả còn gặp một cô bé khôn ngoan, mạnh mẽ và trông giống như bà.

CHINESE

這本帶有插圖的介紹性書籍說明了精彩的漫畫書是如何編成的。首先，漫畫書的作者必須具有豐富的想像力。有了想像力，可以創造出不同凡響的人物和故事情節。其次，這本書告訴您不少關於漫畫創作的竅門。書中說，您應該確定人物是高大、英俊，還是矮小、丑陋。然後，您應該嘗試用不同的風格畫出每個人物，以便確定人物的外貌長相。最後，您應該為人物穿上特別的服裝。您的人物可以穿披肩，帶面具，蹬長靴；也可以穿戴您能想像出任何其他服飾。

CAMBODIAN

" The Library Card" គឺជារឿងប្រលោមលោកអំពីក្មេងប្រុសម្នាក់ឈ្មោះ ម៉ុងគូស ដែលជាអ្នករកឃើញ ស្នូកនៃសត្វល្អិតចំឡែកមួយ។ វាក៏រកឃើញកាតបណ្ណាល័យមួយដែរ។ វាទៅបណ្ណាល័យ បើទោះជាវាមិនដែលទៅ ទីនោះពីមុនមកក៏ដោយ។ នៅទីនោះ វាសួរស្ត្រីម្នាក់អំពីស្នូកសត្វ។ គាត់យកសៀវភៅមួយមកឲ្យវារៀបពីស្នូក។ ម៉ុងគូសរត់ទៅផ្ទះដើម្បីអានសៀវភៅ។ វាដឹងថា ស្នូកមកពីសត្វល្អិតមួយហៅថា ស៊ីកាដា។ ម៉ុងគូសចំណាយពេល មួយយប់អានអំពីសត្វដែលគួរចាប់អារម្មណ៍នេះ។

" At the Library" ជាកំណាព្យមួយអំពីការសប្បាយដោយការអានសៀវភៅ។ អ្នកអានកំណាព្យនិយាយថា សៀវភៅអនុញ្ញាតឲ្យនាងមើលឃើញសមុទ្រនិងចោរសមុទ្រ។ ពេលអាន នាងទៅដល់ទឹកដីដែលសត្វស្លាបចេះ និយាយ, កូនក្មេងចេះហោះ, និងដើមឈើចេះដើរ។ ពេលខ្លះ អ្នកអានក៏ជួបក្មេងស្រីដែលខ្លាំង ហើយចិត្តគំនិតល្អ ដែលមានរូបរាងដូចនាងដែរ។

HAITIAN CREOLE

"The Library Card" se yon woman ki pale sou yon ti gason yo te rele Mongoose ki jwenn yon kokiy nan men yon ensèk etranj. Li jwenn yon kat pou bibliyotèk tou. Byenke li pat janm konn ale la, li deside ale nan bibliyotèk lan. Lè li rive la, li poze yon dam kesyon sou kokiy lan. Dam lan pote yon liv bali pou l ede l aprann kèk bagay sou kokiy lan. Mongoose kouri ale lakay li pou l li liv lan. Li aprann kokiy lan soti nan yon ensèk yo rele lasigal. Mongoose pase tout rès nuit lan ap li osijè kèk kreyati enteresan.

"At the Library" se yon powèm konsènan jwa ki genyen lè w ap li liv. Oratè an di liv yo pèmèt li imajine lanmè yo ak pirat yo. Lè l ap li, li vizite peyi kote zwazo konn pale, kote timoun konn vole, epi kote pye bwa konn mache. Kèlkefwa, oratè an pale an te menm konn rankontre yon tifi ki fò, epi ki saj ki te sanble avèk li..

Name ______________________________ Date ____________________

UNIT 4 • CHAPTER 2

Discovering the Inca Ice Maiden, by Johan Reinhard

ENGLISH

This nonfiction narrative is about an important discovery. Johan Reinhard writes about how he likes to climb mountains. He climbs Ampato, a volcano in South America. During his climb, he finds old pottery and other objects near the top of the volcano. Then he sees a mummy. It is the body of a young girl. This is the first frozen female mummy ever in South America. Reinhard tries to carry the mummy down the mountain. He stops when it becomes too dangerous. The next day, Reinhard goes back to get the mummy. Scientists later study the mummy. They discover that the girl was about 14 years old. She was part of the South American Inca empire. She lived about 500 years ago.

SPANISH

Esta narración histórica es acerca de un descubrimiento importante. Johan Reinhard escribe acerca de su interés por escalar montañas y de su experiencia en Ampato, un volcán de Suramérica. Durante su ascenso, Reinhard descubre cerámica antigua y otros objetos cerca de la cima de la montaña. Luego encuentra la momia de una niña, la cual es la primera momia congelada de una mujer en Suramérica. Reinhard intenta cargar a la momia al bajar de la montaña, pero deja de hacerlo cuando se vuelve demasiado peligroso. Al día siguiente, Reinhard se devuelve para recoger a la momia. Los científicos luego estudian la momia y descubren que la niña murió cuando tenía unos 14 años. Ella formaba parte del imperio inca y vivió hace unos 500 años.

HMONG

Zaj lus no piav txog raws li qhov tau muaj thiab yog ib qho tshawb nrhiav pom uas tseem ceeb. Hohan Reinhard sau txog tias nws nyiam nces roob ruas licas. Nws nce Ampato uas yog ib lub av kub npau-volcano nyob rau yav qabteb Amesliskas. Nws pom ib lub cev tibneeg tuag. Nws yog ib tug me nyuam ntxhais lub cev. No yog thawj lub ce pojniam uas tau khov nabkuab nyob rau qabteb Asmesliskas. Reihard sim nqa nws nqis roob tsuas los. Nws nres theem tos yog thaum nws pom tias kev phem heev tsi zoo mus lawm. Hnub tom qab, Reinhard mam rov qab mus nqa lub cev tuag ntawd. Tom qab no cov kws kawm-scientists mam kawm txog lub cev tuag ntawd. Lawv tau tias tus me nyuam ntxhais ntawd nws muaj 14 xyoos. Nws yog ib tus neeg ntawm haiv neeg Inca uas tau kav nyob rau Asmesliskas Qabteb. Thaum nws tseem muaj txojsia nyob yog li 500 xyoo dhau los lawm.

Name ______________________________ Date ______________________

VIETNAMESE

Truyện phi tiểu thuyết này kể về một khám phá quan trọng. Johan Reinhard viết về thú leo núi của ông. Ông leo núi Ampato, một núi lửa ở Nam Mỹ. Khi leo, ông tìm thấy các đồ gốm cũ và những thứ đồ khác ở gần đỉnh núi lửa. Sau đó ông tìm thấy một xác đóng băng. Đó là xác của một cô bé. Đây là xác nữ đông lạnh đầu tiên được tìm thấy ở Nam Mỹ. Reinhard cố khiêng xác xuống núi. Ông ngừng lại bởi vì tình thế trở nên quá nguy hiểm. Ngày kế tiếp, Reinhard trở lại tìm xác đóng băng. Các nhà khoa học sau đó nghiên cứu về xác này. Họ phát hiện rằng cô bé được 14 tuổi. Cô là một người dân của đế quốc Inca ở Nam Mỹ. Cô sống cách đây 500 năm.

CHINESE

這篇非小說類敘事文講述的是一個重要發現。約翰˙萊恩哈德寫出他如何喜愛攀山活動。他攀登過位於南美洲的安帕托火山。在攀登的時候，他在火山頂附近，找到一些古老的陶器及其他東西。然後，他看見一個木乃伊。那是一個年青女孩的屍體。這是以前在南美洲從未發現過的第一個冰凍女性木乃伊。萊恩哈德嘗試把木乃伊帶下山去。可是，由於太危險，他只能作罷。第二天，他又返回去把木乃伊帶走。稍後，科學家對木乃伊進行了研究。他們發現那女孩子大約十四歲。她生活在南美洲印加帝國的年代。她大約活在距今五百年之前。

CAMBODIAN

រឿងប្រឌិតនេះអធិប្បាយអំពីការរកឃើញដ៏សំខាន់មួយ។ ចូហាន់ រានហាដ សរសេរពីការដែលគាត់ចូលចិត្តឡើងភ្នំ។ គាត់ឡើងភ្នំ អែមផាតូ, ភ្នំភ្លើងនៅទ្វីបអាមេរិកខាងត្បូង។ នៅពេលដែលគាត់ឡើង គាត់រកឃើញឆ្នាំងដីចាស់ៗ និង របស់ផ្សេងៗទៀត នៅជិតកំពូលភ្នំភ្លើង។ បន្ទាប់មកគាត់ឃើញសពដែលមិនរលួយ (mummy)។ វាជាសពក្មេងស្រីម្នាក់។ នេះជាសពស្ត្រីមិនរលួយទីមួយដែលមិនដែលមាននៅទ្វីបអាមេរិកខាងត្បូង។ រានហាដ សាកល្បងកាន់សពចុះពីភ្នំ។ គាត់ឈប់នៅពេលដែលវាចាប់ផ្តើមមានភាពគ្រោះថ្នាក់។ ថ្ងៃបន្ទាប់ រានហាដ ត្រឡប់ទៅយកសពវិញ។ ក្រោយមកអ្នកវិទ្យាសាស្ត្រសិក្សាសព។ គេរកឃើញថា សពជាក្មេងស្រីអាយុប្រហែល ១៤ឆ្នាំ។ នាងជាមនុស្សនៃចក្រភព អាមេរិកកែន អិនកា។ នាងរស់នៅប្រហែល ៥០០ឆ្នាំមុន។

HAITIAN CREOLE

Narasyon sa a ki pa fiktif pale konsènan yon dekouvèt enpòtan. Johan Reinhard ekri sou fason li renmen monte mòn. Li monte mòn Ampato, yon vòlkan nan Amerik di Sid. Pandan l ap monte mòn lan, li jwenn vye potri ak kèk lòt bagay tou pre tèt vòlkan an. Aprè sa li wè yon momi. Se kò yon jèn tifi. Se premye momi fanm konjele yo te dekouvri an Amerik di Sid. Reinhard eseye desann mòn lan ak momi an. Li fè yon kanpe lè sa te kòmanse vin twò danjre. Nan landmen, Reinhard retounen pou l ale chèche momi an. Pita syantifik yo te vin etidye momi an. Yo dekouvri tifi an te genyen apeprè 14 an. Li te yon manm nan Anpir Enka Amerik di Sid lan. Li te viv sa te fè apeprè 500 andesa.

Name ________________________________ Date ____________________

UNIT 4 • CHAPTER 3

The Art of Swordsmanship, by Rafe Martin

ENGLISH

In this folktale, Manjuro wants to become a master swordsman. He wants Banzo to teach him. Banzo is the best swordsman in the country. For the first three years, Banzo tells Manjuro to do chores only. Manjuro is upset and wants to leave Banzo. Manjuro thinks he is not learning anything about becoming a swordsman from Banzo. Then one day Banzo does something different. Banzo surprises Manjuro and hits him with a wooden sword. Banzo does this every day. Soon, Manjuro is alert at all times. He begins to block every blow from the sword with whatever he is holding. Manjuro becomes a great swordsman. Now no one, not even his teacher, can defeat Manjuro.

SPANISH

En este cuento tradicional, Manjuro quiere convertirse en un espadachín diestro. Él quiere que Banzo le enseñe, porque Banzo es el mejor espadachín del país. Los primeros tres años, Banzo le pide a Manjuro que sólo haga quehaceres. Manjuro se enfurece y quiere dejar de trabajar con Banzo. Manjuro piensa que no está aprendiendo nada de Banzo acerca de ser un buen espadachín. Sin embargo, un día Banzo hace algo distinto. Banzo sorprende a Manjuro y le pega con una espada de madera. Banzo comienza a hacer lo mismo todos los días. Pronto, Manjuro está alerta a toda hora y comienza a bloquear todos los golpes con lo que tenga a mano. Así es que Manjuro se vuelve un espadachín diestro. Ahora nadie, ni siquiera su maestro, puede ganarle a Manjuro.

HMONG

Nyob rau hauv zaj dab neeg no, Manjuro xav ua ib tug tub tua ntaj uas keej heev. Nws xav kom Banzo qhia nws. Banzo yog ib tug tub tua ntaj keej tshaj plaws nyob rau lub teb chaws ntawd. Nyob rau ntawm thawj peb xyoos, Banzo tsua yog qhia rau Manjuro ua haujlwm xwb nkauj. Manjuro chim thiab tsi xav nrog Banzo nyob ntxiv lawm. Manjuro xav hais tias nws yeej kawm tsi tau abtsi uas yog txog ua ib tug tub tua ntaj los ntawm Banzo hlo li. Ces muaj ib hnub Banzo txawm ua ib yam uas txawm tsi zoo li qub lawm. Tog nwd Banzo txawm xuas ib tsab ntaj ntoo ntaus Manjuro lawm. Banzo ua li no rau txhua hnub li. Tsi ntev Manjuro txawj ceev faj txhua lub sib hawm lawm. Thaum zoo li ntawd nws txawm pib thaiv tsab ntaj ntawd nrog rau txhua yam uas nws tuav nyob hauv nws txhais tes. Manjuro txawm dhau los ua ib tug tub tua ntaj uas keej heev. Niaj hnub nim no, txawm yog nws tus xib hwb los twb kov tsi yeej Manjuro lawm.

Name ______________________________ Date ______________________

VIETNAMESE

Trong truyện kể dân gian này, Manjuro muốn trở thành một kiếm sĩ điêu luyện. Cậu muốn nhờ Banzo dạy kiếm cho cậu. Banzo là kiếm sĩ bậc nhất trong nước. Trong ba năm đầu, Banzo chỉ sai Majuro làm việc vặt. Majuro rất khổ sở và muốn rời bỏ Banzo. Manjuro tưởng mình không học được điều gì về thuật đánh kiếm từ Banzo. Rồi một ngày nọ Banzo làm một điều khác lạ. Banzo bất chợt đánh cậu bằng một thanh kiếm gỗ. Banzo hằng ngày làm điều này. Chẳng bao lâu sau Manjuro trở nên luôn luôn cảnh giác. Cậu bắt đầu đỡ được mỗi đòn kiếm tấn công bằng bất cứ thứ gì trên tay mình. Manjuro trở thành một kiếm sĩ tuyệt diệu. Giờ đây không một người nào, kể cả thầy của Manjuro, có thể đánh bại được cậu.

CHINESE

這篇非小說類敘事文講述的是一個重要發現。約翰˙萊恩哈德寫出他如何喜愛攀山活動。他攀登過位於南美洲的安帕托火山。在攀登的時候，他在火山頂附近，找到一些古老的陶器及其他東西。然後，他看見一個木乃伊。那是一個年青女孩的屍體。這是以前在南美洲從未發現過的第一個冰凍女性木乃伊。萊恩哈德嘗試把木乃伊帶下山去。可是，由於太危險，他只能作罷。第二天，他又返回去把木乃伊帶走。稍後，科學家對木乃伊進行了研究。他們發現那女孩子大約十四歲。她生活在南美洲印加帝國的年代。她大約活在距今五百年之前。

CAMBODIAN

ក្នុងរឿងល្បើកនេះ ម៉ែនជូរ៉ូ ចង់ក្លាយជាអ្នកជំនាញកាប់ដាវម្នាក់។ គាត់ចង់ឲ្យ បែនហ្សូ បង្រៀនគាត់។ បែនហ្សូ ជាអ្នកកាប់ដាវពូកែម្នាក់នៅក្នុងស្រុក។ បីឆ្នាំដំបូង បែនហ្សូ ប្រាប់ម៉ែនជូរ៉ូឲ្យធ្វើតែកិច្ចការផ្ទះប៉ុណ្ណោះ។ ម៉ែនជូរ៉ូ អាក់អន់ចិត្ត ហើយចង់ចេញពីបែនហ្សូ។ ម៉ែនជូរ៉ូគិតថា គាត់គ្មានបានរៀនអ្វីទាំងអស់ពីបែនហ្សូឲ្យក្លាយជាអ្នកកាប់ដាវ។ បន្ទាប់មក មានថ្ងៃមួយបែនហ្សូធ្វើអ្វីមួយដែលផ្សេងពីមុន។ បែនហ្សូធ្វើឲ្យម៉ែនជូរ៉ូភ្ញាក់ផ្អើល ហើយកាប់គាត់ជាមួយនឹងដាវឈើ។ បែនហ្សូធ្វើបែបនេះរាល់ថ្ងៃ។ មិនយូរប៉ុន្មាន ម៉ែនជូរ៉ូ ដឹងខ្លួនរាល់ៗពេល។ គាត់ចាប់ផ្តើមទប់ទល់វិញបានគ្រប់ពេលដែលកាប់ ដោយប្រើអ្វីដែលគាត់កាន់នៅជាប់ដៃ។ ម៉ែនជូរ៉ូ ក្លាយជាអ្នកកាប់ដាវខ្លាំងពូកែម្នាក់។ ឥឡូវនេះ គ្មាននរណាម្នាក់អាចប្រយុទ្ធឈ្នះគាត់ឡើយ សូម្បីតែគ្រូគាត់ក៏ដោយ។

HAITIAN CREOLE

Nan istwa fòlklò sa a, Manjuro vle vin mèt nan tire epe. Li vle pou Banzo montre l kouman pou l fè sa. Banzo se meyè tirè epe nan peyi an. Pandan premye twa zan yo, Banzo di Manjuro pou li fè ti travay menaje sèlman. Manjuro pa kontan epi li vle vire do bay Banzo. Manjuro panse pa gen anyen l ap aprann la nan men Banzo sou zafè kouman pou tire epe. Epi yon jou Banzo fè yon bagay ki diferan de sa l konn fè. Banzo pran Manjuro pa sipriz epi li frape misye ak yon epe an bwa. Banzo fè sa chak jou. Sa pa pran tan, Manjuro vin toujou alèt. Li kòmanse ka pare tout kout epe yo avèk kèlkeswa sa l gen nan men lan. Manjuro vin yon gran tirè epe. Kounye an pèsonn, pa menm pwofesè l lan, paka defye Manjuro.

Name ______________________ Date ______________________

UNIT 4 • CHAPTER 4

Mae Jemison, Space Scientist, by Gail Sakurai

ENGLISH

This biography is about Mae Jemison. Jemison was the first African-American woman in space. Jemison worked hard to make her dream of becoming an astronaut come true. When she was young, many people told her that an African-American girl could not grow up to be an astronaut. This did not stop Jemison. With the support of her parents, Jemison followed her dream. She went to college and medical school. Then she trained to become an astronaut. On September 12, 1992, Jemison's dream came true. Jemison blasted off in a space shuttle. She spent eight days in space and traveled 3.3 million miles. Jemison did many important experiments while in space. Today, Jemison encourages young people to follow their dreams.

SPANISH

Esta biografía es acerca de Mae Jemison, quien fue la primera mujer afroamericana en viajar al espacio. Jemison trabajó duro para que su sueño de ser astronauta se convirtiera en realidad. Cuando era joven, mucha gente le dijo que una niña afroamericana no podría volverse astronauta. Pero eso no detuvo a Jemison. Con el apoyo de sus padres, Jemison siguió su sueño. Ella fue a la universidad, estudió medicina y luego entrenó para ser astronauta. El 12 de septiembre de 1992, el sueño de Jemison se volvió realidad. Jemison montó en un transbordador espacial. Ella duró ocho días en el espacio y viajó 3.3 millones de millas. Jemison llevó a cabo muchos experimentos importantes en su viaje espacial. Hoy en día, Jemison anima a la gente joven a seguir sus propios sueños.

HMONG

Zaj lus sau tseg no yog hais txog Mae Jemison. Jemison nws yog thawj tug pojniam Asfliskas-Asmeslikas uas caij avposlaus mus sau ntuj. Jemison tau rau siab kawm ntawv heev, qhov nws xav ua ib tug avposlaus mus saum ntuj uas yog astronaut thiaj tau peem tsheej lawm. Thaum nws tseem yog ib tug me ntxhais xwb, coob tug tib neeg tau hais rau nws tias ua ib tug me nyuam ntxhais Asfliskas-Asmesliskas yuav loj hlob mus ua tsi tau ib tug avposlaus mus saum ntuj uas yog astronaut li. Txawm yog lawv tau thuam nws li ntawd los qhov no cheem tsi tau nws Jemison li. Thaum nws niam thiab nws txiv txhawb nws lub zog, Jemison tau rau siab nro kawm thiab ua raws li qhov nws xav tau ntawd. Nws mus kawm ntawv qib siab (college) thiab mus kawm ua kws kho mob. Ces nws mam li mus xyaum ua ib tug mus saum ntuj. Nyob rau lub 9hlis, hnub tim 12, xyoo 1992, Jemison tus npau suav txawm peem tsheej li lawm tiag. Jemison tau caij lub avposlaus ya mus saum ntuj lawm. Nws tau nyob yim hnub saum ntuj thiab tau ya ncig mus los tau 3.3 lab mais deb. Jemison tau kawm thiab sim ntau yam thaum nws nyob saum nruab ntug. Niaj hnub tam sim no Jemison hais kom txhua tug tub hluas ntxhais hluas rau siab sib zog kawm thiaj mus txog lawv tus npau suav.

Name ______________________ Date ______________________

VIETNAMESE

Cuốn tiểu sử này nói về Mae Jemison. Jemison là phụ nữ Mỹ gốc Châu Phi đầu tiên du hành xuyên qua không trung. Jemison làm việc vất vả để biến giấc mơ làm phi hành gia trở thành sự thực. Khi bà còn bé, nhiều người nói rằng một cô bé Mỹ gốc Châu Phi không thể nào lớn lên làm phi hành gia được. Tuy nhiên điều này không làm Jemison nản lòng. Với sự hỗ trợ của cha mẹ, Jemison theo đuổi ước mơ của mình. Bà theo học đại học và trường y khoa. Sau đó bà được huấn luyện trở thành phi hành gia. Vào ngày 12 tháng Chín, 1992, ước mơ của Jemison trở thành hiện thực. Jemison cùng với tàu con thoi vũ trụ được phóng lên không trung. Bà ở tám ngày ngoài không gian vũ trụ và du hành được 3.3 triệu dặm. Jemison thực hiện nhiều thí nghiệm quan trọng khi ở ngoài không trung. Ngày nay, Jemison động viên nhiều thanh niên theo đuổi ước mơ của mình.

CHINESE

這是一本關於梅˙傑米森的傳記。傑米森是第一位登上太空的非洲裔美國女性。傑米森一直努力不懈地要實現她成為太空人的夢想。當她年輕時，很多人告訴她，非洲裔美國女孩子是不可能成為太空人的。但這並沒有阻止傑米森。在她父母的支持下，傑米森追尋她的夢想。她上了大學及醫學院，後來她接受訓練成為太空人。一九九二年九月十二日，傑米森的夢想成真。傑米森乘坐穿梭機升空。她在太空停留了八天，共飛行了三百三十萬英哩。傑米森在太空中做了很多重要的實驗。今天，傑米森鼓勵年青人去追尋他們的夢想。

CAMBODIAN

ប្រវត្តិរូបនេះអំពី ម៉ា ជេមីសុន។ ជេមីសុន គឺជាស្ត្រីអាហ្វ្រិកកែន-អាមេរិកកែន ទីមួយនៅក្នុងលំហរអាកាស។ ជេមីសុន ប្រឹងធ្វើការដើម្បីឲ្យការយល់សប្តិ៍ក្លាយជា អវកាសយានិករបស់គាត់ ទៅជាការពិត។ កាលគាត់ នៅពីក្មេង មនុស្សជាច្រើនប្រាប់គាត់ថា ស្រីអាហ្វ្រិកកែន-អាមេរិកកែន មិនអាចធំឡើងជា អវកាសយានិកទេ។ ការនេះមិនបញ្ឈប់ជេមីសុនបានទេ។ ជាមួយនឹងការគាំទ្ររបស់ឪពុកម្តាយគាត់ ជេមីសុនធ្វើតាមការយល់សប្តិ៍របស់គាត់។ គាត់ទៅរៀននៅមហាវិទ្យាល័យ និង សាលាវេជ្ជសាស្ត្រ។ បន្ទាប់មកគាត់ហ្វឹកហ្វឺនទៅជាអវកាសយានិកម្នាក់។ នៅថ្ងៃទី១២ ខែកញ្ញា ឆ្នាំ១៩៩២ ការយល់សប្តិ៍របស់ជេមីសុនបានក្លាយជាការពិត។ ជេមីសុន ហោះឡើង នៅក្នុងយានអវកាសមួយ។ គាត់ចំណាយពេលប្រាំបីថ្ងៃនៅក្នុងលំហរអាកាស និងធ្វើដំណើរចម្ងាយ ៣.៣ លានម៉ាយ។ ជេមីសុន បានធ្វើការពិសោធន៏សំខាន់ៗជាច្រើននៅពេលនៅក្នុងលំហរអាកាស។ សព្វថ្ងៃ ជេមីសុន លើកទឹកចិត្តឲ្យក្មេងៗធ្វើតាមការយល់សប្តិ៍របស់គេ។

HAITIAN CREOLE

Byografi sa a pale konsènan Mae Jemison. Jemison te premye fanm Afriken-Ameriken nan lespas. Jemison te travay di pou li te ka reyalize rèv li pou l te devni yon astwonòt. Lè li te jèn, anpil moun te di l yon tifi Afriken-Ameriken paka grandi pou l devni yon astwonòt . Sa pat rete Jemison. Ak sipò paran l, Jemison te pousuiv rèv li an. Li te ale nan kolèj epi nan lekòl Medsin. Aprè sa li te resevwa fòmasyon pou l te devni yon astwonòt. Le 12 septanm 1992, rèv Jemison lan te reyalize. Jemison te pati nan lè an nan yon veso espasyal . Li te pase uit jou nan lespas epi li te vwayaje yon distans de 3,3 milyon mil. Jemison te fè anpil eksperyans enpòtan lè li te nan lespas lan. Jodi a, Jemison ap ankouraje tout jèn timoun pou yo pousuiv rèv yo.

Name ______________________________ Date ______________________

UNIT 5 • CHAPTER 1

How Tía Lola Came to (Visit) Stay, by Julia Alvarez

ENGLISH

This selection is from the novel "How Tía Lola Came to (Visit) Stay." Miguel, Juanita, and their mother have just moved from New York City to Vermont. Their aunt, Tía Lola, is coming to visit. The children's mother is excited, but Miguel is unhappy. He is unhappy that his parents got divorced. He is also unhappy about moving away from his friends. Miguel does not want to see Tía Lola. Miguel, Juanita, and their mother go to the airport to meet Tía Lola. At the airport, Miguel calls Tía Lola using the airport microphone. Soon, the children hear an excited shout. It is Tía Lola. When Miguel hugs his aunt, he feels a little better. For that moment, Miguel forgets about feeling unhappy.

SPANISH

Esta es una selección de la novela "How Tía Lola Came to (Visit) Stay". Miguel, Juanita y su madre se acaban de mudar de Nueva York a Vermont, y Tía Lola va a ir a visitarlos. La mamá de los niños está contenta, pero Miguel no lo está. Él está triste porque sus padres se divorciaron y porque tiene que vivir lejos de sus amigos. Así que no quiere ver a Tía Lola. Miguel, Juanita y su madre van al aeropuerto a recibir a Tía Lola. En el aeropuerto, Miguel usa el altavoz del aeropuerto para llamar a Tía Lola. Pronto, los niños oyen una voz feliz. Es la voz de Tía Lola. Cuando Miguel abraza a su tía, él se siente un poco mejor y, por ese momento, se olvida de sentirse triste.

HMONG

Zaj lus no yog xaiv los the phau ntawv "How Tía Lola Came to (Visit) Stay." Hais txog Miguel, Juanita, thiab lawv niam uas nim qhuav khiav ntawm lub nroog New York City mus rau Vermont. Lawv tus phauj, Tía Lola, tseem tab tom tuaj mus saib lawv. Cov me nyuam niam zoo siab heev li, tiam sis Miguel tsi zoo siab. Nws tsi zoo siab vim tias nws niam thiab nws txiv tau sib nrauj lawm. Thiab qhov nws tsi zoo siab ntawd vim tias nws khiav ntawm nws cov phooj ywg mus nyob deb lawm. Miguel tsi xav pom Tía Lola. Miguel siv tshav dav hlau lub paj taub hu nrhiav Tía Lola. Tib pliag xwb ces cov me nyuam txawm nov ib lub suab qw nrov luag ntxhi. Nws yog Tía Lola los sav. Thaum Miguel khawm nkaus nws tus phauj, nws cia li zoo siab zog tuaj. Ces thaum ntawd Miguel txawm nov qab qhov nws tsi zoo siab lawm.

Name ________________________________ Date ________________________

VIETNAMESE

Đây là đoạn trích từ tiểu thuyết "How Tía Lola Came to (Visit) Stay" Miguel, Juanita, và mẹ vừa mới dọn từ Thành Phố New York sang Vermont. Người dì, là Tía Lola, sắp đến thăm. Mẹ của bọn trẻ rất phấn khởi, nhưng Miguel thì lại không được vui. Cậu không vui vì cha mẹ cậu ly dị. Cậu cũng không vui vì phải ở xa bạn bè. Miguel không muốn gặp dì Tía Lola. Miguel, Juanita, và mẹ đến phi trường để đón dì. Tại đó, Miguel dùng micrô của phi trường để gọi dì Tía Lola. Chẳng mấy chốc, bọn trẻ nghe một tiếng la phấn khởi. Dì Tía Lola đấy! Khi Miguel ôm dì, cậu cảm thấy đỡ hơn một chút. Lúc này Miguel quên hẳn cảm giác không vui trước đó.

CHINESE

這個故事選自小說 How Tía Lola Came to (Visit) Stay。米高爾、裘安妮達與他們的母親剛從紐約市搬到佛蒙特。姨媽蘿拉要來看他們。母親很高興，可是米高爾卻不開心，因為他父母離婚了，他又離開了朋友。米高爾不想見到蘿拉姨媽。米高爾、裘安妮達與母親一起去機場接蘿拉姨媽。在機場，米高爾用機場的麥克風呼叫蘿拉姨媽。不一會，孩子們就聽到有人在高興地喊著，原來是蘿拉姨媽。米高爾與姨媽抱在一起，感覺好些了。那一刻，米高爾忘記了不開心的事。

CAMBODIAN

ការជ្រើសនេះគឺបានមកពីប្រលោមលោក " How Tía Lola Came to (Visit) Stay "។ មីគែល, ជូអានីតា, និងម្តាយពួកគេ ទើបតែផ្លាស់ពីទីក្រុងញូយ៉កមកនៅ វ៉រម៉ន។ មីងពួកវា, តៃយ៉ា ឡូឡា, កំពុងមកលេង។ ម្តាយក្មេងទាំងនេះរំភើបណាស់ តែមីគែលមិនរីករាយទេ។ វាមិនរីករាយដោយឪពុកម្តាយវា លែងលះគ្នា។ វាក៏មិនរីករាយដែរ ដែលផ្លាស់ចេញឆ្ងាយពីមិត្តភក្តិវា។ មីគែលមិនចង់ជួបមុខ តៃយ៉ា ឡូឡា ទេ។ មីគែល, ជូអានីតា, និងម្តាយ ទៅវាលចំណតយន្តហោះ ដើម្បីជួប តៃយ៉ា ឡូឡា។ នៅវាលចំណតយន្តហោះ មីគែល ហៅ តៃយ៉ា ឡូឡា តាមមេក្រូនៅចំណតយន្តហោះ។ ភ្លាមនោះ ក្មេងទាំងនេះឮសូរសំឡេងស្រែកដោយ ក្តីរំភើប។ គឺតៃយ៉ា ឡូឡា។ ពេលដែល មីគែល អោបមីងវា វាមានអារម្មណ៍ធូរស្រាលបន្តិច។ ពេលនោះ មីគែលភ្លេចអំពីអារម្មណ៍ដែលមិនរីករាយអស់។

HAITIAN CREOLE

Seleksyon sa a soti nan woman "How Tía Lola Came to (Visit) Stay." Miguel, Juanita, ak manman yo fèk soti New York City pou al rete nan Vermont. Matant yo, Tía Lola, ap vin vizite yo. Manman timoun yo kontan anpil, men Miguel limenm pa kontan. Li pa kontan paske manman l ak papa l te divòse. Li pa kontan tou paske li te deplase kite zanmi l yo. Miguel pa bezwen wè Tía Lola. Miguel, Juanita, ak manman yo ale nan ayewopò an pou rankontre Tía Lola. Nan ayewopò an, Miguel rele Tía Lola nan mikwofòn ayewopò an. Anpil tan pa pase, timoun yo tande yon vwa byen anime. Se Tía Lola. Lè Miguel anbrase matant li, li vin santi l yon ti jan miyò. Pou kounye a, Miguel bliye si li pat kontan.

Name ______________________________ Date ______________________

UNIT 5 • CHAPTER 2

Helen Keller, by George Sullivan, & **The Miracle Worker,** by William Gibson

ENGLISH

Helen Keller is seven years old. She cannot see or hear. In the biography "Helen Keller," the author explains how Helen learns to communicate. Annie is Helen's teacher. She tries to teach Helen to understand words by spelling them with her finger. One day, Annie takes Helen to the water pump. She puts Helen's hand under the stream of water. At the same time, Annie spells the word *water* in Helen's other hand. Helen understands. She learns many more words that day.

The play, "The Miracle Worker," tells the same story. Annie places a water pitcher in Helen's hand. She guides the pitcher so that some water spills onto Helen's hand. Annie writes water on Helen's free hand. Helen understands. Helen touches many things and asks for their names. Helen touches Annie's cheek. Annie spells *teacher.* Helen spells back teacher and Annie nods.

SPANISH

Helen Keller tiene siete años y no puede ver ni oír. En la biografía de Helen Keller, el autor explica cómo hace Helen para aprender a comunicarse. Annie es la maestra de Helen. Para enseñarle a comprender palabras, Annie se las deletrea con el dedo. Un día, Annie lleva a Helen a la fuente de agua. Annie pone la mano de Helen bajo el chorro de agua mientras deletrea la palabra "agua" en la otra mano de Helen. Helen comprende lo que significa la palabra y así ella aprende muchas más palabras ese día.

La obra de teatro llamada "The Miracle Worker" cuenta la misma historia de Helen. Annie pone una jarra con agua en las manos de Helen y mueve la jarra, de manera que cae un poco de agua en la mano de Helen. Annie escribe "agua" en la mano de Helen y ella entiende lo que significa. Helen toca muchas cosas y pregunta por sus nombres. Helen toca la mejilla de Annie y Annie deletrea la palabra "profesora". Helen deletrea "profesora" y Annie dice "sí" con un movimiento de aprobación de la cabeza.

HMONG

Helen Keller muaj xya xyoo. Nws tsi hnov lus thiab tsi pom kev. Nyob rau hauv zaj lus "Helen Keller," uas tus sau tau piav txog nws qhia tej uas Helen xyaum cev lus li cas. Annie yog Helen tus xib hwb qhia ntawv. Helen tus xib hwb qhia kom nws txawj nkag siab cov suab hais lus los ntawm uas siv nws cov ntiv tes sau ib tug ntawv zuj zus. Muaj ib hnub, Annie coj Helen mus rau ntawm lub cav nqus dej. Tus xib hwb muab Helen txhais tes mus txais cov dej uas tab tom txhuav tawv los. Thaum Helen tseem ib sab tes kov dej, Annie ua tes qhia sau qhia rau Helen sab tes tsi kov dej kom nws paub tias dej yog sau li cas. Helen nkag siab huvsi. Hnub ntawd nws kawm ntau lo lus tshiab ntxiv.

Qhov yeeb yam ntawm zaj, "The Miracle Worker" yog qhia txog tib zaj dab neeg li xwb. Annie muab ib tug txau dej tso rau hauv Helen txhais tes. Nws nyem tus txau dej kom dej txeej rau Helen txhais tes. Ces Annie sau los lus tias dej no rau Helen sab tes uas tsi tuav dabtsi. Helen paub. Helen kov ntau yam thiab nug saib lawv ib yog hu li cas. Helen kov Annie lub kauj tsaig. Ces Annie sau qhia tias xib hwb. Helen sau lawv qab hais tias xib hwb ces thaum ntawd Annie co nws taub hau.

Name ____________________ Date ____________________

VIETNAMESE

Helen Keller bảy tuổi. Cô bé bị mù và điếc. Trong cuốn tiểu sử "Helen Keller," tác giả giải thích cách Helen học giao tiếp với người khác. Annie là cô giáo của Helen. Cô cố gắng dạy Helen hiểu từ bằng cách dùng ngón tay để đánh vần. Một ngày nọ, Annie dẫn Helen đến máy bơm nước. Cô đặt tay Helen dưới luồng nước. Cùng lúc đó, Annie đánh vần từ *nước* vào tay kia của Helen. Helen hiểu. Cô bé học thêm nhiều từ vào ngày hôm ấy.

Vở kịch, "The Miracle Worker," kể cùng câu chuyện này. Annie đặt một bình nước vào tay Helen. Cô nghiêng bình sao cho một ít nước đổ vào tay Helen. Annie viết từ *nước* vào tay kia của Helen. Helen hiểu. Cô bé sờ vào nhiều thứ và hỏi tên của chúng. Helen sờ tay vào má Annie. Annie đánh vần *cô giáo*. Helen bắt chước đánh vần *cô giáo* và Annie gật đầu.

CHINESE

海倫・凱勒七歲了，可是她看不見也聽不見。在 Helen Keller 傳記中，作者敘述了海倫是如何學習溝通與表達的。安妮是海倫的老師，她想透過用手指拚寫單詞來教海倫理解單詞的含義。有一天，安妮帶海倫來到水泵旁。她把海倫的手放在水流下面，同時在海倫的另一只手上拚寫出「水」字。海倫就懂了。那天，她還學會了其他不少單詞。

話劇 The Miracle Worker 講述的是同一個故事。安妮把水壺放在海倫手中，將水壺中的一些水倒在海倫手上。安妮在海倫的另一只手上寫下「水」字。海倫就懂了。海倫用手摸到很多東西，然後就會問它們叫什麼。海倫摸到安妮的面頰，安妮就寫出「老師」一詞。海倫學著拚寫出「老師」後，安妮會點頭表示肯定。

CAMBODIAN

ហេឡែន ខែលល័រ មានអាយុប្រាំពីរឆ្នាំ។ នាងមិនអាចមើលឃើញឬស្តាប់ឮអ្វីទេ។ នៅក្នុងប្រវត្តិរូប "Helen Keller", អ្នកនិពន្ធពន្យល់ពីរបៀបដែលហេឡែនរៀនប្រស្រ័យទាក់ទង។ អាននី ជាគ្រូរបស់ ហេឡែន។ គាត់ព្យាយាមបង្រៀនហេឡែនឲ្យយល់ពាក្យ ដោយការសរសេរពាក្យជាមួយម្រាមដៃនាង។ ថ្ងៃមួយ អាននី នាំហេលែនទៅកន្លែងស្នប់បូមទឹក។ គាត់យកដៃហេឡែនទៅដាក់ពីក្រោមទឹកដែលហូរ។ នៅពេលជាមួយ គ្នានោះ អាននី សរសេរពាក្យ *ទឹក* នៅលើដៃម្ខាងទៀតរបស់ហេឡែន។ ហេឡែនយល់។ នាងរៀនពាក្យជាច្រើនថែមទៀតក្នុងថ្ងៃនោះ។

ល្ខោន " The Miracle Worker" ប្រាប់រឿងដូចគ្នា។ អាននី ដាក់ថូរទឹកទៅក្នុងដៃហេឡែន។ គាត់ផ្អៀងថូរ ដែលធ្វើឲ្យទឹកស្រក់ទៅលើដៃហេឡែន។ អាននី សរសេរពាក្យ *ទឹក* នៅលើដៃទំនេររបស់ហេឡែន។ ហេឡែនយល់។ ហេឡែន ប៉ះវត្ថុច្រើនទៀត ហើយសួរពីឈ្មោះវត្ថុនោះ។ ហេឡែនពាល់ថ្ពាល់របស់អាននី។ អាននី សរសេរពាក្យ *គ្រូ* ។ ហេឡែន សរសេរពាក្យ *គ្រូ* តបវិញ ហើយអាននី ងក់ក្បាល។

HAITIAN CREOLE

Helen Keller gen set an. Li paka wè oswa tande. Nan byografi "Helen Keller" an, otè an eksplike kouman Helen te aprann kominike. Pwofesè Helen lan se Annie. Li eseye montre Helen kouman pou l ka konprann mo yo lè li eple yo ak dwèt li. Yon jou, Annie mennen Helen nan yon pomp dlo. Li mete men Helen anba dlo an k ap koule. Anmenmtan, Annie eple mo dlo nan lòt men Helen. Helen konprann. Jou sa a li te aprann anpil mo.

Pyès teyat, "The Miracle Worker," an rakonte menm istwa sa a. Annie mete yon po dlo nan men Helen. Li dirije po dlo a yon fason pou dlo ka tonbe sou men Helen. Annie ekri mo dlo sou men Helen ki vid la. Helen konprann. Helen touche anpil bagay epi li mande kouman yo rele. Helen touche bò figi Annie. Annie eple mo pwofesè. Helen eple mo pwofesè anretou epi Annie fè yon siy ak tèt li.

Name ______________________ Date ______________________

UNIT 5 • CHAPTER 3

Hearing: the Ear

ENGLISH

This informational text explains how people hear sounds. A guitar string vibrates when someone plucks it. When something vibrates, it moves back and forth quickly. Vibrations cause sound. Sound moves in waves. The ear catches these sound waves. The sound waves go down a tube in the ear and cause the eardrum to vibrate. These vibrations go through three ear bones. The ear bones make waves that go to the cochlea. The cochlea is a part of the ear with special cells. These cells change sound waves to electric signals. These signals go to the brain. The brain then tells you what sound you are hearing. In addition to hearing, your ears help you keep your balance.

SPANISH

Este texto informativo explica cómo oye la gente los sonidos. La cuerda de una guitarra vibra cuando uno la toca. Cuando algo vibra, es porque se mueve rápidamente de una dirección a otra. Las vibraciones causan sonidos y los sonidos se mueven como ondas. El oído percibe esas ondas sonoras. Las ondas pasan por un tubo del oído y hacen que vibre el tímpano del oído. Las vibraciones pasan por los huesecillos del oído y estos forman ondas que pasan por el caracol, el cual es una parte del oido que tiene unas células especiales. Esas células cambian las ondas sonoras a señales eléctricas que van al cerebro. Entonces el cerebro le dice a uno los sonidos que está oyendo. Además de oír, el oído nos ayuda a mantener el equilibrio.

HMONG

Ntawm no yog qhia kom sawv daws paub txog qhov tib neeg mloog li cas thiaj hnov tau tej suab. Txoj hlua rau lub kistaj tshee yog thaum leej twg rub tso plhuav. Thaum muaj ib yam abtsi tshee, nws yeej mus los ceev ntsooj. Tej suab tshee ua rau muaj suab nrov. Suab nws nrov tuaj ua tej vuag. Lub pob ntseg nws ntes tau tej vuag li no. Tej suab uas tuaj tsheej vuag no nkag rau lub qhov raj hauv pob ntseg mam li ua rau daim ntxaij puag hauv lub qhov ntsej tshee. Nws tshee mus dhau peb tug txha hauv pob ntseg. Cov pob txha no nrov tsheej vuag tuaj mus rau lub qhov txha mos uas nkhaus li lub qwj yeeg yog hu ua cochlea. Ntawm tus txha mos cochlea no nws yog ib qho ntawm lub pob ntseg uas muaj cov hlab ntsha phij xej heev. Cov hlab ntsha no hloov cov suab uas tuaj tsheej vuag no mus ua fais fab ceeb toom lawm. Ces qhov ceeb toom no mam mus rau hauv cov hlwb. Thaum ntawd cov hlwb mam qhia rau koj tias yog koj nov suab dabtsi. Tshaj dua li qhov hnov suab no, koj lub pob ntseg kuj pab koj lub cev kom nyob tau tus thiab.

VISIONS **READING SUMMARIES Unit 5**

Name ______________________ Date ______________________

VIETNAMESE

Bài viết mang tính chất tài liệu này giải thích làm thế nào con người nghe được âm thanh. Một dây đàn ghita rung khi có người khảy vào dây. Khi rung động, dây chuyển động qua lại rất nhanh. Sự rung động tạo nên âm thanh. Âm thanh di chuyển theo các sóng. Tai bắt được các sóng âm này. Các sóng âm đi vào ống tai và khiến cho màng nhĩ rung động. Những rung động này đi xuyên qua ba xương nhỏ ở tai. Những xương này tạo nên các sóng truyền tới ốc tai. Ốc tai là một bộ phận của tai với các tế bào đặc biệt. Các tế bào này chuyển sóng âm thành các tín hiệu điện. Các tín hiệu này được truyền vào não. Sau đó não cho biết là ta đang nghe âm thanh gì. Ngoài chức năng nghe, tai còn giúp ta giữ thăng bằng.

CHINESE

這篇知識性文章說明人們是如何聽到聲音的。撥動結他弦線，產生了振動。物體振動時，會快速來回移動。振動發出聲音。聲音像波浪般傳動。耳朵接收到這些聲波後，聲波會進入耳道，使耳鼓膜產生振動。這種振動會傳過三塊耳骨，而耳骨會將聲波傳到耳蝸。耳蝸是耳朵中具有特殊細胞的器官。這些細胞將聲波變為電訊號後，再傳到大腦。然後，大腦會告訴您，您聽到了什麼聲音。耳朵除了聽覺功能外，還能幫助您保持平衡。

CAMBODIAN

សៀវភៅពត៌មាននេះពន្យល់ពីរបៀបដែលមនុស្សស្តាប់ឮ។ ខ្សែរចាប៉ី ញ័រពេលណាមានគេកេះវា។ ពេលណាវត្ថុអ្វីមួយដែលញ័រ វាកំរើកចុះឡើងយ៉ាងញាប់។ ភាពញ័របង្កើតជាសំឡេង។ សំឡេងធ្វើដំណើរជា រលក។ ត្រចៀកចាប់រលកសំឡេងទាំងនោះ។ រលកសំឡេងចូលទៅក្នុងបំពង់មួយនៅក្នុងត្រចៀក ហើយបណ្តាលឲ្យសន្ទះក្រដាសត្រចៀកញ័រ។ ភាពញ័រទាំងនេះចូលទៅតាមឆ្អឹងត្រចៀកបី។ ឆ្អឹងត្រចៀកធ្វើឲ្យចូលទៅ កូចលី (cochlea)។ កូចលី គឺជាផ្នែកមួយនៃត្រចៀកដែលមានកោសិកាពិសេស។ កោសិកាទាំងនេះ ដូររលកសំឡេងឲ្យទៅជាចរន្តអេឡិកត្រិក។ ចរន្តទាំងនេះចូលទៅកាន់ខួរក្បាល។ បន្ទាប់មក ខួរក្បាលប្រាប់អ្នកឲ្យដឹងនូវសំឡេងអ្វីដែលអ្នកឮស្វរ។ ថែមពីលើការឮស្វរសំឡេង ត្រចៀកអ្នកជួយអ្នកឲ្យមានលំនឹង។

HAITIAN CREOLE

Tèks enfòmatif sa a eksplike kouman moun fè tande son. Yon kòd gita vibre lè yon moun pase dwèt li sou li. Lè yon bagay vibre, li mouvmante nan direksyon ale vini rapidman. Se vibrasyon yo ki koze son an. Son pwopaje sou fòm ond. Zòrèy ou kapte ond son yo. Ond son yo desann nan yon tib nan zòrèy lan epi li koze vibrasyon tenpan an. Vibrasyon sa yo pase nan twa zo nan zòrèy lan. Zo sa yo pwodui ond ki ale nan yon pati nan zòrèy la yo rele limason. Limason an se yon pati nan zòrèy la ki gen kèk selil espesyal. Selil sa yo konvèti ond son an siyal elektrik. Siyal sa yo ale nan sèvo an. Sèvo an fè w konnen apre sa ki son w ap tande a. Anplis de ede w tande, zòrèy ou yo pèmèt ou kenbe balans ou.

Name ________________________________ Date ____________________

UNIT 5 • CHAPTER 4

The Art of Making Comic Books, by Michael Morgan Pellowski

ENGLISH

This illustrated how-to book explains how good comic books are made. First, a good comic book writer must have a great imagination. This imagination helps create unusual characters and stories. Next, the book gives tips for drawing your own comics. It says you should decide if your character will be big or little, good-looking or ugly. Then, you should try to draw each character in different styles. These different styles will help you decide what your character will look like. Finally, you should give your character special clothing. Your character can wear a cape, a mask, boots, or anything else you can think of.

SPANISH

Este libro didáctico ilustrado explica cómo se hacen los buenos libros de tiras cómicas. Primero que nada, un buen escritor de tiras cómicas debe tener una gran imaginación, para crear ideas de personajes e historias originales. El libro también da consejos de cómo hacer los dibujos y dice que hay que decidir si un personaje va a ser grande o pequeño, bien parecido o feo. Luego, hay que tratar de dibujar a los personajes de diferentes maneras, lo cual te ayudará a decidir cómo va a ser cada personaje. Al final, le debes dar a cada personaje un vestido especial, como por ejemplo, una capa, una máscara, botas, o cualquier otra cosa que se te ocurra.

HMONG

Phau ntawv no qhia kiag rau kom yus paub ua thiab piav qhia txog tias cov phau ntawv kos duab uas yog comic hais lus tso dag ntawd shaib nws tsim tau tiav zoo npaum li cas. Ua ntej tshaj plaws, tus sau yuav tsum yog ib tug muaj tswv yim. Lub tswv yim no pab tsim tau tej tug yam ntxwv thiab tej zaj lus uas zoo txawv heev. Ntxiv mus, phau ntawv nws qhia cov tswv yim rau nej siv kos duab thiab rau nej tus kheej. Nws qhia hais tias koj yuav tsum tau txiav txim siab saib koj yuav cia tus duab koj kos loj puad los sis cia me, kos kom zoo nkauj puas los kos ua ib niag phem ncawb. Ces koj yuav tsum tau sim kos cov duab ntawd kom nyias zoo txawv nyias. Qhov uas nws ib daim nyias zoo txawv nyias no yuav pab tau rau koj xaiv saib koj xav tau tu yeeb yam zoo li cas. Tag li no lawd ces koj yuav tsum tau ua khaub ncaws phij xej rau tus duab ntawd. Koj muab mom rau tus duab ntawd ntoo, ua ib daim looj ntsej muag, rau khau looj tagnrho rau pem plab hlaub, los yog lwm yam uas koj xav tau tias zoo.

VISIONS **READING SUMMARIES Unit 5**

Name ______________________________ Date ____________________

VIETNAMESE

Cuốn sách hướng dẫn có tranh minh họa này giải thích cách đặt và vẽ một cuốn truyện tranh hay. Trước tiên, tác giả viết truyện tranh giỏi phải giàu trí tưởng tượng. Trí tưởng tượng giúp dựng lên những câu chuyện và nhân vật khác thường. Kế tiếp, quyển sách đưa ra các hướng dẫn vẽ truyện tranh. Theo sách cho biết, em nên quyết định xem nhân vật của mình to hay nhỏ, đẹp hay xấu. Sau đó, em nên cố gắng vẽ mỗi nhân vật theo một số phong cách khác nhau để giúp xác định ngoại hình của nhân vật. Cuối cùng, em nên cho nhân vật mang quần áo đặc thù. Nhân vật của em có thể mang áo choàng không tay, mặt nạ, giày ống, hoặc bất cứ thứ gì khác mà em nghĩ ra được.

CHINESE

這本帶有插圖的介紹性書籍說明了精彩的漫畫書是如何編成的。首先，漫畫書的作者必須具有豐富的想像力。有了想像力，可以創造出不同凡響的人物和故事情節。其次，這本書告訴您不少關於漫畫創作的竅門。書中說，您應該確定人物是高大、英俊，還是矮小、丑陋。然後，您應該嘗試用不同的風格畫出每個人物，以便確定人物的外貌長相。最後，您應該為人物穿上特別的服裝。您的人物可以穿披肩，帶面具，蹬長靴；也可以穿戴您能想像出任何其他服飾。

CAMBODIAN

សៀវភៅរបៀបគូររូបនេះ ពន្យល់ពីរបៀបធ្វើសៀវភៅរឿងរូបល្អៗ។ ដំបូង អ្នកនិពន្ធសៀវភៅរឿងរូបមួយត្រូវតែបង្កើតការស្រមៃ។ ការស្រមៃនេះជួយបង្កើតតួរនិងសាច់រឿង។ បន្ទាប់មក សៀវភៅនេះផ្តល់ល្បិចគូររូបសំរាប់សៀវភៅរបស់អ្នកផ្ទាល់។ វានិយាយថា អ្នកគួរសំរេចថាតើតួររបស់អ្នកគួរមានរូបរាងតូចឬធំ, រូបល្អស្អាតឬរូបអាក្រក់។ បន្ទាប់មក អ្នកគួរសាកគូររូបតួមួយៗដោយបែបផ្សេងៗពីគ្នា។ បែបផ្សេងៗគ្នានេះ នឹងជួយអ្នកឲ្យសំរេចថាតើតួរបស់អ្នកនឹងមានរូបដូចម្តេច។ ទីបញ្ចប់ អ្នកគួរផ្តល់ដល់តួនូវសំលៀកបំពាក់សំខាន់។ តួររបស់អ្នក អាចពាក់មួក, ពាក់មុខ, ស្បែកជើងកវែង, ឬអ្វីផ្សេងទៀតដែលអ្នកគិតឃើញ។

HAITIAN CREOLE

Manyèl ilistre sa eksplike kouman yo ekri bon liv komik yo. Toudabò, ekriven yon bon liv komik dwe gen anpil imajinasyon. Imajinasyon ede w kreye karaktè ak istwa ekstraòdinè. Ansuit, liv lan bay kèk sijesyon sou kouman pou desine pwòp komik ou yo. Liv lan fè konnen ou dwe deside si karaktè w lan ap gwo oswa piti, bèl oswa lèd. Ansuit, ou ta dwe desine chak karaktè nan yon estil diferan. Estil diferan sa yo pral ede w detèmine a kisa karaktè w lan pral sanble. Finalman, ou ta dwe mete rad espesyal sou karaktè w lan. Karaktè w lan ka gen yon mask, bòt, oswa nenpòt lòt bagay ou ka imajine.

Name ______________________________ Date ______________________

UNIT 6 • CHAPTER 1

The Lewis and Clark Expedition

ENGLISH

This excerpt from a textbook is about two famous explorers of the American West. This area was called the Louisiana Territory. In the early 1800s, President Thomas Jefferson wanted to learn more about the American West. He sent Meriwether Lewis and William Clark to explore it. In 1804, Lewis and Clark left from St. Louis, Missouri. They traveled along the Missouri River. They hired a fur trapper and his Native American wife, Sacagawea. Sacagawea helped Lewis and Clark talk to Native Americans they met along the way. Lewis and Clark faced many dangers, such as bears. They also saw many natural wonders, such as mountains. They returned to St. Louis in 1806. They wrote about the land and made maps of the area.

SPANISH

Esta selección de un libro es acerca de dos exploradores famosos del oeste americano. La región del oeste era conocida como el Territorio de Louisiana. A comienzos del siglo XIX, el Presidente Thomas Jefferson quizo aprender más acerca del oeste americano y envió a Meriwether Lewis y a William Clark a explorarlo. En 1804, Lewis y Clark salieron de St. Louis, Missouri y navegaron por el río Missouri. En el camino, contrataron a un cazador de pieles y a su esposa indígena llamada Sacagawea. Sacagawea ayudó a Lewis y a Clark a hablar con los indígenas que encontraron en su camino. Lewis y Clark tuvieron que enfrentar muchos peligros, como osos, y vieron muchas bellezas naturales, como las grandes montañas del oeste. Regresaron a St. Louis en 1806 y escribieron acerca de los territorios que exploraron e hicieron mapas de ellos.

HMONG

Zaj lus no yog rho tawm hauv ib phau ntawv los, yog hais txog ob tus neeg nto moo uas tau ncig saib teb chaw nyob rau sab hnub poob teb chaws Asmesliskas. Sab teb chaws no yav thaud yog hu ua Av Louisiana. Nyob rau thaum uas nim qhuav tawm plaws thawj ob peb xyoos ntawm 1800 ntawd, tus nom Thomas Jefferson xav kawm txog cov neeg Asmesliskas nyob rau sab hnub poob kom paub zoo ntxiv. Nws thiaj tau xa Meriwether Lewis thiab William Clark mus kawm txog. Nyob rau xyoo 1804, Lewis thiab Clark tau sawv kev ntawm lub zos St. Louis xeev Missouri mus lawm. Nkawv taug raws ntug dej Missouri mus. Nkawv tau ntiav ib tug kws cuab tsiaj yuav plaub thiab nws tus pojniam Khab Amesliskas uas yog Sacagawea nrog nkawv mus. Sacagawea ua tug pab txhais lus rau Lewis thiab Clark nkawv thaum lawv ntsib cov neeg Khab Asmesliskas. Lewis thiab Clark tau ntsib ntau yam kas ndas xws li cov dais. Lawv kuj pom ntau yam uas lub ntuj tau tsim muaj, xws li tej toj roob hoov peg. Nkaws rov qab los rau St. Louis yog xyoo 1806. Nkawv tau sau thiab tsim tau ib co meemteb txog sab tebchaws ntawd.

Name ______________________________ Date ______________________

VIETNAMESE

Đây là đoạn trích từ sách giáo khoa nói về hai nhà thám hiểm nổi tiếng đã đến miền Tây Mỹ. Khu vực này được gọi là Lãnh Thổ Louisiana. Vào đầu những năm 1800, Tổng Thống Thomas Jefferson muốn tìm hiểu về Tây Mỹ. Ông phái Meriwether Lewis và William Clark tới đó thám hiểm. Vào năm 1804, Lewis và Clark rời St. Louis, Missouri. Họ đi dọc theo Sông Missouri. Họ thuê một người đánh bẫy thú và vợ người Mỹ Da Đỏ, là Sacagawea. Sacagawea giúp Lewis và Clark nói chuyện với những người Mỹ Da Đỏ họ gặp trên đường đi. Lewis và Clark đương đầu với nhiều mối nguy hiểm, chẳng hạn như gấu. Họ cũng chứng kiến nhiều kỳ quan thiên nhiên chẳng hạn như các dãy núi. Họ trở về St. Louis vào năm 1806. Họ viết bài và vẽ bản đồ vùng đất này.

CHINESE

這是關於美國西部兩位有名探險家的課本摘錄。西元 19 世紀早期，湯瑪士•傑佛遜總統想更了解美國西部，便派馬修•路易士和威廉•克拉克兩人去探索這個當時稱之為路易士安那區的地方。1804 年，路易士和克拉克從密蘇里州的聖路易市出發，沿著密西西比河走，他們僱了一個專獵動物毛皮的獵人和他那位名叫沙卡加慧的印地安妻子。沙卡加慧幫助路易士和克拉克與沿途遇到的印地安人溝通。路易士和克拉克遇到過許多危險，譬如遇到熊等，但也看到了山脈等許多自然奇觀。他們在 1806 年回到聖路易，寫了有關路易士安那地區自然環境的書籍並製作了地圖。

CAMBODIAN

សេចក្តីនេះបានមកពីសៀវភៅមួយដែលនិយាយអំពីអ្នករុករកទឹកដីអាមេរិកប៉ែកខាងលិច ដ៏ល្បីពីរនាក់។ តំបន់នេះហៅថា ទីតាំងល្វីសាណា ។ នៅដើមសតវត្សទី ១៩ ប្រធានាធិបតេយ្យ ថូម៉ាស ជេហ្វ័រសុន ចង់ដឹងថែមទៀតពីទឹកដីអាមេរិកប៉ែកខាងលិច។ គាត់បញ្ជូនឲ្យ មើរីសវ៉ាហ្ស័រ លេវីស និង វីលីយ៉ាំ ក្លាក ទៅរុករកទីនោះ។ ក្នុងឆ្នាំ ១៨០៤ លេវីស និង ក្លាក ចាកចេញពី សេនល្វីស, រដ្ឋមីសសួរី។ គេធ្វើដំណើរតាមបណ្តោយស្ទឹងមីសសួរី។ គេជួលអ្នកដាក់អន្ទាក់សត្វយករោម និង ភរិយាគាត់ជាតិភ្នងអាមេរិក, ឈ្មោះ សាកាខាវី។ សាកាខាវី ជួយលេវីស និង ក្លាក ក្នុងការនិយាយជាមួយពួកភ្នងអាមេរិក ដែលគេជួបតាមផ្លូវ។ លេវីស និង ក្លាក ជួបគ្រោះថ្នាក់ជាច្រើន ដូចជាខ្លាឃ្មុំ។ គេបានជួបធម្មជាតិចម្លែកៗជាច្រើន ដូចជាភ្នំ។ គេត្រឡប់ទៅសេនល្វីស វិញក្នុងឆ្នាំ ១០៨៦។ គេបានសរសេរអំពីទឹកដីនោះ ហើយបានគូរផែនទីនៃតំបន់នោះ។

HAITIAN CREOLE

Ekstrè sa a ki sòti nan yon manyèl pale osijè de eksploratè fame nan lwès Amerik. Zòn sa te rele teritwa Louisiana. Nan kòmansman lane 1800 yo, Prezidan Thomas Jefferson te bezwen aprann plis bagay sou lwès Amerik. Li voye Meriwether Lewis ak William Clark al eksplore zòn lan. An 1804, Lewis ak Clark kite St. Louis, Missouri. Yo vwayaje bò larivyè Missouri an. Yo te anboche yon trapè fouri ak madanm li, Sacagawea, ki te yon endyèn Ameriken natif natal. Sacagawea te ede Lewis ak Clark pale ak endyen ameriken natif natal yo te rankontre sou wout lan. Lewis ak Clark te rankontre anpil danje, tankou ous yo. Yo te wè anpil bèl mèvèy lanati tou, tankou mòn yo. Yo retounen St. Louis an 1806. Yo te ekri osijè peyi an epi yo te fè kat jeyografik pou zòn lan.

Name ______________________ Date ______________________

UNIT 6 • CHAPTER 2

A Wrinkle in Time, by Madeleine L'Engle

ENGLISH

This excerpt from a science fiction novel is about two children, Meg and Charles. They are searching for their father with the help of their friend Calvin. Their father is a scientist. He disappeared while doing secret work on a tesseract. A tesseract is a way to travel through space and time. The children meet three mysterious women along the way—Mrs. Which, Mrs. Whatsit, and Mrs. Who. The women help Meg and Charles search for their father. The women explain that they will travel using a tesseract. When it is time to travel, the women fade into the air. Then the children fade away, too. Everything is silent. Suddenly, Meg is a flat shape. She hears the women say that they must go on and quickly leave that place. When everyone reappears, they are on a distant star.

SPANISH

Esta selección de una novela de ciencia ficción es acerca de dos niños: Meg y Charles. Ellos buscan a su padre con la ayuda de su amigo Calvin. Su padre es un científico que desapareció mientras hacía trabajo en secreto en un teseractor. Un teseractor es una manera de viajar a través del tiempo y el espacio. Los niños se encuentran con tres mujeres misteriosas a lo largo del camino: la señora Which, la señora Whatsit y la señora Who, quienes ayudan a Meg y a Charles a buscar a su padre. Las mujeres les explican que viajarán por un teseractor. Cuando se llega la hora de viajar, las mujeres desaparecen en el aire. Luego, los niños también desaparecen y todo queda en silencio. De pronto, Meg es una figura plana. Ella escucha a las mujeres decir que deben irse de prisa y dejar ese lugar. Cuando todos vuelven a aparecer, se encuentran en una estrella distante.

HMONG

Zaj lus no yog rho tawm hauv ib phau ntawv uas yog ib lub tswv yim sau hais txog ob tug me nyuam, Meg thiab Charles. Nkawv tus phooj ywg Calvin pab nkawv nrhiav nkawv txiv. Nkawv txiv yog ib tug kws tshawb nrhiav kawm uas yog hu tias scientist. Nws tau ploj lub caij uas nws tab tom ua haujlwm zais nkoos tsi pub twg paub los tsim ib lub ua plaub ceg cig pom kev uas yog hu ua tesseract. Tesseract yog ib txog kev rau yus mus saum ntuj thiab hla cai nyoog. Cov me nyuam ntsib peb tug pojniam uas yog tus niam Which, niam Whatsit, thiab niam Who ua rau lawv tsi paub xav li. Cov pojniam ntawd kuj pab nrog Meg thiab Charles nkawv nrhiav nkawv txiv huvsi. Cov pojniam piav tias lawv yuav siv lub tesseract ua kev mus los. Thaum uas txog lub caij sawv kev ce cov pojniam ntawd cia li ploj zuj zug rau saum tej fuab cua li xwb. Ces cov me nyuam ploj zuj zug thiab. Txhua yam cia li ntsiag twb to. Tog nwd Meg txawm pliab luav tag lawm. Nws hnov cov pojniam hais tias lawv yuav tau mus ces txawm tawm ceev nrooj ntawm qhov chaw ntawd mus lawm. Thaum lawv txhua tug rov tshwm los lawv nyob deb npaum li lub hnub qub lawm.

Name ______________________________ Date ______________________

VIETNAMESE

Đây là đoạn trích từ một cuốn tiểu thuyết khoa học viễn tưởng nói về hai đứa trẻ, Meg và Charles. Các em đi tìm cha với sự giúp đỡ của người bạn tên Calvin. Cha của các em là một khoa học gia. Ông ta mất tích trong lúc thực hiện các nghiên cứu bí mật về khối bốn chiều (tesseract). Khối bốn chiều là một phương thức du hành xuyên qua không gian và thời gian. Trên đường đi, bọn trẻ gặp ba người đàn bà bí ẩn-Bà Which, Bà Whatsit, và Bà Who. Những người đàn bà này giúp Meg và Charles tìm cha mình. Các bà giải thích rằng họ sẽ du hành qua một khối bốn chiều. Đã đến lúc ra đi, những người đàn bà biến dần vào không khí. Sau đó các đứa trẻ cũng biến theo. Mọi thứ đều im lặng. Bỗng nhiên, Meg thấy mình trở thành một hình phẳng. Cô nghe những người đàn bà nói rằng họ phải tiếp tục cuộc hành trình và nhanh chóng rời khỏi nơi này. Khi mọi người hiện ra lại, họ có mặt tại một vì sao rất xa.

CHINESE

這是從一本科幻小說選錄出來的故事，敘述兩個叫做麥琅和查理的小孩，藉朋友卡文幫助，找尋父親。他們的父親是個科學家，在一次超立方體秘密工作中消失。超立方體是一種穿越空間與時間的旅行方法。兩個小孩在途中遇到三個神秘女人，她們是「那個太太」、「這是什麼太太」和「誰太太」。她們也幫麥琅和查理尋父，並且向他們解釋要用超立方體旅行，但到出發時，那三個女人卻在空氣中逐漸消失。之後小孩也跟著消失，這時萬寂無聲，麥琅突然變扁，她聽到那些女人講必須前進並且要趕快離開這個地方。當大家重新出現時，他們已經在一個遙遠的星球上了。

CAMBODIAN

សេចក្តីនេះបានមកពីប្រលោមលោកប្រឌិតខាងវិទ្យាសាស្ត្រមួយ ដែលនិយាយអំពីក្មេងពីរនាក់។ មេក និង ឆាលី។ ពួកគេសាវជ្រាវរកឪពុកគេ ដោយមានជំនួយពីពីមិត្តរបស់គេ ឈ្មោះ ខាលវិន។ ឪពុកគេជាអ្នកប្រាជ្ញ វិទ្យាសាស្ត្រ។ គាត់បាត់ខ្លួនក្នុងពេលសាវជ្រាវដំណើរ តេសសឺរាក់។ តេសសឺរាក់ ជាមធ្យោបាយមួយសំរាប់ធ្វើដំណើរ តាមរយៈលំហរអាកាសនិងពេលវេលា។ ក្មេងៗបានជួបស្ត្រីអាថ៌កំបាំងបីនាក់នៅតាមផ្លូវ- អ្នកស្រី មួយណា, អ្នកស្រី អ្វីទៅ, និងអ្នកស្រី នរណា។ ស្ត្រីទាំងនោះជួយ មេក និង ឆាលី សាវជ្រាវរកឪពុកគេ។ ស្ត្រីពន្យល់ថា ពួកគេនឹង ធ្វើដំណើរដោយប្រើ តេសសឺរាក់។ ពេលចេញដំណើរត្រូវមកដល់ ស្ត្រីទាំងនោះរលាយបាត់ទៅក្នុងខ្យល់តែម្តង។ បន្ទាប់មកក្មេងទាំងនោះក៏រលាយទៅដែរ។ អ្វីៗស្ងាត់ឈឹង។ មួយរំពេចនោះ មេក មានរូបរាងសំប៉ែត។ នាងឮ ស្ត្រីនិយាយប្រាប់ថា ពួកគេត្រូវតែចាកចេញទីនោះភ្លាម។ ពេលដែលអ្នកទាំងអស់លេចចេញរូបរាងឡើងវិញ ពួកគេនៅលើផ្កាយមួយឆ្ងាយ។

HAITIAN CREOLE

Ekstrè sa a ki soti nan yon woman syans fiksyon pale osijè de timoun, Meg ak Charles. Y ap chèche papa yo epi zanmi yo Calvin ap ede yo. Papa yo se te yon syantifik. Li te disparèt pandan li t ap travay ansekrè sou yon teserak. Yon teserak se yon fason pou vwayaje atravè lespas ak letan. Timoun yo rankontre ak twa dam misterye sou wout lan—Madan Kilès, Madan Kisa, epi Madan Kiyès. Dam yo ede Meg ak Charles chèche papa yo. Dam yo eksplike yo pral vwayaje ak yon teserak. Lè moman an rive pou vwayaj lan, dam yo disparèt nan lè a. Aprè sa timoun yo vin disparèt tou. Vin gen yon silans konplè. Toudenkou, Meg vin tounen yon fòm plat. Li tande dam yo k ap di yo dwe kontinye ale epi kite zòn lan rapidman. Lè tout moun reparèt, yo tounen yon zetwal byen lwen.

Name ______________________________ Date ____________________

UNIT 6 • CHAPTER 3

I Have a Dream, by Martin Luther King Jr.

ENGLISH

In this speech, given in 1963, Martin Luther King Jr. talks about his dream. His dream is that all Americans will treat one another equally. His dream is for his children to live in a land where people will not judge them based on their skin color. He wants all boys and girls to hold hands like brothers and sisters. King wants people of all races to respect one another. He says that if this happens, the United States will be a nation where everyone is equal. When this happens, he says, people of every race will live in peace.

SPANISH

En este discurso, dado en 1963, Martin Luther King Jr. cuenta su sueño. Su sueño es que todos los americanos se traten como iguales los unos con los otros y que los niños vivan en un mundo en el que las personas no sean juzgadas en base al color de su piel. Él quiere que todos los niños y niñas se tomen de la mano como hermanos y hermanas, y que las personas de todas las razas se respeten entre sí. Él dice que si eso llega a ocurrir, los Estados Unidos será un país donde todos serán iguales y las personas de todas las razas vivirán en paz.

HMONG

Nyob rau hauv nws cov lus uas tau hais rau xyoo 1963, Martin Luther King Jr. qhia txog nws tus npau suav. Nws tus npau suav ntawd yog xav kom txhua tug neeg Asmesliskas ib leeg saib taus ib leeg. Nws tus npau suav yog xav kom nws cov me nyuam tau nyob ib daim av uas tib neeg tsi txhob txiav txim raws li nws daim nqaij tawv lub xim xoos. Nws xav tau txhua tug tub ntxhais sib tuav tes li lawv yog nkauj muam nraug nus. King xav tau txhua haiv neeg ib leeg fwm ib leeg. Nws hais tias yog qhov no tshwm sim, lub teb chaws United States yuav yog ib lub teb chaws uas txhua tus yuav muaj lub vaj huam sib luag. Thaum qhov no tshwm sim lawm, nws hais, txhuav yam tibneeg yuav nyob rau txoj kev thaj yeeb.

Name ______________________________ Date ______________________

VIETNAMESE

Trong bài diễn văn vào năm 1963, Martin Luther King Jr. thuyết trình về ước mơ của ông. Ước mơ của ông là mọi người dân Mỹ đối xử bình đẳng với nhau, là con cháu ông sống trên một vùng đất nơi đó không có ai phán xét chúng dựa trên màu da. Ông muốn tất cả trẻ em nam và nữ nắm tay nhau như thể anh chị em. Ông King muốn những người thuộc tất cả các chủng tộc đều tôn trọng nhau. Ông nói rằng nếu điều này trở thành hiện thực, Hoa Kỳ sẽ trở thành một quốc gia nơi đó ai ai cũng bình đẳng. Nếu điều này trở thành hiện thực, ông nói thêm, thì mọi người thuộc các chủng tộc khác nhau sẽ sống trong hòa bình.

CHINESE

小馬丁•路德•金在這篇 1963 年的演講詞中，訴說了他的夢想，他夢想所有美國人都能彼此平等相待，他夢想他的孩子住在一片國土上，而該國的人不用膚色來判斷人，他想所有的男孩和女孩像是兄弟姊妹一般手拉手，他想不同種族的人會互相敬重。他說如果這樣的願望可以實現，美國就能變成一個人人平等的國家，他也說當這樣的願望實現時，各種族的人便能過和平生活。

CAMBODIAN

នៅក្នុងសន្ទរកថានេះ, ធ្វើឡើងឆ្នាំ ១៩៦៣, ម៉ាធិន លូធ័រ ឃីង ជូនញ័រ និយាយពីការស្រមៃរបស់គាត់។ ការស្រមៃរបស់គាត់គឺ ជនជាតិអាមេរិកទាំងអស់នឹងប្រព្រឹត្តចំពោះគ្នាទៅវិញទៅមកដោយស្មើភាព។ ការស្រមៃរបស់គាត់គឺសំរាប់កូនគាត់ ដើម្បីរស់នៅលើទឹកដីដែលមិនឲ្យតម្លៃទៅលើពណ៌សម្បុរស្បែកនោះទេ។ គាត់ចង់ឲ្យក្មេងប្រុសស្រីទាំងអស់កាន់ដៃគ្នា បីដូចជាបងប្អូន។ ឃីង ចង់ឲ្យមនុស្សគ្រប់សញ្ជាតិ គោរពគ្នាទៅវិញទៅមក។ គាត់និយាយថា បើការនេះកើតឡើងមែន ប្រទេសអាមេរិកនឹងក្លាយជាប្រទេសដែលមនុស្សមានភាពស្មើគ្នា។ គាត់និយាយថា កាលណាការនេះកើតឡើង មនុស្សគ្រប់សញ្ជាតិនឹងរស់នៅក្នុងសុខសន្តិភាព។

HAITIAN CREOLE

Nan diskou l lan, ki te fèt an1963, Martin Luther King Jr. pale osijè rèv li an. Rèv li se pou tout Ameriken trete youn lòt egal ego. Rèv li se pou l wè pitit li yo ap viv nan yon peyi kote moun pa pral jije moun sou koulè po yo. Li vle pou tout tigason ak tout tifi kenbe men kòm frè ak sè. King vle pou moun tout ras respekte youn lòt. Li di si sa rive fèt, Etazini pral vrèman tounen yon nasyon kote tout moun egal ego. Lè sa va rive fèt, li di, moun tout ras pral viv anpè.

Name ______________________________ Date ______________

UNIT 6 • CHAPTER 4

Lyndon Baines Johnson: Our Thirty-Sixth President, by Melissa Maupin & Speech to the Nation: July 2, 1964, by Lyndon Baines Johnson

ENGLISH

"Lyndon Baines Johnson: Our Thirty-Sixth President" is a biography of Lyndon Johnson. He became president of the United States after John F. Kennedy died in 1963. Johnson promised to carry out Kennedy's goals. One goal was to pass a civil rights act. Johnson signed the Civil Rights Act of 1964. It ended laws that kept African-Americans out of some public places.

In his "Speech to the Nation: July 2, 1964," President Johnson tells Americans that he will sign the Civil Rights Act of 1964. He says that Americans of all races have died protecting our freedom. He says that Americans believe all people are equal. He also says that many are not treated equally because of their race. Johnson believes the Civil Rights Act of 1964 will change this unequal treatment. It will give every American the same chance to live freely.

SPANISH

"Lyndon Baines Johnson: Our Thirty-Sixth President" es una biografía de Lyndon Johnson, quien se volvió presidente de los Estados Unidos después de que John F. Kennedy falleciera en 1963. Johnson prometió llevar a cabo las metas de Kennedy. Una de ellas era la de pasar un acta de los derechos civiles para los ciudadanos. Johnson firmó el Acta de Derechos Civiles de 1964, que acabó con leyes que no permitían a los afroamericanos estar en muchos lugares públicos.

En el discurso "Speech to the Nation: July 2, 1964", el President Johnson le dice a los americanos que él va a firmar el Acta de Derechos Civiles de 1964. Johnson dice que americanos de todas las razas han muerto para proteger nuestra libertad y que los americanos creen que todas las personas son iguales. También dice que muchas personas no son tratadas por igual, dado su raza. Johnson cree que el Acta de Derechos Civiles de 1964 cambiará ese trato no equitativo que reciben algunos, y que le dará a cada americano la oportunidad de vivir libremente.

HMONG

"Lyndon Baines Johnson: Our Thirty-Sixth President" yog sau hais txog Lyndon Johnson. Tom qab John F. Kennedy tau tuag nyob rau xyoo 1963 tag lawd, nws tau los ua tug nom rau lub teb chaws United States no. Johnson tau cog lus tseg tias nws yuav khaws coj Kennedy cov hom phiaj ua ntxiv. Ib yam ntawm cov hom phiaj ntawd yog yuav tsum tau muaj ib tsab cai civil rights act. Johnson tau xee tsab cai Civil Rights Act no rau xyoo 1964. Thaum muaj txojcai no lawm, lwm txoj cai uas txwv tsi pub Asflikas-Amesliskas mus rau qee qhov chaw cia li tsi muaj ntxiv lawm.

Nyob rau hauv nws cov lus uas "Speech to the Nation: July 2, 1964," tus nom Johnson hais rau Amesliskas tias nws yuav xee tsab cai Civil Rights Act ntawm xyoo 1964. Nws hais tias txhua hais neeg ntawm hauv teb chaws Asmesliskas tau mus tuag tiv thaiv rau peb txoj kev ywj pheej. Nws hais tias cov neeg Asmesliskas yeej ntseeg tias txhua tus neeg yeej muaj cai sib txig sib npaug. Tsi tag li ntawd nws tseem hais tias coob leej yeej tau raug lwm tus saib tis taus vim tib qhov lawv txawv haiv xwb. Johnson ntseeg hais tias txojcai Civil Rights Act ntawm xyoo 1964 yuav hloov tej kev tsi sib saib tau no. Nws yuav muab lub sib hawm rau txhua tug Asmesliskas nyob ywj siab hlo.

VISIONS **READING SUMMARIES Unit 6**

Name ______________________________ Date ______________________

VIETNAMESE

"Lyndon Baines Johnson: Our Thirty-Sixth President" là một cuốn tiểu sử về Lyndon Johnson. Ông trở thành tổng thống Mỹ sau khi John F. Kennedy mất vào năm 1963. Johnson hứa là sẽ thực hiện các mục tiêu của Kennedy. Một trong các mục tiêu là thông qua đạo luật về quyền công dân. Johnson ký Đạo Luật Quyền Công Dân năm 1964. Đạo luật này bác bỏ các luật cấm người Mỹ gốc Châu Phi đến một số nơi công cộng.

Trong bài "Diễn Văn Quốc Gia: 2 Tháng Bảy, 1964," Tổng Thống Johnson hứa với dân Mỹ là ông sẽ ký Đạo Luật Quyền Công Dân năm 1964. Ông nói rằng dân Mỹ thuộc mọi chủng tộc khác nhau đã hy sinh cho quyền tự do của chúng ta. Ông nói rằng dân Mỹ tin rằng mọi người đều bình đẳng. Ông cũng nói rằng nhiều người không được đối xử bình đẳng chỉ vì chủng tộc của họ. Johnson tin rằng Đạo Luật Quyền Công Dân năm 1964 sẽ thay đổi sự đối xử bất bình đẳng này. Đạo luật sẽ cho mọi người dân Mỹ có cơ hội sống tự do.

CHINESE

Lyndon Baines Johnson: Our Thirty-Sixth President 這本書是林登　詹森的傳記。詹森在 1993 年約翰•甘迺迪逝世後成為美國總統，他承諾會繼承甘迺迪遺志，其中之一便是通過一項人權法案。詹森簽署了「1964 年人權法案」，廢除了在某些公共場所排斥非州裔美國人的法律。

詹森總統在他的 Speech to the Nation: July 2, 1964 演講詞中告訴美國人，他將簽署「1964 年人權法案」。他說各種族的美國人都曾為了保衛我們的自由而犧牲性命，而且美國人相信所有人都是平等的。他也說有很多人因為他們的種族而受到不平等待遇。詹森相信，「1964 年人權法案」會改變這種不平等待遇，會給每個美國人相同機會來過自由生活。

CAMBODIAN

"Lyndon Baines Johnson: Our Thirty-Sixth President" ជាប្រវត្តិរូបរបស់ លីនដុន ចនសុន។ គាត់លើងជាប្រធានាធិបតេយ្យនៃប្រទេសអាមេរិក ក្រោយពី ចន អែវ កេននីឌី ស្លាប់នៅ ឆ្នាំ១៩៦៣។ ចនសុន សន្យានឹងបន្តគោលការណ៍របស់ កេននីឌី។ គោលការណ៍គឺសំរេចច្បាប់សិទ្ធិក្នុងស្រុក។ ចនសុន ចុះហត្ថលេខាលើច្បាប់ សិទ្ធិក្នុងស្រុក ឆ្នាំ១៩៦៤។ វាជាច្បាប់ដែលបញ្ចប់ការឃាត់ជនជាតិ អាហ្វ្រិកកែន-អាមេរិកកែន ឲ្យនៅខាងក្រៅកន្លែងសាធារណៈខ្លះ។

នៅក្នុង "Speech to the Nation: July 2, 1964" របស់គាត់, ប្រធានាធិបតេយ្យ ចនសុន ប្រាប់អាមេរិកកាំងថា គាត់នឹងចុះហត្ថលេខាលើច្បាប់ សិទ្ធិក្នុងស្រុក ឆ្នាំ១៩៦៤។ គាត់និយាយថា អាមេរិកកាំងគ្រប់សញ្ជាតិ បានស្លាប់ក្នុងការការពារសេរីភាពរបស់យើង។ គាត់និយាយថា អាមេរិកកាំង មានជំនឿថា មនុស្សគ្រប់រូបមានភាពស្មើគ្នា។ គាត់ក៏និយាយដែរថា មនុស្សជាច្រើនមិនបានទទួលការប្រព្រឹត្តទៅលើឲ្យបានស្មើគ្នាទេ ដោយសារតែសញ្ជាតិរបស់គេ។ ចនសុន មានជំនឿថា ច្បាប់សិទ្ធិក្នុងស្រុកឆ្នាំ១៩៦៤ នឹងដូរការប្រព្រឹត្តទៅលើមិនស្មើគ្នានេះ។ ច្បាប់នេះនឹងផ្តល់ឲ្យអាមេរិកកាំងមានសិទ្ធិស្មើគ្នា ដើម្បីរស់ដោយសេរី។

HAITIAN CREOLE

"Lyndon Baines Johnson: Our Thirty-Sixth President" se yon byografi Lyndon Johnson. Li te vin prezidan Etazini aprè John F. Kennedy te mouri an 1963. Johnson te pwomèt li pral kontinye pousuiv objektif Kennedy yo. Youn nan objektif sa yo se te pou pase yon lwa sou dwa sivil. Johnson te siyen Lwa sou Dwa Sivil lan 1964 lan. Lwa sa a te mete fen a lwa ki te anpeche Afriken-Ameriken ale nan plas piblik yo.

Nan diskou l lan "Speech to the Nation: 2 juillet 1964," Prezidan Johnson fè Ameriken yo konnen entansyon l pou l siyen Lwa sou Dwa Sivil 1964 lan. Li te fè konnen Ameriken tout ras te mouri pouka defann libète nou. Li di Ameriken kwè nan egalite moun. Li te fè konnen tou gen anpil moun yo pa trete ak egal ego akòz ras yo. Johnson kwè Lwa sou Dwa Sivil 1964 lan pral chanje tretman inegal sa a. Lwa sa a pral bay chak Ameriken menm chans pou l viv an libète.

School-Home Connection
Sharing Visions

UNIT 1 Challenges

Name ______________________

Date ______________________

Dear Family,

In class, we learned about challenges people face. ______________ *(student's name)* would like to share with you the stories we read.

The Race, by Jennifer Trujillo, & **The Camel Dances,** by Arnold Lobel A girl competes in a horse race, and a camel wants to be a ballet dancer.

Hatchet, by Gary Paulsen A teenage boy must find a way to make a fire and survive alone in the wilderness.

Antarctic Adventure, by Meredith Hooper A group of brave men are shipwrecked in Antarctica and must find a way to return to civilization.

Yang the Youngest, by Lensey Namioka A young boy tries to adjust to life in a new country and in a new school.

The Scholarship Jacket, by Marta Salinas A teenage girl must prove that she deserves to win a the school's academic award—a scholarship jacket.

We would also like you to take a few moments to participate in an interview about challenges to share with the class. Thank you for your support.

Sincerely,

______________________ *(Teacher)*

INTERVIEW

1. Name of person being interviewed: ______________________
2. Question: What big challenge have you faced?

   Answer: ______________________

   ____
3. Question: Why was it a challenge?

   Answer: ______________________

   ____
4. Question: What did you do to meet the challenge?

   Answer: ______________________

   ____
5. (Student: *Ask one question of your own.*)

   Question: ______________________

   Answer: ______________________

School-Home Connection
Sharing Visions
UNIDAD 1 Retos

Nombre ______________________

Fecha ______________________

Estimada familia:

En nuestra clase, aprendimos acerca de los retos que confronta la gente. A ______________________ *(nombre del estudiante)* le gustaría compartir con usted las historias que leímos.

The Race, por Jennifer Trujillo, & **The Camel Dances,** por Arnold Lobel Una niña compite en una carrera de caballos, y un camello quiere ser bailarina.

Hatchet, por Gary Paulsen Un niño debe hallar la manera de encender una hoguera y de sobrevivir por sí mismo en el bosque.

Antarctic Adventure, por Meredith Hooper Un grupo de hombres valientes ha naufragado en la Antártica y debe hallar la manera de regresar a la civilización.

Yang the Youngest, por Lensey Namioka Un niño trata de ajustarse a vivir en un nuevo país y a asistir a una nueva escuela.

The Scholarship Jacket, por Marta Salinas Una niña debe comprobar que se merece ganar un premio escolar: una chamarra de la escuela.

Ahora nos gustaría que participara en una entrevista acerca de retos, para luego compartirla con el resto de la clase. Muchas gracias por su apoyo.

Cordialmente,

______________________ *[Maestra(o)]*

ENTREVISTA

1. Nombre de la persona siendo entrevistada: ______________________
2. Pregunta: Cuéntame de un gran reto que hayas tenido.

   Respuesta: ______________________

   ____
3. Pregunta: ¿Por qué lo consideraste un reto?

   Respuesta: ______________________

   ____
4. Pregunta: ¿Qué hiciste para confrontar el reto?

   Respuesta: ______________________

   ____
5. (Estudiante: *Haz una pregunta tuya.*)

   Pregunta: ______________________

   Respuesta: ______________________

School-Home Connection
Sharing Visions
BÀI SỐ 1 Những Thách Thức

Tên ______________________

Ngày ______________________

Kính Gởi Gia Đình,

Trong lớp, chúng tôi đã tìm hiểu những thách thức mà con người phải đương đầu. ______________ *(tên học sinh)* muốn chia xẻ với quý vị những câu chuyện chúng tôi đã đọc.

The Race, tác gia Jennifer Trujillo, & **The Camel Dances,** tác gia pa Arnold Lobel tác giả Arnold Lobel Một cô bé tranh tài trong cuộc đua ngựa, và một chị lạc đà muốn trở thành diễn viên múa balê.

Hatchet, tác gia Gary Paulsen Một cậu thiếu niên phải tìm cách nhóm lửa và một mình tồn tại nơi vùng đất hoang vu.

Antarctic Adventure, tác gia Meredith Hooper Một nhóm chàng trai dũng cảm bị đắm thuyền ở Nam Cực và phải tìm đường trở lại xã hội văn minh.

Yang the Youngest, tác gia Lensey Namioka Một cậu bé cố gắng thích nghi với cuộc sống ở một quốc gia mới và trường học mới.

The Scholarship Jacket, tác gia Marta Salinas Một cô thiếu niên phải chứng tỏ là cô xứng đáng được nhận giải thưởng học tập của trường —một chiếc áo khoác phần thưởng.

Chúng tôi cũng xin quý vị dành một ít thời giờ để tham dự cuộc phỏng vấn về những thách thức mà quý vị đã từng đương đầu để trình bày với lớp học. Xin cám ơn sự hỗ trợ của quý vị.

Trân trọng,

______________________ *(Giáo viên)*

PHỎNG VẤN

1. Tên người được phỏng vấn: ______________________
2. Hỏi: Xin cho biết một thách thức lớn mà quý vị đã phải đương đầu.

   Đáp: ______________________

   ____
3. Hỏi: Tại sao đó lại là một thách thức?

   Đáp: ______________________

   ____
4. Hỏi: Quý vị đã làm gì để đối phó được với thách thức này?

   Đáp: ______________________

   ____
5. (Học sinh: *Tự đặt một câu hỏi.*)

   Hỏi: ______________________

   Đáp: ______________________

School-Home Connection
Sharing Visions

YAM 1 Tej nyuaj rau yus

Npe ______________________

Vasthib ______________________

Nyob zoo,

Nyob rau hauv hoob tsev kawm ntawv no, peb tau kawm txog tej yam nyuaj uas tej tibneeg niaj hnub tau ntsib thiab tau raug. ______________ *(Menyuam npe)* xav muab cov dab neeg uas peb tau kawm lawd coj los qhia rau nej sub nej thiaj nrog nws paub thiab.

The Race, los ntawm Jennifer Trujillo, & **The Camel Dances,** los ntawm Arnold Lobel Yog hais txog ib tug me ntxhais caij nees sib xeem, thiab tus ntxhuav xav ua tug seev cev uas yog siv ntsis taw.

Hatchet, los ntawm Gary Paulsen Yog hais txog ib tug tub hluas uas nws yuav tsum tau nrhiav kev rauv kom tau ib cub hluav taws thiab yuav ua cas nws thiaj ciaj tau siav nyob rau tom hav zoov nuj txeeg.

Antarctic Adventure, los ntawm Meredith Hooper Yog qhia txog ib pab txivneej uas muaj peevxwm uas tau caij ib lub nkoj mus daig nyob rau Antarctica thiab qhov uas lawv yuav tsum tau nrhiav kev rov qab los tsev.

Yang the Youngest, los ntawm Lensey Namioka Zaj no yog hais txog ib tug Menyuam tub hloov nws tus yam ntxwv kom haum lub teb chaw tshiab uas nws tau khiav mus nyob thiab rau hauv nws lub tsev kawm ntawv tshiab.

The Scholarship Jacket, los ntawm Marta Salinas Yog hais txog ib tug ntxhais uas yuav tsum muaj pov thawj qhia tias nws tsim nyog yog tus yeej tsev kawm ntawv qhov khoom plig ua kev zoo siab rau tus kawm keej—nws yog ib lub tsho tiv no.

Ntxiv no, peb xav thov nej siv sib hawm me ntsis los pab teb cov lus xam phaj uas yog nug txog yam nyuaj uas nej tau ntsib thiab tau raug uas xav qhia kom peb lub hoob qhia ntawv kom tau nrog nej kawm thiab paub ua ke. Ua tsaug rau nej txoj kev txhawb pab no.

Xee npe,

______________________ *(Xib hwb)*

COV LUS NUG

1. Lub npe ntawm tus neeg uas pab teb cov lus xam phaj no: ______________________
2. Lo lus nug: Qhov nej tau ntsib thiab tau raug uas nyuaj tshaj plaws yog dabtsi?

   Lo lus teb: ______________________

3. Lo lus nug: Yog vim li cas ho nyuaj?

   Lo lus teb: ______________________

4. Lo lus nug: Koj tau keb li cas xwb thiaj keb dhau qho ke nyuaj ntawd lawm?

   Lo lus teb: ______________________

5. (Rau tus menyuam lubxiv nug: *Koj yuav tau nug ib los ua koj tug.)*

   Lo lus nug: ______________________

   Lo lus teb: ______________________

School-Home Connection
Sharing Visions
第一單元：挑戰

姓名：________________________
日期：________________________

各位尊敬的家庭成員：

在課堂上，我們學習了有關挑戰的內容。 ____________ *（學生名字）*想與各位分享我們上課時讀過的故事。

The Race, by Jennifer Trujillo & **The Camel Dances,** by Arnold Lobel 前者講及一位參加賽馬的女孩，後者描述一隻想成為芭蕾舞蹈家的駱駝。

Hatchet, by Gary Paulsen 描述一位少年如何獨自在荒野中想辦法生火來保著性命。

Antarctic Adventure, by Meredith Hooper 描述一群勇敢的人在南極沉船之後，如何找尋路徑返回文明世界。

Yang the Youngest, by Lensey Namioka 描述一個男童如何在新國家與新學校適應新生活。

The Scholarship Jacket, by Marta Salinas 描述一位少女需要證實自己值得贏取學校的學術獎——一件學術榮譽外套。

我們還希望各位能抽出時間參與一項有關挑戰的訪問，與全班同學一起分享。感謝各位的支持。

順祝安康，

____________________ *（教師）*

訪談

1. 接受訪問者的姓名：

   ____

2. 問：請問您面臨過的最大挑戰為何？
   答：________________________

   ____

3. 問：為何它對您而言是個挑戰？
   答：________________________

   ____

4. 問：請問您如何面對挑戰？
   答：________________________

   ____

5. （學生：*請提出一個你自己的問題。*）
   問：________________________
   答：________________________

School-Home Connection
Sharing Visions
ជំពូក ១ ការប្រឹងប្រកួតប្រជែង

ឈ្មោះ ______________________

កាលបរិច្ឆេទ ______________________

ជូនចំពោះគ្រួសារ.

នៅក្នុងថ្នាក់ យើងរៀនអំពីការប្រឹងប្រកួតប្រជែងធ្វើអ្វីមួយដែលមនុស្សជួបប្រទះ។ ______________ (ឈ្មោះសិស្ស) ចង់ប្រាប់អ្នកអំពីរឿង ដែលយើងបានអាន។

The Race, by Jennifer Trujillo, & **The Camel Dances,** by Arnold Lobel
ក្មេងស្រីប្រណាំងសេះ និង សត្វអូដ_ចង់ ក្លាយជាអ្នករាំបាឡេ

Hatchet, by Gary Paulsen ក្មេងប្រុសជំទង់ម្នាក់ត្រូវរកមធ្យោបាយធ្វើឲ្យកើតមានភ្លើង ហើយតស៊ូរស់ម្នាក់ឯងនៅក្នុងព្រៃស្ងាត់។

Antarctic Adventure, by Meredith Hooper ក្រុមបុរសក្លាហានមួយ ដែលសំពៅខ្លួនបាក់ធ្លាយនៅទ្វីបអង់តាក់ទិកាហើយត្រូវ រកផ្លូវត្រឡប់ទៅកាន់អរិយធម៌វិញ។

Yang the Youngest, by Lensey Namioka
ក្មេងប្រុសម្នាក់សាកល្បងជូរទម្លាប់ឲ្យទៅតាមការរស់នៅក្នុងប្រទេសថ្មីមួយ និង សាលារៀនថ្មីមួយ។

The Scholarship Jacket, by Marta Salinas ក្មេងស្រីជំទង់ម្នាក់ ត្រូវបង្ហាញថានាងត្រូវបានឈ្នះរង្វាន់សិក្សាប្រចាំសាលា- អាវចាកកែក អាហារូបករណ_។

យើងក៏ចង់ឲ្យអ្នកចំណាយពេលវេលាមួយភ្លែត ដើម្បីចូលរួមការសម្ភាសមួយអំពីការប្រឹងប្រែងខិតខំ ដើម្បីប្រាប់សិស្សនៅក្នុងថ្នាក់។ សូមអរគុណ ចំពោះការគាំទ្ររបស់អ្នក។

ដោយសោះស្ម័គ្រ

______________________ (គ្រូបង្រៀន)

ការសម្ភាស

១, ឈ្មោះអ្នកដែលត្រូវគេសម្ភាស: ______________________

២, សំនួរ: តើអ្វីដែលជាការខិតខំប្រឹងប្រែងដែលអ្នកធ្លាប់បានប្រឈមមុខ?
ចម្លើយ: ______________________

៣, សំនួរ: ហេតុអ្វីបានជាការនេះធ្វើឲ្យអ្នកខិតខំប្រកួត?
ចម្លើយ: ______________________

៤, សំនួរ: តើអ្នកធ្វើអ្វីខ្លះដើម្បីតម្រូវទៅតាមការខិតខំប្រកួតនេះ?
ចម្លើយ: ______________________

៥, (សិស្ស: សួរសំនួរមួយរបស់ខ្លួនឯង)
សំនួរ: ______________________
ចម្លើយ: ______________________

School-Home Connection
Sharing Visions
INITE 1 Pwoblèm

Non ______________________

Dat ______________________

Chè Fanmi,

Nan klas, nou te pale sou pwoblèm moun rankontre. ______________ *(non elèv lan)* ta renmen pataje avèk ou kèk nan istwa nou te li yo.

The Race, ekri pa Jennifer Trujillo, ak **The Camel Dances,** ekri pa Arnold Lobel Yon tifi pral patisipe nan yon kous cheval, epi yon chamo vle devni yon dansè balè.

Hatchet, ekri pa Gary Paulsen Yon jèn tigason dwe jwenn yon fason pou li limen yon dife epi siviv poukont li nan rak bwa yo.

Antarctic Adventure, ekri pa Meredith Hooper Bato yon gwoup mesye brav koule nan Antartik la epi yo dwe jwenn yon fason pou yo retounen nan peyi sivilize.

Yang the Youngest, ekri pa Lensey Namioka Yon jèn tigason eseye ajiste l ak lavi nan yon nouvo peyi ak yon nouvo lekòl.

The Scholarship Jacket, ekri pa Marta Salinas Salinas Yon jèn tifi dwe pwouve li merite pou li gaye prim akademik lekòl lan—yon djakèt pou bous detid.

Nou ta renmen pou ou pran yon ti moman pou patisipe nan yon entèvyou osijè kèk pwoblèm ou ka pataje ak klas lan. Mèsi pou sipo w.

Sensèman,

______________________ *(Pwofesè)*

ENTÈVYOU

1. Non moun w ap entèvyoure a: ______________________
2. Kesyon: A ki gwo pwoblèm ou te fè fas?

   Repons: ______________________

3. Kesyon: Poukisa sa te yon pwoblèm?

   Repons: ______________________

4. Kesyon: Kisa ou te fè pou rezoud pwoblèm lan?

   Repons: ______________________

5. (Elèv: *Poze yon kesyon paw.*)

   Kesyon: ______________________

   Repons: ______________________

School-Home Connection
Sharing Visions
UNIT 2 Changes

Name ______________________

Date ______________________

Dear Family,

In class, we have been learning about changes. ______________________ *(student's name)* would like to share with you the stories we read.

Why Do Leaves Change Color in the Fall? This article explains how leaves change with the seasons.

Elizabeth's Diary, by Patricia Hermes A young girl and her family travel from England to the New World in the early 1600s. They make their new home in Jamestown, Virginia.

And Now Miguel, by Joseph Krumgold A teenage boy wants to be a man so that he can take his herd of sheep to the Sangre de Cristo Mountains.

Tuck Triumphant, by Theodore Taylor A family in the United States is excited to meet the young boy from Korea that they have adopted.

The Journal of Jesse Smoke, by Joseph Bruchac, & **Ancient Ways** by Elvania Toledo A Cherokee teenager describes how his people are forced from their lands. A poem describes how Native American life has changed.

We would also like you to take a few moments to participate in an activity about changes to share with the class. Thank you for your support.

Sincerely,

______________________ *(Teacher)*

Are there any changes that you would like to make at home? These can be simple changes, such as rearranging your furniture. These can be bigger changes, such as who should cook dinner.

1. Ask each person at home to think of a change he or she would like to make. List them in the box.
2. Vote on one change that you all agree to make.

____

____

3. Explain what each person will do to help make the change.

____

____

____

____

4. In thirty days, review this plan to see if you were successful in making the change.

Person	Change

School-Home Connection
Sharing Visions
UNIDAD 2 Cambios

Nombre ______________________

Fecha ______________________

Estimada familia:

En nuestra clase, hemos estado aprendiendo acerca de los cambios. A ______________ *(nombre del estudiante)* le gustaría compartir con usted las historias que leímos.

Why Do Leaves Change Color in the Fall? Este artículo explica cómo cambian las hojas durante las estaciones del año.

Elizabeth's Diary, por Patricia Hermes Una niña y su familia viajan desde Inglaterra a Norteamérica a comienzos del siglo XVII, y se radican en Jamestown, Virginia.

And Now Miguel, por Joseph Krumgold Un joven quiere ser un hombre para que pueda ser pastor de ovejas en las Montañas Sangre de Cristo.

Tuck Triumphant, por Theodore Taylor Una familia en los Estados Unidos está muy ansiosa por conocer a un niño coreano que han adoptado.

The Journal of Jesse Smoke, por Joseph Bruchac, & **Ancient Ways** por Elvania Toledo Un joven cheroquí describe cómo su pueblo fue forzado a abandonar sus tierras. Un poema describe los cambios que han ocurrido en las vidas de los indígenas norteamericanos.

Ahora nos gustaría que participara en una actividad acerca de cambios, para luego compartirla con el resto de la clase. Muchas gracias por su apoyo.

Cordialmente,

______________________ *[Maestra(o)]*

¿Hay algunos cambios que te gustaría hacer en casa? Puede que sean cambios pequeños, como reorganizar los muebles, o puede que sean cambios más grandes, como cambiar la persona encargada de preparar la cena.

1. Pide a todos en casa que piensen en cambios que les gustaría hacer. Luego escríbelos en la caja.

2. Voten por un cambio que a todos les gustaría hacer. ______________________

   ____

3. Expliquen lo que hará cada persona para llevar a cabo el cambio.

   ____

   ____

   ____

4. En treinta días, revisen el plan para ver si lograron hacer el cambio esperado.

Persona	Cambio

VISIONS NEWSLETTER Unit 2

School-Home Connection
Sharing Visions
BÀI SỐ 2 Những Thay Đổi

Tên ____________________

Ngày ____________________

Kính Gởi Phụ Huynh,

Trong lớp, chúng tôi đang tìm hiểu về những thay đổi. ____________________ *(tên học sinh)* muốn chia xẻ với quý vị những câu chuyện chúng tôi đã đọc.

Why Do Leaves Change Color in the Fall? Bài viết này giải thích tại sao lá cây đổi màu theo mùa.

Elizabeth's Diary, tác gia Patricia Hermes Một cô bé cùng gia đình dời nhà từ Anh Quốc sang Tân Thế Giới vào đầu những năm 1600. Họ định cư tại Jamestown, Virginia.

And Now Miguel, tác gia Joseph Krumgold Một cậu thiếu niên muốn lớn lên thành đàn ông để có thể dẫn bầy cừu đến Dãy Núi Sangre de Cristo.

Tuck Triumphant, tác gia Theodore Taylor Một gia đình tại Hoa Kỳ nôn nóng muốn gặp cậu bé người Hàn Quốc mà họ đã nhận nuôi.

The Journal of Jesse Smoke, tác gia Joseph Bruchac, & **Ancient Ways** tác gia Elvania Toledo Một thiếu niên Cherokee mô tả dân tộc mình bị ép buộc rời bỏ đất đai của mình như thế nào. Một bài thơ mô tả những cách mà cuộc sống của Thổ Dân Mỹ đã thay đổi.

Chúng tôi xin quý vị dành một ít thời giờ để tham dự cuộc phỏng vấn về những thay đổi để trình bày với lớp học. Xin cám ơn sự hỗ trợ của quý vị.

Trân trọng,

____________________ *(Giáo viên)*

Em có muốn thay đổi gì ở nhà hay không? Đây có thể là những thay đổi đơn giản, chẳng hạn như sắp xếp lại bàn ghế tủ giường, mà cũng có thể là những thay đổi lớn hơn chẳng hạn như ai nên nấu bữa tối.

1. Yêu cầu mỗi người trong nhà nghĩ ra một điều mình muốn thay đổi. Liệt kê vào ô bên phải.
2. Đưa ra biểu quyết một thay đổi mà mọi người đều đồng ý.
   ____
   ____
3. Giải thích xem mỗi người phải làm gì để đưa đến thay đổi đó. ____________________
   ____
   ____
   ____
4. Trong vòng ba mươi ngày, hãy xem xét lại kế hoạch này để xem em đã thay đổi được chưa.

Người	Sự Thay Đổi

VISIONS NEWSLETTER Unit 2

School-Home Connection
Sharing Visions
YAM 2 Txog hloov

Npe ____________________

Vasthib ____________________

Nyob zoo,

Nyob rau hauv hoob, peb tau kawm txog yam uas nws hloov. ____________________ *(Menyuam npe)* xav muab tej dab neeg uas peb tau nyeem nyob hauv hoob lawd coj los qhia rau nej sub nej thiaj nrog nws paub.

Why Do Leaves Change Color in the Fall? Zaj lus no nws piav qhia txog tias tej nplooj nws hloov raws tej caij nyoog.

Elizabeth's Diary, los ntawm Patricia Hermes Piav txog ib tug me ntxhais thiab nws tsev neeg kev khiav teb chaw Askiv tuaj mus rau ib lub Tebchaw Tshiab nyob rau thawj ob peb xyoos ntawm xyoo 1600 tawm plaws ntawd. Lawv muab lub zos Jamestown xeev Virginia ua lawv lub chaw nyob tshiab.

And Now Miguel, los ntawm Joseph Krumgold Hais txog ib tug tub hluas uas xav dhau lso ua ib tug txiv neej sub nws thiaj coj tau yaj mus noj zaub pem cov roob Sangre de Cristo Mountains.

Tuck Triumphant, los ntawm Theodore Taylor Yog hais txog ib tsev neeg nyob rau Asmesliskas teb no uas tau kub siab lug tuaj mus tos ib tug menyuam tub Kauslim uas lawv nim qhua tau lees txais coj los tu.

The Journal of Jesse Smoke, los ntawm Joseph Bruchac, & **Ancient Ways** los ntawm Elvania Toledo Yog hais txog ib tug tub hluas Cherokee piav qhia txog ntawm nws haiv neeg tau raug ntiab tawm hauv lawv tej av teb av chaws mus. Ib zaj lus uas qhia txog tias lub neej ntawm cov neeg Khab Amesliskas tau hloov licas.

Ntxiv no mus, peb xav thov nej siv sib hawm ib pliag los pab teb cov lus nram qab no uas yog txog yam hloov txawv pub rau cov menyuam lubxiv. Ua tsaug rau nej txoj kev txhawb pab no.

Xee npe,

____________________ *(Xib hwb)*

Pos muaj tej yam nyob rau tom tsev uas koj xav hloov? Tej xav hloov no txawm yog tej yam me thiab yooj yim hloov los yog tag huvsi, xws li tias muab tej rooj tog txav hloov chaw xwb lo kuj yog tag. Tej yam los uas xav hloov txauv xws li tias sib hloo ua noj los kuj yog tib si thiab.

1. Nug ib tug hauv tsev zuj zug saib yam uas nws xav hloov nyob rau hauv tsev yog dabtsi. Khij ib lub vajvoos npov thiab sau tej yam uas xav hloov ntawd rau hauv.
2. Xaiv ib yam uas yog nej sawvdaws puav leej pom zoo xav hloov. ____________________
3. Piav qhia saib nej ib tug yuav pab ua yam twg pab txog ntawm qhov xav hloov no.

   ____

   ____
4. Tom qab puv pebcaug hnub lawm, rov qab los kuaj xyuas qhov kev nej tau npaj hloov no saib nej puas tau ua tiav.

Npe cov neeg xav hloov	Yam xav hloov

VISIONS NEWSLETTER Unit 2

School-Home Connection
Sharing Visions
第二單元：改變

姓名：______________________

日期：______________________

各位尊敬的家庭成員：

在課堂上，我們學習了有關改變的內容。______________（學生名字）想與各位分享我們上課時讀過的故事。

Why Do Leaves Change Colors in the Fall? 這篇文解釋樹葉如何隨季節變色。

Elizabeth's Diary, by Patricia Hermes 這個故事講及十六世紀初期，一個女童與家人從英格蘭搬到新大陸，在維珍尼亞州的詹姆士鎮建立新居。

And Now, Miguel, by Joseph Krumgold 這個故事講及一位少年急於長大成人，以便帶他的羊群去基度山。

Tuck Triumphant, by Theodore Taylor 這個故事講及一家美國人，為與他們由韓國領養的男童見面而興奮。

The Journal of Jesse Smoke, by Joseph Bruchac & **Ancient Ways,** by Elvania Toledo 前者由一個切羅基族少年描述其族人如何被逼離開自己的土地；後者則是一首詩，描述美國原住民生活的改變經過。

我們還希望各位能抽出時間參與一項有關改變的活動，與全班同學一起分享。感謝各位的支持。

順祝安康，

______________________（教師）

您家中是否有些您想要改變的地方？這些可以是簡單的改變，例如重新擺設家具等；也可以是比較重大的改變，例如改變負責煮飯的人。

1. 請詢問家中每一個人，請他們將想要做的改變列在表格中：
2. 請投票選出一個你們大家都同意做的改變：

   ____

   ____

3. 請說明各人將如何幫手做這個改變：

   ____

   ____

   ____

   ____

4. 30天之後，請評量一下這個計劃，以檢討你們所做的改變是否成功。

姓名	想做的改變

School-Home Connection
Sharing Visions
ជំពូក ២ ការផ្លាស់ប_រ

ឈ្មោះ ______________________

កាលបរិច្ឆេទ ______________________

ជូនចំពោះគ្រួសារ.

នៅក្នុងថ្នាក់ យើងរៀនអំពីការផ្លាស់ប_រ។ ____________________ (ឈ្មោះសិស្ស) ចង់ប្រាប់អ្នកអំពីរឿង ដែលយើងបានអាន។

Why Do Leaves Change Color in the Fall?
អត្ថបទនេះពន្យល់ពីរបៀបដែលស្លឹកឈើដូរទៅតាមរដូវ។

Elizabeth's Diary, by Patricia Hermes
ក្មេងស្រីម្នាក់និងគ្រួសារនាងធ្វើដំណើរពីប្រទេសអង់គ្លេសទៅកាន់ ពិភពថ្មី នៅដើមសតវត្សទី១៧។ ពួកគេធ្វើផ_ះថ្មីមួយនៅទីក្រុង ចេមថោន. រដ_វីជីនញ៉ា។

And Now Miguel, by Joseph Krumgold ក្មេងប្រុសជំទង់ម្នាក់ចង់ក្លាយទៅជាមនុស្សធំ ដើម្បីវាបាននាំហ្វូងចៀមវាឡើង ទៅកាន់ភ្នំ សែនគ្រី ដី គ្រីសេ_។

Tuck Triumphant, by Theodore Taylor គ្រួសារមួយនៅអាមេរិក គេរំភើបដោយបានជួបក្មេងប្រុសម្នាក់មកពីកូរ៉េ ដែលពួក គេបានសុំមកចិញ្ចឹម។

The Journal of Jesse Smoke, by Joseph Bruchac, & **Ancient Ways** by Elvania Toledo
ក្មេងជំទង់ជនជាតិ ជូរូគី អធិប្បាយពីប្រជាជនរបស់វាដែលត្រូវគេបង្ខំឲ្យចាកចេញពីទឹកដី។ កំណាព្យមួយនិយាយអំពីការដែលជីវិតរបស់ជនជាតិដើមអាមេរិក ត្រូវ បានផ្លាស់ប_រ។

យើងក៏ចង់ឲ្យអ្នកចំណាយពេលវេលាមួយភ្លែត ដើម្បីចូលរួមសកម្មភាពមួយអំពីការផ្លាស់ប_រ ដើម្បីប្រាប់សិស្សនៅក្នុងថ្នាក់។ សូមអរគុណចំពោះ ការគាំទ្ររបស់អ្នក។

ដោយសេចក្ដីស្មោះត្រង់

____________________ (គ្រូបង្រៀន)

តើមានការផ្លាស់ប_រណាមួយដែលអ្នកចង់ធ្វើនៅផ_ះឬទេ? ទាំងនេះអាចជាការផ្លាស់ប_រតែមួយមុខ. ដូចជា ការដូរកន្លែងតុទូរកៅអី។ ទាំងនេះអាច ជាការផ្លាស់ប_រដ៏ធំ. ដូចជា អ្នកណាដែលគួរចំអិនម្ហូបអាហារ។

មនុស្ស	ការផ្លាស់ប_រ

១, សួរមនុស្សម្នាក់ៗនៅក្នុងផ_ះ ឲ្យគិតពីការផ្លាស់ប_រអ្វីមួយដែលគេចង់ធ្វើ។ ចុះបញ្ជីឈ្មោះកិច្ចការទាំងនេះនៅក្នុងប្រអប់មួយ

២, បោះឆ្នោតរើសការផ្លាស់ប_រមួយ ដែលអ្នកទាំងអស់គ្នាយល់ស្របថានឹងធ្វើ។

____

____

៣, ពន្យល់ម្នាក់ៗ ពីអ្វីដែលគេនឹងធ្វើ ដើម្បីជួយក្នុងការផ្លាស់ប_រនេះ។

____

____

៤, ក្នុងរយៈសាមសិបថ្ងៃ ពិនិត្យកិច្ចការនេះសារឡើងវិញ ដើម្បីមើលថាតើអ្នកទទួលជោគជ័យទេ ក្នុងការផ្លាស់ប_រនេះ។

School-Home Connection
Sharing Visions
INITE 2 Chanjman

Non ______________________

Dat ______________________

Chè Fanmi,

Nan klas, nou te pale sou chanjman ki konn fèt. ______________ *(non elèv lan)* ta renmen pataje avèk ou kèk nan istwa nou te li yo.

Why Do Leaves Change Color in the Fall? Atik sa eksplike kijan fèy yo chanje lè sezon yo ap chanje.

Elizabeth's Diary, ekri pa Patricia Hermes Yon jèn tifi ak fanmi li ap vwayaje soti an Angletè pou ale nan Nouvo Monn lan nan kòmansman lane 1600 yo. Yo etabli yo nan Jamestown, Virginia.

And Now Miguel, ekri pa Joseph Krumgold Yon jèn tigason bezwen vin yon nonm pou li ka mennen twoupo mouton l lan nan mòn Sangre de Cristo.

Tuck Triumphant, ekri pa Theodore Taylor fanmi Ozetazini kontan anpil pou yo rankontre yon tigason Koreyen yo te adopte.

The Journal of Jesse Smoke, ekri pa Joseph Bruchac, ak **Ancient Ways** ekri pa Elvania Toledo Yon jèn gason Cherokee dekri kouman y ap fòse pèp li a kite tè yo. Yon powèm dekri kouman lavi Endyen Ameriken natif natal vin chanje.

Nou ta renmen pou ou pran yon ti moman pou patisipe nan yon aktivite osijè chanjman ki konn fèt pouka pataje sa ak klas lan. Mèsi pou sipò w.

Sensèman,

______________ *(Pwofesè)*

Èske gen okenn chanjman ou ta renmen fè lakay ou? Sa ka kèk chanjman trè senp, tankou rearanje mèb nan kay lan. Sa ka pi gwo chanjman tankou kilès ki ta dwe fè manje nan kay lan.

1. Mande chak moun nan kay la pou l panse sou yon chanjman li ta renmen fè. Mete lis lan nan bwat la.
2. Vote sou yon chanjman tout moun dako pou fè.

   ____

   ____

3. Eksplike sa chak moun pral fè ki pral ede fè chanjman an.

   ____

   ____

   ____

   ____

4. Nan trant jou, revize plan sa a pou wè si nou te gen siksè pou fè chanjman an.

Moun nan	Chanjman an

School-Home Connection
Sharing Visions
UNIT 3 Courage

Name ______________________________

Date ______________________________

Dear Family,

In class, we learned about people who showed courage. ____________________ *(student's name)* would like to share with you the stories we read.

Life Doesn't Frighten Me, by Maya Angelou This poem describes frightening things and how the author faces them.

Matthew A. Henson, by Wade Hudson This is an excerpt from the biography of the first African-American to reach the North Pole.

Anne Frank: The Diary of a Young Girl A teenage Jewish girl describes how her family is forced to hide from the Nazis during World War II.

Lance Armstrong: Champion Cyclist, by George W. Bush The president of the United States praises Lance Armstrong for his courage in his Tour de France wins and his battle with cancer.

Earthquake, by Huynh Quang Nhuong A man remembers the day that a strong earthquake demolished much of his village in Vietnam.

We would also like you to take a few moments to share with the class information about a person in your family or culture who showed courage. Thank you for your support.

Sincerely,

__________________________ *(Teacher)*

Talk about a person in your family or culture who has shown courage.

1. Who is this person? ______________________________

____

2. What did he or she do that showed courage? ______________________________

____

____

3. How does this person's courage influence you? ______________________________

____

____

4. Where can we learn more information about this person? ______________________________

____

____

School-Home Connection
Sharing Visions
UNIDAD 3 Valentía

Nombre ____________________

Fecha ____________________

Estimada familia:

En nuestra clase, aprendimos acerca de personas que demuestran valentía. A ____________________ *(nombre del estudiante)* le gustaría compartir con usted las historias que leímos.

Life Doesn't Frighten Me, por Maya Angelou Este poema describe cosas que dan miedo y la manera en que la autora las confronta.

Matthew A. Henson, por Wade Hudson Esta es una selección de la biografía del primer afroamericano que logró llegar al Polo Norte.

Anne Frank: The Diary of a Young Girl Una joven judía describe cómo su familia se ve obligada a esconderse de los nazis durante la Segunda Guerra Mundial.

Lance Armstrong: Champion Cyclist, por George W. Bush El presidente de los Estados Unidos elogia a Lance Armstrong por su valentía en su triunfo en el *Tour de France* y en su batalla personal contra el cancer.

Earthquake, por Huynh Quang Nhuong Un hombre recuerda el día en que un terremoto fuerte destruyó gran parte de su aldea en Vietnám.

Ahora nos gustaría que compartiera con la clase información acerca de una persona de su familia o comunidad que haya mostrado valentía. Muchas gracias por su apoyo.

Cordialmente,

____________________ *[Maestra(o)]*

Hablen acerca de una persona de tu familia o de tu comunidad que haya demostrado valentía.

1. ¿Quién es esa persona? ____________________

2. ¿Qué hizo él o ella que demuestra valentía? ____________________

3. ¿Cómo les afecta el haber aprendido acerca de la valentía de esa persona? ____________________

4. ¿Dónde podemos obtener más información acerca de esa persona? ____________________

School-Home Connection
Sharing Visions
BÀI SỐ 3 Sự Can Đảm

Tên ______________________

Ngày ______________________

Kính Gởi Phụ Huynh,

Trong lớp, chúng tôi tìm hiểu về những người đã chứng tỏ lòng can đảm. ______________ *(tên học sinh)* muốn chia xẻ với quý vị những câu chuyện chúng tôi đã đọc.

Life Doesn't Frighten Me, tác gia Maya Angelou Bài thơ này mô tả những sự việc đáng sợ và làm thế nào tác giả đã đối phó được.

Matthew A. Henson, tác gia Wade Hudson Đây là một đoạn trích từ tiểu sử của người Mỹ gốc Châu Phi đầu tiên đã đặt chân đến Bắc Cực.

Anne Frank: The Diary of a Young Girl Một cô thiếu niên người Do Thái kể chuyện gia đình mình bắt buộc phải trốn bọn Quốc Xã Đức trong suốt Thế Chiến Thứ Hai.

Lance Armstrong: Champion Cyclist, tác gia George W. Bush Tổng Thống Mỹ đề cao lòng can đảm của Lance Armstrong đã thắng cuộc đua Tour de France cũng như đối phó với bệnh ung thư.

Earthquake, tác gia Huynh Quang Nhuong Một người đàn ông hồi tưởng lại cái ngày mà một trận động đất mãnh liệt đã tàn phá phần lớn ngôi làng của ông tại Việt Nam.

Chúng tôi xin quý vị dành một ít thời giờ để kể về một người can đảm trong gia đình hay dân tộc của quý vị nhằm trình bày với lớp học. Xin cám ơn sự hỗ trợ của quý vị.

Trân trọng,

______________________ *(Giáo viên)*

Hãy kể về một người can đảm trong gia đình hay dân tộc của em.

1. Người này là ai? ______________________

____

2. Người này đã làm gì để chứng tỏ lòng can đảm? ______________________

____

____

3. Lòng can đảm của người này có ảnh hưởng như thế nào đến em? ______________________

____

____

4. Chúng tôi có thể tìm đâu ra thêm thông tin về người này? ______________________

____

____

School-Home Connection
Sharing Visions
YAM 3 Txog tsab peevxwm

Npe ________________________________

Vasthib ________________________________

Nyob zoo,

Nyob rau hauv hoob, peb tau kawm txog cov tib neeg uas nws coj tus yam ntxwv tawm plaws qhia tias nws muaj tsab peevxwm. ________________________ *(Menyuam npe)* xav muab zaj no los qhia rau nej paub sub nej tau nrog peb kawm ua ke.

Life Doesn't Frighten Me, los ntawm Maya Angelou Zaj lus no yog piav txog tej yam uas txaus ntshai thiab qhia txog tias tus sau zaj no nws raug ntsib licas.

Matthew A. Henson, los ntawm Wade Hudson Zaj dab neeg no yog rho tawm hauv phau ntawv uas sau qhia txog thawj tug Asfliskas-Asmesliskas uas tau mus txog rau pem qaum ntiajteb xaub los yog hu ua North Pole.

Anne Frank: The Diary of a Young Girl Yog ib tug ntxhais Yusndais piav txog nws tsev neeg tau raug quab yuam mus khiav nkaum cov Nazis thaum Tsov Rog Ntiajteb Zaum Ob los yog World War II.

Lance Armstrong: Champion Cyclist, los ntawm George W. Bush Qhia txog tus nom lub teb chaws United States no tau qhuas txog Lance Armstrong rau qhov uas nws muaj tsab peevxwm heev nyob rau thaum nws yeej kev xeem luv thij Tour de France thiab qhov uas nws sib zog peem yeej kev mob khaabxawm los sis cancer.

Earthquake, los ntawm Huynh Quang Nhuong Ib tug txiv neej tseem nco txog hnub av qeeg nyob rau Nyablaj Teb uas tau ua rau nws lub zos nroog tas.

Peb xav thov nej siv sib hawm ib pliag los qhia rau cov menyuam lubxiv txog ib tug hauv nej tsev neeg los yog hauv nej haiv neeg ua nws tau muaj tsab peevxwm. Ua tsaug rau nej txoj kev txhawb pab no.

Xee npe,

________________________ *(Xib hwb)*

Qhia txog ib tug uas nyob hauv nej tsev neeg los yog hauv nej haiv neeg uas tau muaj tsab peevxwm.

1. Tus neeg no nws yog leejtwg? ________________________

2. Tus pojniam los txiv neej no tau ua dabtsi es ho hais tau tias nws muaj tsab peevxwm? ________________________

3. Tsab peevxwm tus neeg no muaj puas yaum tau koj los sis puas txhawb tau koj lub zog? ________________________

4. Peb yuav nrhiav kawm txog tus neeg no nyob rau qhov twg thiaj nrhiav tau? ________________________

VISIONS NEWSLETTER Unit 3

School-Home Connection
Sharing Visions
第三單元：勇氣

姓名：______________________

日期：______________________

各位尊敬的家庭成員：

在課堂上，我們學習了有關勇氣的內容。 ____________ *（學生名字）*想與各位分享我們上課時讀過的故事。

Life Doesn't Frighten Me, by Maya Angelou 這首詩描述作者所害怕的事物，又描述作者如何勇敢面對這些事物。

Matthew A. Henson, by Wade Hudson 這是一本傳記摘錄，介紹第一位到達北極的非洲裔美國人。

Anne Frank: A Diary of a Young Girl 在這書中，一位猶太少女描述家人如何在二次世界大戰中被逼躲避納粹。

Lance Armstrong: Champion Cyclist, by George W. Bush 美國總統在書中稱讚蘭思 • 阿姆斯壯贏得環法單車賽冠軍時所表現的勇氣，亦讚美他對抗癌症的勇氣。

Earthquake, by Huynh Quang Nhuong 這本書描述一位男士對越南大地震的回憶，地震當日，他的村子大部份遭地震摧毀。

我們還希望各位能抽出時間參與一項有關勇氣的活動，與全班同學一起分享。感謝各位的支持。

順祝安康，

____________________ *（教師）*

請談一下您的家人或歷史文化中曾表現勇氣的人物。

1. 那個人是誰？______________________

2. 他做了甚麼表現勇氣的事？______________________

3. 這個人的勇氣如何影響您？______________________

4. 我們在何處可以取得更多有關這個人的資料？______________________

School-Home Connection
Sharing Visions
ជំពូក ៣ សេចក្ដីក្លាហាន

ឈ្មោះ ______________________

កាលបរិច្ឆេទ ______________________

ជូនចំពោះគ្រួសារ.

នៅក្នុងថ្នាក់ យើងរៀនអំពីមនុស្សដែលបង្ហាញនូវសេចក្ដីក្លាហាន។ ______________ (ឈ្មោះសិស្ស) ចង់ប្រាប់អ្នកអំពីរឿង ដែលយើងបានអាន។

Life Doesn't Frighten Me, by Maya Angelou កំណាព្យនេះនិយាយអំពីអ្វីដែលគួរខ្លាច និងរបៀបដែលអ្នកនិពន្ធប្រឈមមុខនឹងអ្វី ដែលគួរឲ្យខ្លាចនោះ

Matthew A. Henson, by Wade Hudson នេះជាសេចក្ដីដែលដកស្រង់ពីប្រវត្តិរូបរបស់ អាហ្វ្រិកកែន-អាមេរិកកែនទី១ ដែលបាន ទៅដល់ប៉ូលខាងជើង។

Anne Frank: The Diary of a Young Girl ក្មេងស្រីជំទង់ជាតិជ្វីសម្នាក់ រៀបរាប់អំពីការដែលគ្រួសារនាងត្រូវបានបង្ខំខ្លួនឲ្យលាក់ខ្លួនពួន ពីពួក ណាស៊ីស នៅពេលសង្គ្រាមលោកលើកទី២។

Lance Armstrong: Champion Cyclist, by George W. Bush ប្រធានាធិបតីយអាមេរិក សរសេរ ឡែន អាមស្រ្តង អំពីសេចក្ដីក្លាហានរបស់គាត់នៅក្នុងការប្រណាំងកង់ ថួរដឺហ្វ្រង់ បានជោគជ័យ ហើយនិងប្រយុទ្ធទប់ទល់នឹងជម្ងឺមហារីករបស់ គាត់។

Earthquake, by Huynh Quang Nhuong បុរសម្នាក់ចងចាំនូវថ្ងៃដែលការរំជួយផែនដីដ៏ធំមួយ បានបំផ្លាញភូមិគាត់យ៉ាងច្រើន នៅ ប្រទេសវៀតណាម។

យើងក៏ចង់ឲ្យអ្នកចំណាយពេលវេលាមួយភ្លែត ដើម្បីជាពត៌មានស្ដីរាប់ថ្នាក់រៀនអំពីមនុស្សម្នាក់នៅក្នុងគ្រួសារឬក្នុងប្រពៃណីយ៍របស់អ្នក ដែល បង្ហាញនូវសេចក្ដីក្លាហាន។ សូមអរគុណចំពោះការគាំទ្ររបស់អ្នក។

ដោយសោះស្ម័គ្រ

______________________ (គ្រូបង្រៀន)

និយាយអំពីមនុស្សម្នាក់នៅក្នុងគ្រួសារឬប្រពៃណីយ៍អ្នក ដែលបានបង្ហាញនូវសេចក្ដីក្លាហាន។

១, តើមនុស្សនេះជានរណា? ______________________

២, តើគាត់ធ្វើអ្វី ដែលបានបង្ហាញសេចក្ដីក្លាហាននេះ? ______________________

៣, តើសេចក្ដីក្លាហានរបស់ជននេះមានឥទ្ធិពលយ៉ាងណាចំពោះអ្នក? ______________________

៤, តើយើងអាចរៀនថែមនូវពត៌មានពីជននេះ នៅឯណាបាន? ______________________

School-Home Connection
Sharing Visions
INITE 3 Kouraj

Non ______________________

Dat ______________________

Chè Fanmi,

Nan klas, nou te pale osijè moun ki te montre kouraj. ____________ *(non elèv lan)* ta renmen pataje avèk ou kèk nan istwa nou te li yo.

Life Doesn't Frighten Me, ekri pa Maya Angelou Powèm sa a dekri kèk pwoblèm efreyan epi jan otè a te fè fas a yomenm.

Matthew A. Henson, ekri pa Wade Hudson Se yon ekstrè ki soti nan byografi premye Afriken- Ameriken ki te rive nan Pòl Nò.

Anne Frank: The Diary of a Young Girl Yon tifi Jwif dekri kouman yo te fòse fanmi li kache pandan Dezyèm Gè Mondyal la.

Lance Armstrong: Champion Cyclist, ekri pa George W. Bush Prezidan Etazini an fè lwanj pou Lance Armstrong pou kouraj li pou viktwa li te ranpòte nan Tour de France lan epi pou lit li te mennen kont kansè.

Earthquake, ekri pa Huynh Quang Nhuong mesye sonje jou yon gwo tranbleman de tè te prèske demoli vilaj li an nèt nan Vyetnam.

Nou ta renmen tou pou pran yon ti moman pou pataje ak klas la enfòmasyon konsènan yon moun nan fanmi w oswa kilti w ki te montre kouraj. Mèsi pou sipò w.

Sensèman,

____________________ *(Pwofesè)*

Pale konsènan yon moun nan fanmi w oswa kilti w ki te montre kouraj.

1. Kilès moun sa ye? ______________________________

2. Kisa li te fè ki te montre li gen kouraj? ______________________________

3. Kijan kouraj moun sa a enfliyanse w? ______________________________

4. Ki kote ou ka aprann plis bagay sou moun sa a? ______________________________

School-Home Connection
Sharing Visions
UNIT 4 Discoveries

Name ______________________

Date ______________________

Dear Family,

In class, we learned about discoveries. ________________ *(student's name)* would like to share with you the stories we read.

The Library Card, by Jerry Spinelli, & **At the Library,** by Nikki Grimes A teenager finds a library card and visits the library for the first time. A poem describes how books excite the imagination.

Discovering the Inca Ice Maiden, by Johan Reinhard While climbing a volcano in the Andes Mountains, two men discover the frozen mummy of a 14-year-old Inca girl.

The Art of Swordsmanship, by Rafe Martin A young man becomes a master swordsman with the help of a great teacher.

Mae Jemison, Space Scientist, by Gail Sakurai This biography of Mae Jemison describes how she became an astronaut.

We would also like you to take a few moments to participate in an activity about discoveries to share with the class. Thank you for your support.

Sincerely,

______________________ *(Teacher)*

Think of a place in your community that you have never visited and that you would like to discover.

1. What new place would you like to discover? ______________________

2. Why? ______________________

3. What do you think you can learn at this place? ______________________

If possible, arrange a time to visit this place together. After the visit, answer these questions.

4. What did you do? ______________________

5. What did you discover about this place? ______________________

6. Will you return for a second visit? Why or why not? ______________________

School-Home Connection
Sharing Visions

UNIDAD 4 Descubrimientos

Nombre ______________________

Fecha ______________________

Estimada familia:

En nuestra clase, aprendimos acerca de descubrimientos. A ____________ *(nombre del estudiante)* le gustaría compartir con usted las historias que leímos.

The Library Card, por Jerry Spinelli, & **At the Library,** por Nikki Grimes Un niño se encuentra una tarjeta para la biblioteca y visita la biblioteca por primera vez. Un poema describe la manera en que los libros estimulan la imaginación.

Discovering the Inca Ice Maiden, por Johan Reinhard Mientras escalaba un volcán en la Cordillera de los Andes, un hombre descubre la momia congelada de una niña inca de 14 años de edad.

The Art of Swordsmanship, por Rafe Martin Un joven se convierte en un espadachín diestro con la ayuda de un gran maestro.

Mae Jemison, Space Scientist, por Gail Sakurai Esta biografía de Mae Jemison describe lo que hizo ella para convertirse en astronauta.

Ahora nos gustaría que participara en una actividad acerca de descubrimientos, para luego compartirla con el resto de la clase. Muchas gracias por su apoyo.

Cordialmente,

____________________ *[Maestra(o)]*

Piensen en un lugar en su comunidad que nunca hayan visitado y que les gustaría llegar a conocer.

1. ¿Qué lugar nuevo les gustaría descubrir? ______________________

____

2. ¿Por qué? ______________________
3. ¿Qué creen que pueden aprender de ese lugar? ______________________

____

Si es posible, determinen cuando podrían ir a conocer ese lugar. Después de visitar el lugar, contesten las siguientes preguntas.

4. ¿Qué hicieron en ese lugar? ______________________
5. ¿Qué descubrieron en ese lugar? ______________________

____

6. ¿Volverán a ir al lugar? ¿Por qué sí o por qué no? ______________________

____

School-Home Connection
Sharing Visions
BÀI SỐ 4 Những Khám Phá

Tên ______________________________

Ngày ______________________________

Kính Gởi Phụ Huynh,

Trong lớp, chúng tôi đã tìm hiểu về những khám phá. ____________________ *(tên học sinh)* muốn chia xẻ với quý vị những câu chuyện chúng tôi đã đọc.

The Library Card, tác gia Jerry Spinelli, & **At the Library,** tác gia Nikki Grimes Một thiếu niên tìm thấy một thẻ thư viện và đến thư viện lần đầu tiên. Một bài thơ mô tả những cuốn sách khơi gợi trí tưởng tượng như thế nào.

Discovering the Inca Ice Maiden, tác gia Johan Reinhard Trong lúc leo núi lửa ở dãy núi Andes, hai người đàn ông phát hiện xác đóng băng của một cô bé người Inca 14 tuổi.

The Art of Swordsmanship, tác gia Rafe Martin Một chàng trai trẻ trở thành một kiếm sĩ điêu luyện nhờ sự giúp đỡ của một thầy dạy tuyệt vời.

Mae Jemison, Space Scientist, tác gia Gail Sakurai Tiểu sử của Mae Jemison mô tả làm thế nào bà ta trở thành một phi hành gia.

Chúng tôi xin quý vị dành một ít thời giờ để tham gia một hoạt động về những khám phá nhằm trình bày với lớp học. Xin cám ơn sự hỗ trợ của quý vị.

Trân trọng,

____________________ *(Giáo viên)*

Hãy nghĩ đến một nơi trong cộng đồng mà em chưa từng đến và muốn đến khám phá.

1. Em muốn khám phá nơi mới nào? ______________________________

____

2. Tại sao? ______________________________

3. Em nghĩ rằng em có thể học hỏi được gì ở nơi này? ______________________________

____

Nếu được, hãy sắp xếp thời giờ để cùng nhau đến thăm nơi này. Sau chuyến viếng thăm, hãy trả lời những câu hỏi sau đây.

4. Em đã làm gì? ______________________________

5. Em đã khám phá gì về nơi này? ______________________________

____

6. Em có muốn đến đây lần thứ hai hay không? Tại sao hoặc tại sao không? ______________________________

____

School-Home Connection
Sharing Visions
YAM 4 Tshawb nrhiav pom

Npe ______________________

Vasthib ______________________

Nyob zoo,

Nyob rau hauv hoob, peb tau kawm txog kev tshawb nrhiav pom. ______________ *(Menyuam npe)* xav muab cov dab neeg peb tau nyeem lawd coj los qhia rau nej sub nej thiaj paub txog tias peb kawm li cas.

The Library Card, los ntawm Jerry Spinelli, & **At the Library,** los ntawm Nikki Grimes Yog hais txog ib tug menyuam uas khaws tau ib daim npav qiv ntawv los sis yog library card thiab tau mus xyuas lub chaw qiv thiab saib ntawv ntawd nyob rau nws thawj zaug xwb. Ib zaj lus txog cov phau ntawv ua rau yus kub siab xam pom ntau yam.

Discovering the Inca Ice Maiden, los ntawm Johan Reinhard Thaum sam swm nce ib lub roob av npau uas yog Andes Mountains, ob tug txiv neej ntawd nkawv pom ib lub cev menyuam ntxhais tuag uas tau khov lawm. Nws yog haiv neeg Inca thiab muaj hnub nyoog 14 xyoos.

The Art of Swordsmanship, los ntawm Rafe Martin Ib tug tub hluas dhau los ua ib tug kws tua ntaj vim yog muaj tus xib hwb txawj tes taws.

Mae Jemison, Space Scientist, los ntawm Gail Sakurai Phau ntawv sau txog Mae Jemison no nws piav qhia txog tias ua li cas nws thiaj tau ua ib tug caij avposlaus mus saum ntuj uas yog astronaut.

Ntxiv ntawm rau ntawm no, peb xav thov nej siv sib hawm ib pliag los koom txog rau qhov kev tshawb nrhiav pom no es pab teb cov lus nram qab no rau cov menyuam lubxiv. Ua tsaug rau qhov nej pab txhawb nqa no.

Xee npe,

______________________ *(Xib hwb)*

Xav saib hauv nej lub zos puas muaj ib qhov chaw uas nej tsi tau mus xyuas hlo li uas nej xav mus saib nws muaj dabtsi.

1. Qhov chaw tshiab uas nej xav mus saib yog dabtsi? ______________________

____

2. Yog vim licas nej thiaj xav mus saib qhov chaw no? ______________________

3. Nej xav hais tias nej yuav kawm tau dabtsi los ntawm qhov chaw no? ______________________

____

Yog hais tias tau, nrhiav ib lub sib hawm mus xyuas qhov chaw no ua ib ke. Tom qab nej tau mus saib tag lawd, ces pab teb cov lus nram qab no.

4. Thaum nej mus txog nej ua licas xwb? ______________________

5. Nej pom tau tias qhov chaw no nws muaj dabtsi xwb? ______________________

____

6. Nej puas rov qab mus xyuas ib zaug ntxiv? Yog vim li cas hov xav rov mus dua los yog tsi xav mus lawm?

____

School-Home Connection
Sharing Visions

第四單元：新發現

姓名：____________________

日期：____________________

各位尊敬的家庭成員：

在課堂上，我們學習了有關新發現的內容。 ________________ *（學生名字）*想與各位分享我們上課時讀過的故事。

The Library Card, by Jerry Spinelli & **At the Library,** by Nikki Grimes 前者描述一位少年拾到一張借書證後，第一次去圖書館；後者是一首詩，描述書籍如何啓發想像力。

Discovering the Inca Ice Maiden, by Johan Reinhard 描述兩位男士攀登安地斯山脈的火山時，發現一個十四歲印加少女已結凍的木乃伊。

The Art of Swordsmanship, by Rafe Martin 描述一位青年男子如何在一位好老師的協助下成爲劍術大師。

Mae Jemison, Space Scientist, by Gail Sakurai 這是梅•傑米森的傳記，描述她如何成爲太空人。

我們還希望各位能抽出時間參與一項有關新發現的活動，與全班同學一起分享。感謝各位的支持。

順祝安康，

____________________ *（教師）*

請想想您的社區內，有無您未曾去過而想去探究的地方？

1. 您想去探究的新地方在何處？____________________

2. 爲甚麼您要去這個地方？____________________

3. 您認爲您在這個地方可以學到甚麼？____________________

如有可能，請安排時間一同去這個地方；回來後，請回答下列問題。

4. 您做了些甚麼？____________________

5. 您在這個地方發現了甚麼？____________________

6. 您會再去嗎? 爲甚麼?____________________

School-Home Connection
Sharing Visions
ជំពូក ៤ ការរុករកឃើញ

ឈ្មោះ ______________________

កាលបរិច្ឆេទ ______________________

ជូនចំពោះគ្រួសារ.

នៅក្នុងថ្នាក់ យើងរៀនអំពីការរុករកឃើញ។ ______________________ (ឈ្មោះសិស្ស) ចង់ប្រាប់អ្នកអំពីរឿងដែលយើងបានអាន។

The Library Card, by Jerry Spinelli, & **At the Library,** by Nikki Grimes ក្មេងជំទង់ម្នាក់រកឃើញកាតបណ្ណាល័យមួយ ហើយក៏ទៅបណ្ណាល័យជាលើកទីមួយ។ កំណាព្យអធិប្បាយពីសៀវភៅដែលធ្វើឲ្យរំភើបដល់ការស្រមៃ។

Discovering the Inca Ice Maiden, by Johan Reinhard ពេលឡើងភ្នំភ្លើងនៅភ្នំ អែនដែស បុរសពីរនាក់រកឃើញសាក សពមិនរលួយដែលរឹងកក នៃក្មេងស្រីជាតិអ៊ិនកា អាយុ ១៤ឆ្នាំ។

The Art of Swordsmanship, by Rafe Martin បុរសក្មេងម្នាក់ក្លាយទៅជាអ្នកជំនាញកាប់ដាវ ដោយការជួយពីគ្រូជ_ខ្លាំងពូកែម្នាក់។

Mae Jemison, Space Scientist, by Gail Sakurai ព្រាក្រភា ប្រវត្តិរូបនៃ ម៉ា ជេនីសុន អធិប្បាយអំពី របៀបបែបណា ដែលនាងបានក្លាយទៅជា អវកាសយាននិក។

យើងក៏ចង់ឲ្យអ្នកចំណាយពេលវេលាមួយភ្លេត ដើម្បីចូលរួមសកម្មភាពមួយអំពីការរុករកឃើញ ដើម្បីប្រាប់សិស្សនៅក្នុងថ្នាក់។ សូមអរគុណចំពោះ ការគាំទ្ររបស់អ្នក។

ដោយស្មោះស្ម័គ្រ

______________________ (គ្រូបង្រៀន)

គិតពីកន្លែងណាមួយដែលអ្នកមិនធ្លាប់ទៅ ហើយដែលជាកន្លែងអ្នកចង់ឃើញ។

១, កន្លែងថ្មីណាដែលអ្នកចង់ទៅឃើញ ______________________

____

២, ហេតុអ្វី? ______________________

៣, អ្វីដែលអ្នកគិតថាអ្នកអាចរៀនសូត្រអំពីទីកន្លែងនេះ? ______________________

____

បើអាច សូមចាត់ចែងពេលដើម្បីទៅកន្លែងនេះទាំងអស់គ្នា។ ក្រោយពីទៅឃើញហើយ សូមឆ្លើយសំនួរទាំងនេះ។

៤, តើអ្នកបានធ្វើអ្វីខ្លះ? ______________________

៥, តើអ្នករកឃើញអ្វីខ្លះនៅទីនេះ? ______________________

____

៦, តើអ្នកនឹងវិលទៅជាលើកទី២ទេ? ហេតុអ្វីបានទៅ ឬ ហេតុអ្វីមិនទៅ? ______________________

____

School-Home Connection
Sharing Visions
INITE 4 Dekouvèt

Non ______________________

Dat ______________________

Chè Fanmi,

Nan klas, nou te pale konsènan kèk dekouvèt. ______________ *(non elèv lan)* tarenmen pataje avèk ou kèk nan istwa nou te li yo.

The Library Card, ekri pa Jerry Spinelli, ak **At the Library,** ekri pa Nikki Grimes Yon jèn adolesan jwenn yon kat bibliyotèk epi li ale vizite bibliyotèk lan pou lapremyè fwa. Yon powèm dekri ki jan liv kapab anrichi imajinasyon moun.

Discovering the Inca Ice Maiden, ekri pa Johan Reinhard Pandan y ap monte yon vòlkan nan Mòn And yo, de mesye dekouvri momi yon tifi Enka 14 an.

The Art of Swordsmanship, ekri pa Rafe Martin Yon jèn gason vin mèt nan tire epe gras ak èd yon gran pwofesè.

Mae Jemison, Space Scientist, ekri pa Gail Sakurai Byografi Mae Jemison sa a dekri kouman li te fè pou l devni yon astwonòt.

Nou ta renmen pou pran yon ti moman pou patisipe nan yon aktivite osijè kèk dekouvèt pouka pataje sa ak klas lan. Mèsi pou sipò w.

Sensèman,

______________ *(Pwofesè)*

Panse a yon kote nan kominote w lan ou poko janm vizite epi ou ta renmen dekouvri.

1. Ki nouvo kote ou ta renmen dekouvri? ______________
2. Rezon? ______________
3. Kisa ou panse ou ka aprann la? ______________

Si sa posib, aranje yon lè pou nou vizite kote sa a ansanm. Aprè vizit lan, reponn a kesyon sa yo.

4. Kisa nou te fè? ______________
5. Kisa nou te dekouvri konsènan kote sa a? ______________
6. N ap retounen ankò? Pouki rezon oswa poukwa pa? ______________

School-Home Connection
Sharing Visions
UNIT 5 Communication

Name ______________________________

Date ______________________________

Dear Family,

In class, we learned about communication. ____________________ *(student's name)* would like to share with you the stories we read.

How Tía Lola Came to (Visit) Stay, by Julia Alvarez A teenage boy is nervous about a visit from his aunt who doesn't speak English.

Helen Keller, by George Sullivan, & **The Miracle Worker,** by William Gibson A young deaf and blind girl learns how to communicate with the world for the first time.

Hearing: The Ear This article describes the functions of the ear and its role in communication.

The Art of Making Comic Books, by Michael Morgan Pellowski This book describes the features of a comic strip and how to begin creating one.

We would also like you to take a few moments to participate in an interview about communication to share with the class. Thank you for your support.

Sincerely,

____________________________ *(Teacher)*

INTERVIEW

1. Name of person being interviewed: ______________________________
2. Question: What ways do you use to communicate with other people?

   Answer: ______________________________

   ____
3. Question: What are some inventions that have made communication easier?

   Answer: ______________________________
4. Question: What do you think is the best form of communication? Why?

   Answer: ______________________________

   ____
5. Question: Which form of communication could you live without? Why?

   Answer: ______________________________

   ____
6. (Student: *Ask one question of your own.*)

   Question: ______________________________

   Answer: ______________________________

School-Home Connection
Sharing Visions

UNIDAD 5 Comunicación

Nombre ______________________

Fecha ______________________

Estimada familia:

En nuestra clase, aprendimos acerca de communication. A ______________________ *(nombre del estudiante)* le gustaría compartir con usted las historias que leímos.

How Tía Lola Came to (Visit) Stay, por Julia Alvarez Un niño está nervioso acerca de la visita de su tía que no habla inglés.

Helen Keller, por George Sullivan, & **The Miracle Worker,** por William Gibson Una niña sordomuda se aprende a comunicar con el mundo por primera vez.

Hearing: The Ear Este artículo describe las funciones del oído y su papel en la comunicación.

The Art of Making Comic Books, por Michael Morgan Pellowski Este libro describe las características de una tira cómica y de cómo comenzar a crear una.

Ahora nos gustaría que participara en una entrevista acerca de la comunicación, para luego compartirla con el resto de la clase. Muchas gracias por su apoyo.

Cordialmente,

______________________ *[Maestra(o)]*

ENTREVISTA

1. Nombre de la persona siendo entrevistada: ______________________
2. Pregunta: ¿Qué métodos utilizas para comunicarte con otras personas?

   Respuesta: ______________________

   ____
3. Pregunta: ¿Cuáles son algunos inventos que han facilitado la comunicación?

   Respuesta: ______________________
4. Pregunta: ¿Cuál crees tú que es la mejor manera de comunicarse? ¿Por qué?

   Respuesta: ______________________

   ____
5. Pregunta: ¿Qué forma de comunicación podrías dejar de usar? ¿Por qué?

   Respuesta: ______________________

   ____
6. (Estudiante: *Haz una pregunta tuya.*)

   Pregunta: ______________________

   Respuesta: ______________________

School-Home Connection
Sharing Visions
BÀI SỐ 5 Sự Giao Tiếp

Tên ______________________________

Ngày ______________________________

Kính Gởi Phụ Huynh,

Trong lớp, chúng tôi đã tìm hiểu về việc giao tiếp. ____________________ *(tên học sinh)* muốn chia xẻ với quý vị những câu chuyện chúng tôi đã đọc.

How Tía Lola Came to (Visit) Stay, tác gia Julia Alvarez Một cậu thiếu niên lo lắng về việc một người dì không biết nói tiếng Anh sắp sửa đến thăm.

Helen Keller, tác gia George Sullivan, & **The Miracle Worker,** tác gia William Gibson Một cô bé điếc và mù bắt đầu học cách giao tiếp với thế giới xung quanh.

Hearing: The Ear Bài viết này mô tả chức năng của tai và vai trò của tai trong việc giao tiếp.

The Art of Making Comic Books, tác gia Michael Morgan Pellowski Cuốn sách này mô tả các đặc trưng của thể loại truyện tranh cũng như hướng dẫn cách đặt và vẽ truyện.

Chúng tôi xin quý vị dành một ít thời giờ để tham dự một cuộc phỏng vấn về sự giao tiếp nhằm trình bày với lớp học. Xin cám ơn sự hỗ trợ của quý vị.

Trân trọng,

____________________ *(Giáo viên)*

PHỎNG VẤN

1. Tên người được phỏng vấn: ______________________________
2. Hỏi: Quý vị giao tiếp với người khác bằng những cách nào?

   Đáp: ______________________________

   ____
3. Hỏi: Hãy cho biết một số phát minh đã giúp việc giao tiếp dễ dàng hơn.

   Đáp: ______________________________
4. Hỏi: Theo quý vị nghĩ, dạng giao tiếp nào là tốt nhất? Tại sao?

   Đáp: ______________________________

   ____
5. Hỏi: Còn dạng giao tiếp nào mà quý vị nghĩ là không cần thiết? Tại sao?

   Đáp: ______________________________

   ____
6. (Học sinh: *Tự đặt một câu hỏi.*)

   Hỏi: ______________________________

   Đáp: ______________________________

School-Home Connection
Sharing Visions
YAM 5 Kev sib fij

Npe ______________________

Vasthib ______________________

Nyob zoo,

Nyob rau hauv hoob, peb tau kawm txog kev sib fij. ______________ *(Menyuam npe)* xav muab coj los qhia rau nej txog tias cov dab neeg peb tau kawm lawd yog dabtsi.

How Tía Lola Came to (Visit) Stay, los ntawm Julia Alvarez Hais txog ib tug tub hluas uas nws ntshai txog ntsib nws tus phauj vim tias nws tus phauj uas yuav tuaj xyuas nws ntawd tsi paub hais lus Askiv.

Helen Keller, los ntawm George Sullivan, & **The Miracle Worker,** los ntawm William Gibson Hais txog ib tug ntxhais hluas dig muag thiab tsi pom kev uas xyaum hais lus rau sawvdaws thawj zaug.

Hearing: The Ear Zaj no yog piav qhia tias lub pob ntseg ua haujlwm licas thiab nws lub luag haujlwm ntawm kev txuas lus yog licas.

The Art of Making Comic Books, los ntawm Michael Morgan Pellowski Phau ntawv no nws piav qhia tias kev kos duab nws muaj dabtsi thiab piav qhia kom yus txawj pib tsim.

Ntxiv ntawm no mus, peb xav thov nej siv sib hawm ib pliag los koom rau kev xam phaj txog kev txuas lus pub rau cov menyuam lubxiv. Ua tsaug rau nej kev pab txhawb nqa no.

Xee npe,

______________ *(Xib hwb)*

COV LUS XAM PHAJ

1. Npe ntawm tus neeg tau xam phaj teb cov lus no: ______________
2. Lus nug: Seem kev koj siv txuas lus piav qhia rau lwm leej lwm tug yog dabtsi?

   Lo lus teb: ______________

   ____
3. Lus nug: Qee yam ntawm cov kev uas tau tsim muaj los mus pab kom txoj kev sib txuas lus los yog tham lus no kom yooj yim sib txuas lus me ntsis yog yam twg rau yam twg?

   Lo lus teb: ______________
4. Lo lus nug: Seem kev rau sib txuas lus uas yooj yim tshaj plaws yog seem twg thiab yog vim licas?

   Lo lus teb: ______________

   ____
5. Lo lus nug: Seem kev sib txuas lus twg yog seem uas txawm tias koj tsi siv los koj tseem nyob tau? Qhia saib yog vim licas?

   Lo lus teb: ______________

   ____
6. (Rau tus menyuam: *Koj nug ib los lus ua koj ntiag tus.)*

   Lo lus nug: ______________

   Lo lus teb: ______________

School-Home Connection
Sharing Visions
第五單元：溝通

姓名：________________________
日期：________________________

各位尊敬的家庭成員：

在課堂上，我們學習了有關溝通的內容。________________ *（學生名字）*想與各位分享我們上課時讀過的故事。

How Tía Lola Came to (Visit) Stay, by Julia Alvarez 這個故事描述一個少年因不會講英文的姑姐要來訪問而緊張。

Helen Keller, by George Sullivan & **The Miracle Worker,** by William Gibson 這些故事描述一個既聾又盲的女童，她第一次學習如何與世界溝通。

Hearing, The Ear 這篇文描述耳朵的功能，亦談及耳朵在溝通方面擔任的角色。

The Art of Making Comic Books, by Michael Morgan Pellowski 這本書描述連環漫畫的特色，亦描述如何開始製作連環漫畫。

我們還希望各位能抽出時間參與一項有關溝通的訪問，與全班同學一起分享。感謝各位的支持。

順祝安康，

________________________ *（教師）*

訪談

1. 接受訪問者的姓名：

   ____

2. 問：您以哪些方式與他人溝通？

   答：____

   ____

3. 問：哪些發明使溝通更方便？

   答：____

   ____

4. 問：您認爲最好的溝通方式是甚麼？爲甚麼?

   答：____

   ____

5. 問：您認爲哪一種溝通方式是缺少也無妨？爲甚麼?

   答：____

   ____

6. （學生：*請提出一個你自己的問題。）*

   問：____

   答：____

School-Home Connection
Sharing Visions
ជំពូក ៥ ការប្រស្រ័យទាក់ទង

ឈ្មោះ ______________________
កាលបរិច្ឆេទ ______________________

ជូនចំពោះគ្រួសារ.

នៅក្នុងថ្នាក់ យើងរៀនអំពីការប្រស្រ័យទាក់ទង។ ______________________ (ឈ្មោះសិស្ស) ចង់ប្រាប់អ្នកអំពីរឿងដែលយើងបានអាន។

How Tía Lola Came to (Visit) Stay, by Julia Alvarez
ក្មេងប្រុសម្នាក់មានការជ្រួលច្របល់ចិត្ត–ដោយសារមីងវាដែលមិនចេះភាសាអង់គ្លេសមកលេង។

Helen Keller, by George Sullivan, & **The Miracle Worker,** by William Gibson
ក្មេងស្រីគរខ្វាក់ម្នាក់ រៀនប្រស្រ័យទាក់ទងជាមួយពិភពលោកជាលើកទី១។

Hearing: The Ear អត្ថបទនេះនិយាយអំពីមុខងាររបស់ត្រចៀក ហើយនិងតួនាទីវាក្នុងការប្រស្រ័យទាក់ទង។

The Art of Making Comic Books, by Michael Morgan Pellowski
សៀវភៅនេះនិយាយអំពីផ្នែកសំខាន់ៗនៃសៀវភៅរឿងរូប ហើយនិងរបៀបធ្វើសៀវភៅនេះមួយ។

យើងក៏ចង់ឲ្យអ្នកចំណាយពេលវេលាមួយភ្លែត ដើម្បីចូលរួមការសម្ភាសមួយអំពីការប្រស្រ័យទាក់ទង ដើម្បីប្រាប់សិស្សនៅក្នុងថ្នាក់។ សូមអរគុណចំពោះការគាំទ្ររបស់អ្នក។

ដោយសោះស្ម័គ្រ

______________________ (គ្រូបង្រៀន)

ការសម្ភាស

១, ឈ្មោះអ្នកដែលត្រូវគេសម្ភាស: ______________________

២, សំនួរ: តើអ្នកប្រើមធ្យោបាយបែបណាដើម្បីទាក់ទងទៅមនុស្សផ្សេងទៀត?
ចម្លើយ: ______________________

____

៣, សំនួរ: តើវត្ថុអ្វីខ្លះដែលគេសាវជ្រាវបង្កើតសំរាប់ការទាក់ទងគ្នាឲ្យបានងាយស្រួល?
ចម្លើយ: ______________________

៤, សំនួរ: តើអ្នកគិតថាបែបណាមួយដែលល្អជាងគេសំរាប់ការទាក់ទង? ហេតុអ្វី?
ចម្លើយ: ______________________

____

៥, សំនួរ: តើការទាក់ទងបែបណាមួយដែលអ្នកអាចរស់នៅដោយមិនត្រូវការវា? ហេតុអ្វី?
ចម្លើយ: ______________________

____

៦, (សិស្ស: សួរសំនួរមួយដោយខ្លួនឯង)
សំនួរ: ______________________
ចម្លើយ: ______________________

School-Home Connection
Sharing Visions
INITE 5 Kominikasyon

Non ______________________

Dat ______________________

Chè Fanmi,

Nan klas, nou te pale osijè kominikasyon. ______________ *(non elèv lan)* ta renmen pataje avèk ou kèk nan istwa nou te li yo.

> **How Tía Lola Came to (Visit) Stay,** ekri pa Julia Alvarez Yon jèn tigason sou kiviv akòz matant li ki pa pale anglè k ap vin vizite l.
>
> **Helen Keller,** ekri pa George Sullivan, ak **The Miracle Worker,** ekri pa William Gibson Yon jèn tifi ki soud epi ki avèg ap aprann kominike ak antouraj li pou lapremyè fwa.
>
> **Hearing: The Ear** Atik sa dekri tout fonksyon zorèy moun ak wòl yo jwe nan kominikasyon.
>
> **The Art of Making Comic Books,** ekri pa Michael Morgan Pellowski Liv sa a dekri karakteristik yon liv komik epi kijan pou kreye youn.

Nou ta renmen tou pou pran yon ti moman pou patisipe nan yon entèvyou osijè kominikasyon pouka pataje sa ak klas lan. Mèsi pou sipò w.

Sensèman,

______________ *(Pwofesè)*

ENTÈVYOU

1. Non moun w ap entèvyoure a: ______________
2. Kesyon: Ki fason ou kominike ak lot moun?

   Repons: ______________

3. Kesyon: Ki envansyon ou panse ki te fè kominikasyon vin pi fasil?

   Repons: ______________

4. Kesyon: Kisa ou panse ki meyè metòd kominikasyon? Pouki rezon?

   Repons: ______________

5. Kesyon: Ki metòd kominikasyon ou panse ou ta ka viv san li? Pouki rezon?

   Repons: ______________

6. (Elèv: *Poze kesyon paw.*)

   Kesyon: ______________

   Repons: ______________

School-Home Connection
Sharing Visions

UNIT 6 Frontiers

Name ______________________

Date ______________________

Dear Family,

In class, we learned about frontiers. ______________ *(student's name)* would like to share with you the stories we read.

The Lewis and Clark Expedition In 1804, two explorers led an expedition across North America to explore the West.

A Wrinkle in Time, by Madeleine L'Engle Three young people journey through space.

I Have a Dream, by Martin Luther King Jr. Dr. King calls for equal rights for African-Americans.

Our 36th President, by Melissa Maupin, & **Speech to the Nation 7/2/64,** by Lyndon B. Johnson President Johnson gives a speech about the importance of the Civil Rights Act.

We would also like you to take a few moments to participate in an activity about frontiers to share with the class. Thank you for your support.

Sincerely,

______________________ *(Teacher)*

In this unit, we have learned about frontiers in the past, present, and the future. Fill in the chart with as many frontiers as you can think of.

Frontiers		
Historical Frontiers	**Present-Day Frontiers**	**Future Frontiers**
The Old West	The International Space Station	Other planets

Which of these frontiers would you most like to visit? Why?

____

____

____

School-Home Connection
Sharing Visions
UNIDAD 6 Fronteras

Nombre ______________________

Fecha ______________________

Estimada familia:

En nuestra clase, aprendimos acerca de las fronteras. A ______________________ *(nombre del estudiante)* le gustaría compartir con usted las historias que leímos.

The Lewis and Clark Expedition En 1804, dos exploradores dirigieron una expedición a través de Norte América para explorar el oeste.

A Wrinkle in Time, por Madeleine L'Engle Tres niños viajan en el espacio.

I Have a Dream, por Martin Luther King Jr. Dr. King hace un llamado para que los afroamericanos tengan igualdad de derechos.

Our 36th President, por Melissa Maupin, & **Speech to the Nation 7/2/64,** por Lyndon B. Johnson El Presidente Johnson da un discurso acerca de la importancia del Acta de Derechos Civiles.

Ahora nos gustaría que participara en una actividad acerca de las fronteras, para luego compartirla con la clase. Muchas gracias por su apoyo.

Cordialmente,

______________________ *[Maestra(o)]*

En esta unidad, hemos aprendido acerca de las fronteras en el pasado, el presente y el futuro. Llenen la tabla con tantas fronteras como se les ocurran.

Fronteras		
Fronteras históricas	**Fronteras modernas**	**Futuras fronteras**
El Viejo Oeste	La Estación Espacial Internacional	Otros planetas

¿A cuál de las fronteras en la tabla les gustaría visitar más? ¿Por qué?

____

____

____

School-Home Connection
Sharing Visions
BÀI SỐ 6 Những Người/Nơi Tiên Phong

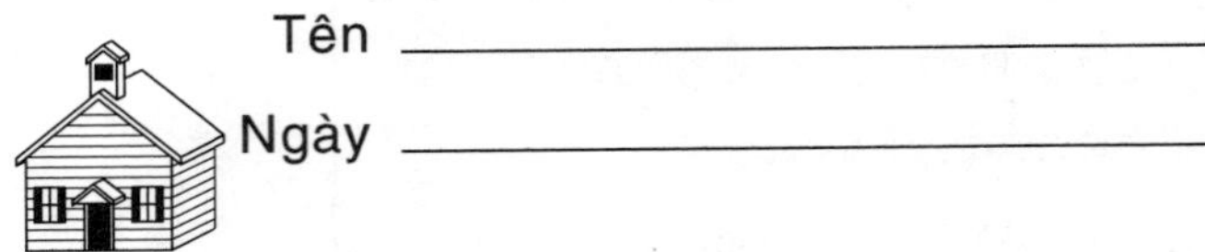

Tên ______________________

Ngày ______________________

Kính Gởi Phụ Huynh,

Trong lớp, chúng tôi đã tìm hiểu về những người/nơi tiên phong. ______________ *(tên học sinh)* muốn chia xẻ với quý vị những câu chuyện chúng tôi đã đọc.

The Lewis and Clark Expedition Vào năm 1804, hai nhà thám hiểm đã dẫn đầu một cuộc hành trình xuyên qua Bắc Mỹ đến thám hiểm miền Tây.

A Wrinkle in Time, tác gia Madeleine L'Engle Ba thiếu niên du hành xuyên qua không trung.

I Have a Dream, tác gia Martin Luther King Jr. Tiến sĩ King kêu gọi quyền bình đẳng cho Người Mỹ gốc Châu Phi.

Our 36th President, tác gia Melissa Maupin, & **Speech to the Nation 7/2/64,** tác gia Lyndon B. Johnson Tổng Thống Johnson diễn thuyết về tầm quan trọng của Đạo Luật Quyền Dân Sự.

Chúng tôi xin quý vị dành một ít thời giờ để tham gia một hoạt động về những người/vùng tiên phong nhằm trình bày với lớp học. Xin cám ơn sự hỗ trợ của quý vị.

Trân trọng,

______________________ *(Giáo viên)*

Trong bài học này, chúng tôi tìm hiểu về những người/nơi tiên phong trong quá khứ, hiện tại, và tương lai. Hãy điền vào bảng càng nhiều nơi tiên phong càng tốt.

Các Nơi Tiên Phong		
Các Nơi Tiên Phong Lịch Sử	**Các Nơi Tiên Phong Hiện Tại**	**Các Nơi Tiên Phong Tương Lai**
Miền Tây Mỹ hồi mới khai phá	Trạm Vũ Trụ Quốc Tế	Các hành tinh khác

Em thích đến thăm nơi tiên phong nào nhất trong số những nơi liệt kê trên đây? Tại sao?

____

____

____

School-Home Connection
Sharing Visions

YYAM 6 Av tshiab

Npe ______________________

Vasthib ______________________

Nyob zoo,

Nyob rau hauv hoob, peb tau kawm txog daim av tshiab. ______________ *(Menyuam npe)* xav muab cov dab neeg peb tau kawm lawd los piav qhia rau nej sub nej thiaj nrog peb paub ua ke.

The Lewis and Clark Expedition Nyob rau xyoo 1804, muaj ob tug neeg uas tau coj ib pab txiv neej hla Qaumteb Asmesliskas mus xyuas teb chaws rau sab Hnubpoob.

A Wrinkle in Time, los ntawm Madeleine L'Engle Txog peb tus neeg uas tau mus saum qaum ntuj.

I Have a Dream, los ntawm Martin Luther King Jr. Dr. King hu kom muaj vaj huam sib luag rau cov Asfliskas-Asmesliskas.

Our 36th President, los ntawm Melissa Maupin, & **Speech to the Nation 7/2/64,** los ntawm Lyndon B. Johnson President Johnson tau muab lus tseem ceeb txog ntawm txojcai Civil Rights Act.

Ntxiv no mus, peb thov nej siv sib hawm ib pliag los koom tes rau kev xam phaj txog ntawm lub teb chaws tshiab pub rau peb cov menyuam lubxiv hauv hoob. Ua tsaug ntau rau nej kev pab txhawb nqa no.

Xee npe,

______________________ *(Xib hwb)*

Nyob rau yam no, peb tau kawm txog tej teb chaws tshiab yam dhau los lawd, txog tam sim no, thiab yav pem suab huvsi lawm. Rau cov npe teb chaws tshiab rau daim ntawv los sis meem teb raws li koj xav tau tawm.

Tebchaws nujtxeeg :		
Tej tebchaws nujtxeeg tshiab	**Nujtxeeg Tshiab Niaj-Hnub no**	**Nujtxeeg Tshiab Pemsuab**
Sab Tebchaws Hnub Poob Thau	Tsev Saum Ib Nta Ntuj Rau Txhualub Tebchaws	Lwm lub Ntiajteb

Lub twg yog lub teb chaws tshiab uas ua li cas los qhov ntau koj yuav tau mus xyuas? Thiab piav saib yog vim cas?

____

____

____

School-Home Connection
Sharing Visions
第六單元：新領域

姓名：______________________

日期：______________________

各位尊敬的家庭成員：

在課堂上，我們學習了有關開拓新領域的內容。______________（學生名字）想與各位分享我們上課時讀過的故事。

The Lewis and Clark Expedition 這本書描寫兩位探險家，他們在 1804 年時，橫越北美洲探索美國西部。

A Wrinkle in Time, by Madeleine L'Engle 這本書描寫三個年輕人的太空旅行。

I Have a Dream, by Martin Luther King Jr. 金博士在這本書中呼籲爲非洲裔美國人爭取平等權利。

Our 36th President, by Melissa Maupin & **Speech to the Nation 7/2/64,** by Lyndon B. Johnson 詹森總統演講「民權法案」的重要性。

我們還希望各位能抽出時間參與一項有關開拓新領域的活動，與全班同學一起分享。感謝各位的支持。

順祝安康，

______________________（教師）

在這個單元中，我們學到了有關過去、現在與未來新領域的故事；請盡您所能，想些新領域填入下面表格中：

新領域		
歷史上的新領域	目前的新領域	未來的新領域
美國西部	國際太空站	其他行星

這些新領域中，您最想去哪個？爲甚麼？

____

____

____

School-Home Connection
Sharing Visions

ជំពូក ៦
កន្លែងដែលមនុស្សមិនទាន់ទៅដល់

ឈ្មោះ ______________________________

កាលបរិច្ឆេទ ______________________________

ជូនចំពោះគ្រួសារ.

នៅក្នុងថ្នាក់ យើងរៀនអំពីកន្លែងដែលមិនទាន់ទៅដល់។ ____________________ (ឈ្មោះសិស្ស) ចង់ប្រាប់អ្នកអំពីរឿងដែលយើងបានអាន។

The Lewis and Clark Expedition ឆ្នាំ១៨០៤
អ្នករុករកពីរនាក់ដឹកនាំការរុករកមួយកាត់ទ្វីបអាមេរិកខាងត្បូង ដើម្បីរកមើលប៉ែក ខាងលិច។

A Wrinkle in Time, by Madeleine L'Engle មនុស្សក្មេងបីនាក់ធ្វើដំណើរក្នុងលំហរអាកាស។

I Have a Dream, by Martin Luther King Jr. បណ្ឌិត ឃីង ស្រែកសុំសិទ្ធិសេរីភាពគ្នាសំរាប់ ជនជាតិ អាហ្វ្រិកកែន អាមេរិកកែន។

Our 36th President, by Melissa Maupin, & **Speech to the Nation 7/2/64,** by Lyndon B. Johnson ប្រធានាធិបតេយ្យ ចនសុន ថ្លែងសន្ទរកថាអំពីសារៈសំខាន់នៃច្បាប់សិទ្ធិក្នុងស្រុក។

យើងក៏ចង់ឲ្យអ្នកចំណាយពេលវេលាមួយភ្លែត ដើម្បីចូលរួមសកម្មភាពអំពីកន្លែងដែលមិនទាន់ទៅដល់ ដើម្បីប្រាប់សិស្សនៅក្នុងថ្នាក់។ សូមអរគុណចំពោះការគាំទ្ររបស់អ្នក។

ដោយស្មោះស្ម័គ្រ

______________________________ (គ្រូបង្រៀន)

នៅក្នុងជំពូកនេះ យើងរៀនអំពីព្រំដែនពីអតីតកាល. បច្ចុប្បន្នកាល. និងអនាគតកាល។ បំពេញនៅក្នុងតារាងនេះ នូវកន្លែងដែលមនុស្ស មិនទាន់ទៅដល់ ដែលអ្នកអាចគិតឃើញ។

កន្លែងមនុស្សមិនទាន់ទៅដល់		
កន្លែងជាប្រវត្តិសាស្រ្ត	**កន្លែងមិនទាន់ទៅដល់- បច្ចុប្បន្ន**	**កន្លែងមិនទាន់ទៅដល់នាអនាគត**
ប៉ែកខាងលិចអាមេរិក	ស្ថានីយ_អន្តរជាតិនៅលំហរអាកាស	ពិភពផ្សេងទៀត

តើកន្លែងណាមួយក្នុងចំណោមទាំងអស់នេះ ដែលអ្នកចង់ទៅឃើញ? ហេតុអ្វី?

____

____

____

VISIONS NEWSLETTER Unit 6

School-Home Connection
Sharing Visions
INITE 6 Fwontyè yo

Non ______________________________

Dat ______________________________

Chè Fanmi,

Nan klas, nou te pale de frontyè yo. ____________________ *(non elèv lan)* ta renemen pataje avèk ou kèk nan istwa nou te li yo.

The Lewis and Clark Expedition An 1804, de eksploratè te mennen yon ekspedisyon atravè Amerik di Nò pou al eksplore Lwès.

A Wrinkle in Time, ekri pa Madeleine L'Engle Twa jèn moun ap vwayaje nan lespas.

I Have a Dream, ekri pa Martin Luther King Jr. Dr. King mande pou gen egalite dwa moun pou Afriken-Ameriken yo.

Our 36th President, ekri pa Melissa Maupin, ak **Speech to the Nation 7/2/64,** ekri pa Lyndon B. Johnson Prezidan Johnson bay yon diskou sou enpòtans Lwa Sivil sou Dwa Moun lan genyen.

Nou ta renmen tou pou pran yon ti tan pou patisipe nan yon aktivite osijè fwontyè yo pouka pataje sa ak klas lan. Mèsi pou sipò w.

Sensèman,

______________________________ *(Pwofesè)*

Nan inite sa a, nou te pale de frontyè yo nan lepase, leprezan, ak lavni. Ranpli tablo an ak otan fwontyè ou ka imajine.

Fwontyè yo		
Fwontyè Istorik	**Fwontyè yo Kounye an**	**Fwontyè yo nan Lavni**
Lwès nan Lepase	Estasyon Espasyal Entènasyonal	Lòt Planet yo

Kilès nan fwontyè sa yo ou panse ou pi ka gen chans pou vizite? Pouki rezon?

____

____

____

Name ______________________________ Date ____________________

UNIT 1 • CHALLENGES

Antarctic Survival

TORNQUIST (REPORTER): In 1914, Sir Ernest Shackleton set out with 27 other men to do what had never been done: sail to the Antarctic, then cross the frozen continent by dogsled.

They never made it, but their two-year odyssey is considered one of the greatest tales of survival in the 20th century.

WOMAN: I think that must have been about as close to hell as you can come, but the men there were of a very different caliber.

TORNQUIST: 80 years later, Shackleton's journey is chronicled through the 150 photographs and film clips taken by the ship's photographer, Frank Hurley, now on display at the American Museum of Natural History.

MAN: We get a sense of what it was like right at the start, before—before the real outlines of understanding of the environment of Antarctica were understood.

TORNQUIST: Just one day away from the Antarctic continent, Shackleton's ship, the *Endurance,* became trapped in ice.

WOMAN: All the ice—sea ice was sort of jammed against the continent. It had nowhere else to disperse, and the *Endurance* was jammed right there in it.

TORNQUIST: The crew lived onboard for ten months, only to abandon ship when the *Endurance* was crushed by ice. Before it sank, photographer Frank Hurley saved his negatives.

WOMAN: He returned to the wreck of the Endurance and dove into the water and retrieved the canister of his negatives from his submerged darkroom.

TORNQUIST: For five months, the men camped on the drifting ice floes until the ice gave way. Then they took three lifeboats and sailed to Elephant Island. There was little hope of being found, so Shackleton and five of his men got into one of the boats and headed for South Georgia Island, a treacherous 800-mile trip in the South Atlantic that took 17 days.

WOMAN: What Shackleton is being celebrated for is that the thing that counts at the end of the day is human life.

TORNQUIST: Shackleton reached South Georgia Island where he got help. He returned to rescue his entire crew.

Cynthia Tornquist, CNN, New York.

Name ______________________ Date ______________________

UNIT 2 • CHANGES

Struggling with Nature

UTLEY (REPORTER): It lay at sea level, exposed, offering no defense against the Gulf of Mexico. In 1900, Galveston, Texas, was a booming, growing city of more than 25,000, a wealthy city of fine Victorian homes and substantial indestructible buildings.

After all, the head of the U.S. Weather Bureau's office in Galveston, Isaac Cline, had said that any fear that a hurricane could seriously threaten the community was an absurd delusion.

HISTORIAN: He believed he knew it all. He believed he understood the weather. He believed he understood all there was to know about the weather.

THURM: They were skilled at looking at the sky and the sea.

UTLEY: Harvey Thurm is the Hurricane Program Leader for the National Weather Service's Eastern Region. He understands what Isaac Cline was thinking . . . or not thinking.

THURM: Since the hurricane was so infrequent visiting a particular location, it was very easy to say that a distant storm or the hint of a distant storm was not going to come your way because the history was in—on your side.

UTLEY: In 1900, Isaac Cline didn't have the tools to see out over the horizon. There were, of course, no airplanes or satellites, not even communications from the ships at sea. So Cline had to go down to the shoreline in Galveston and observe what was happening, and what he saw was baffling and ominous.

A north wind was blowing which normally would have calmed the sea. Something out there, though, was building up high swells and waves. Cline was worried, but only the Weather Bureau's headquarters in Washington was authorized to issue a storm alert.

HISTORIAN: Well, he sent a message to Washington saying that these were phenomena that had—had never before been observed in Galveston. And the response, frankly, was—was not terribly satisfying. Washington sent no warning of a severe storm at all to Galveston that day.

UTLEY: On the afternoon of September 6, 1900, the hurricane hit, pushing a deadly wall of water into the city. One-third of Galveston's buildings were destroyed, the rest severely damaged. Waterfront mansions and hotels and the people in them were swept away by the surging sea. So was the Bath Avenue School, the Sacred Heart Church, the Galveston Orphan's Home with its 90 children inside, and this entire middle-class neighborhood.

Communication was cut with the rest of the nation, which knew something terrible had occurred, but not how terrible. The 1,000 estimated dead would climb to more than 8,000. It was, and remains, the worst natural disaster in American history. And what happened to the man who didn't and, perhaps, couldn't see it coming, Isaac Cline?

HISTORIAN: After the hurricane, all he studied was hurricanes, and he became obsessed with warning. It was clear that he felt that he bore some of the guilt.

UTLEY: A personal guilt he carried through life, for Isaac Cline's home was destroyed too. He, his three daughters, and his brother survived a harrowing night floating on debris. The body of his wife, who was pregnant, was found three weeks later amid the destruction of a city that was and is Galveston.

Garrick Utley, CNN.

Name ______________________ Date ______________

UNIT 3 • COURAGE

A Teenager's Brave Journey

WOODS (REPORTER): This is Brandy Mobley. She's 16 years old, and she's braver than you are, whoever you are. But then, Brandy has always confronted life with the odds against her. She was born without arms or legs. For years, she was routed from one foster home to another, never quite connecting. This pretty youngster has amazed everyone with her patient desire for peer acceptance and independence.

WOMAN: This is a girl with a lot of self-determination, someone who said to herself, "This isn't the way I want my life, and I'm going to change it." She's very bright, and very, very academically gifted.

WOODS: She is able to compete because she taught herself to write with what started out to be a partial foot but serves as a precious hand, a tiny appendage whose use has accelerated her lust for self-reliance.

INTERVIEWER: How far have you come, let's say, in the past five years?

MOBLEY: Oh, a lot. Now I bathe myself and—and get around and, you know, can—can reach things a lot—pick up things a lot more.

INTERVIEWER: You're not angry with what life has done to you, with what fate has done to you?

MOBLEY: Oh, no. There's a reason for everything. I don't think that it's a punishment to—for me to be like this. I think that there's—maybe I'm like this to teach other people—to teach other people things about themselves.

WOODS: After school, three days a week, Brandy motors through the neighborhood to the Lucey Mortgage Company where she has a part-time job, a job she pursued all by herself.

And her boss, Lorcan Lucey, says he never had the first qualm about hiring her.

LUCEY: No, never did. I never thought twice about it. It's not just great for Brandy; it's great for the rest of us. For morale purposes or just opening up our own eyes.

WOODS: As a ward of South Carolina's Department of Social Services, Brandy lives in a group home with four other girls. Next year after graduation, she hopes to attend college. The future is a little hazy right now, but not even marriage and a family is out of the question, says Brandy.

MOBLEY: I would like for it to happen. I won't dwell on it if it doesn't, but I'm sure it will. Sometimes I wonder what—what I would like for my ultimate goal to be, but no, I don't—I don't really know yet.

Larry Woods, CNN, Charleston.

Name ______________________ Date ______________________

UNIT 4 • DISCOVERIES

Exploring Space

MAN: We've gone for main engine start. We have main engine start.

NARRATOR: Since the first launch 17 ½ years ago, the Space Shuttle program has soared to tremendous heights.

MAN: And the shuttle has cleared the tower.

NARRATOR: And it has fallen to cavernous lows.

[God Bless America plays]

There have been 91 shuttle missions prior to Glenn's flight. Crews have spent a total of 783 days in orbit performing experiments, launching satellites, retrieving satellites, and repairing them. They've practiced building a space station and linked up with the Russian Mir space station to learn what it's like to live and work on one.

[men speaking Russian]

NARRATOR: With the deployment of the Hubble Space Telescope in 1990, the shuttle helped astronomers look out into the heavens, and over the years, astronauts have returned to Hubble to give it an even clearer view.

ASTRONAUT #1: The doors just swung open.

ASTRONAUT #2: Sure did.

NARRATOR: The space shuttle has provided a number of firsts for the U.S. space program. Sally Ride became the first American woman to fly in space in 1983. Nine years later, the crew of *Endeavour* included the first African-American woman in space, the first Japanese astronaut, and the first married couple on the same flight.

The shuttle has offered scientists from around the world the opportunity to work in space and to show people in their homeland the peculiarities and the benefits of working in weightlessness.

[man speaking Japanese]

JEMISON: —and you're going to put a little circle up at the top of the filter paper—like that. Fill it in . . . does everybody see?

NARRATOR: Dr. Mae Jemison rode her training in science and medicine all the way into outer space as the first African-American woman to orbit Earth.

BOY: One teaspoon.

JEMISON: Okay, that's one teaspoon.

BOY: And we—I need two, so I'll—

JEMISON: Oh, do you? Is your stuff mixed up?

GIRL: Yeah.

JEMISON: Are you happy with it?

GIRL: Yeah.

JEMISON: Okay.

NARRATOR: Now she's traveling the country to promote the kind of science education that brings out the natural enthusiasm children have for exploring the world around them.

JEMISON: What happens when they get into school is, all of a sudden, they're told, "Don't do that anymore." Right? They're told to look in a textbook, memorize something, and then parrot it back, and so we—they don't get to use their own creativity.

Name ____________________ Date ____________________

UNIT 5 • COMMUNICATION

Sharing Cultures

FLORCRUZ (REPORTER): Dodging bikes and cars, Jenny Nattingly is learning the art of harmonious coexistence. She is one of a growing colony of young Americans who are learning China's history and culture.

NATTINGLY: When I first got here, I was a little nervous, you know, because—going to China.

FLORCRUZ: Instead of a police state, she finds a society that has cast off old stereotypes and is embracing consumerism.

With help from her foster family, she is learning to speak in the right tone and write in neat strokes, tools which give her a close-up look at this society.

MAN: Over time, they realize that this is just another place—where people get up, eat breakfast, go to work. And they become acclimated, and suddenly, it's—you know, it feels like home.

FLORCRUZ: But sharing one roof can lead to cultural clashes.

NATTINGLY: My host mother knocks on the door and immediately opens the door. And it's funny, 'cause sometimes, it scares me, and they're like, "Oh, I'm so sorry."

FLORCRUZ: Although she likes Chinese food, her foster parents have had to adapt to her eating habits.

[host father speaking Chinese]

TRANSLATOR: Jenny does not like eating leftovers, so now we just cook half the chicken and refrigerate the other half for the next meal.

FLORCRUZ: Meeting halfway has meant bliss, a useful lesson for two nations that have locked horns for so many years.

For 16-year-old Jenny, much of China and the world is revealed while crossing a street.

NATTINGLY: It's just, like, you go with, like, you know, when everyone else is going. Everything is more, like, I've—like, laid-back, and I've really learned to be, you know, more patient and understanding. I'm like, "This is what it's like to not be understood," you know?

FLORCRUZ: More and more young Americans are investing in careers related to China. They understand the growing importance of knowing the language, culture, and mind-set of one of the most dynamic and complex nations.

Jaime FlorCruz, CNN, Beijing.

Name ______________________________ Date ______________________

UNIT 5 • COMMUNICATION

Exploring a Lost Language

LAMONT (REPORTER): Anastasia Majel has been dead for nearly 60 years, but it seems her Indian spirit and wisdom has never died. You see, she is teaching these people the lost language of Acjachemen. It is the language of the Juaneño Indians.

Anastasia Majel died in 1938, but in the two years prior to her death, a government anthologist documented the Acjachemen language by tape-recording hundreds of hours of Majel. It is a language no one speaks anymore, that is, until now.

ALL: Ól-va-tëk-mal.

LAMONT: The tapes were recently discovered by Majel's descendents in a cardboard box in the Smithsonian Institution. They are scratchy recordings, but they are saving the language of the Juaneño Indians.

WOMAN: It went underground. The language did go underground. There were many who spoke it, and they did not want to pass it on at that time because they wanted us to survive, and they wanted us to be happy. They didn't want us to live in a world of prejudice.

LINGUIST: Well, language is intimately tied to culture. Culture is the way of thinking, feeling, acting, and living that any human population has. So therefore, when you try to—when language itself is erased, a portion of the rationale for cultural existence is also erased.

LAMONT: But the tape-recordings of Anastasia Majel, very fortunately, had not been erased.

MAN #1: The first time I heard her voice, it was—it was—it was spiritual to me.

LAMONT: And spiritual for these people as well. Once a month in San Juan Capistrano, California, a group of Juaneño men and women gather to carefully listen to Majel's words and learn.

MAN #2: I think that's the point, you know, to be able to say, "Well, I'm Indian, and I can talk the language."

LAMONT: And now it is a language that can, once again, be passed along to the next generation of Juaneño Indians, thanks to Anastasia Majel.

Greg Lamont, CNN, reporting.

UNIT 6 • FRONTIERS

A New Beginning

CLARK (REPORTER): A short drive from the hurried pace and modern buildings of Dallas is a picturesque area that offers a window to the past.

PENN: I remember when a little—as a little kid, there was a big post right here, and it's gone now.

CLARK: This is the land where Andy Penn's family settled nearly 140 years ago. It's now part of a Texas state park and will soon be open to the public as an example of farm life a century ago.

WOMAN: It's very important that our children and their children know that—what had happened, like, 100 years ago.

CLARK: In the mid-1850s, the Penns came to Texas from Illinois in a covered wagon. John Wesley Penn built this home for his family in 1859 and started farming the surrounding land.

PENN: There was a tremendous amount of hard work in building what's up there and—'cause they didn't have power saws, and they didn't have power drills, and they didn't have all these modern conveniences.

CLARK: You can see the axe marks in the logs used to construct the barns. On a granary wall, the Penn name was cut in by hand, and inside the barn, there's an old schoolhouse and a log cabin. They were moved there from their original location and were used for storage.

PENN: Penns were pretty much good about reusing things, and they moved those up there and then built that barn around them, essentially.

CLARK: The family sold the farm in 1970. It was eventually acquired by the Army Corps of Engineers. They built a lake and provided money to turn the farm into an exhibit.

Working from old photos, the Texas Parks Department is renovating the farm. Once the buildings are finished, some of the trees will be cleared so the farm will look like it once did.

PENN: You know, in a way, that's my family's, but it's everybody's too. If you go back far enough, anybody that came from the country around here goes back to something, maybe not like that, but something, an old family settlement of some kind.

CLARK: And in that sense, Penn Farm is everyone's farm. It's part of the roots of this country.

Tony Clark, CNN, Cedar Hill, Texas.

Name ______________________ Date ______________________

UNIT 1 Challenges

CNN Video

Antarctic Survival In 1914, Sir Ernest Shackleton and his crew set off to explore Antarctica in the ship the *Endurance.* This video clip shows the challenges they faced.

Before Viewing

What do you know about Antarctica? Use a KWL Chart to take notes and organize your ideas. Complete the first two columns before you view the video. Then complete the third column after you view and listen to the video.

Topic: *Antarctica*		
Know What do I already know about the topic?	**Want to Know** What do I want to know about the topic?	**Learned** What did I learn about the topic?

While Viewing

First Viewing

Watch and listen to "Antarctic Survival." What is the main idea? What details support the main idea? As you watch the video, take brief notes.

Second Viewing

Make a note for any section that you did not understand. Listen carefully to these sections when you view the video a third time.

Third Viewing

1. As you watch the video, take notes of the important events on a piece of paper.
2. Do you now understand the whole video? If not, ask your teacher for clarification.

After Viewing

Discussion

1. What is the main purpose of this video? Does the filmmaker want to entertain, to inform, or to persuade?
2. What perspective (opinion) of Ernest Shackleton does the filmmaker present? Is Shackleton shown to be courageous or reckless?
3. Use a Venn Diagram to compare and contrast the video "Antarctic Survival" with "Antarctic Adventure" on page 31 of your textbook. How are they similar? How are they different?

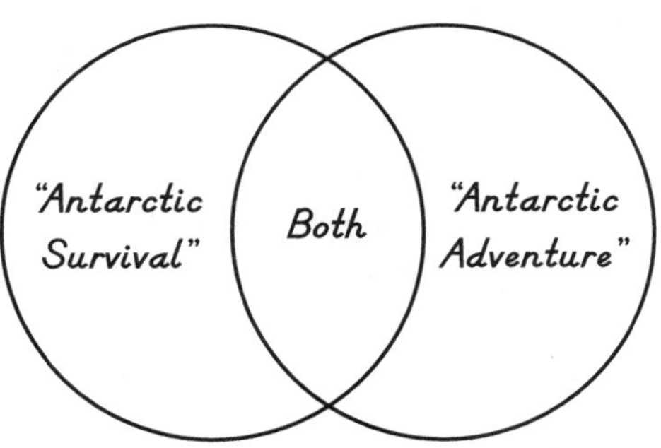

Activities

1. Work with a partner. Compare your perception of the important events with your partner's. Why did you choose these events?
2. On your own, summarize your list of important events. Present your summary to the class.
3. Go back to your KWL Chart and complete the third column.

Name ______________________________ Date ______________________

CNN Video

UNIT 2 Changes

Struggling with Nature Galveston was a growing city in Texas in 1900. Then a hurricane struck and changed the city forever. This video clip shows the effects of the worst natural disaster in U.S. history.

Before Viewing

Work in a small group. Use your prior knowledge to prepare for the video clip. Have you ever experienced a flood, a hurricane, a tornado, or another natural disaster? Talk about what it was like before and after the disaster. If you haven't, try to imagine what it would be like.

While Viewing

First Viewing

Listen and watch carefully for the narrator's message. Work in pairs to summarize your understanding of the narrator's message.

Second Viewing

Listen carefully to learn about Isaac Cline. What facts do you learn about him? What perspectives (opinions) do you hear about him? Fill in the Two-Column Chart.

Isaac Cline	
Facts	**Opinions**

Third Viewing

1. As you watch the video, add more facts and opinions about Isaac Cline to your chart.
2. Do you understand the points of view in the video? Ask your teacher to clarify words and review what the speakers said.

After Viewing

Discussion

1. How does the narrator persuade you? Did Isaac Cline do enough to help the people of Galveston?
2. What words or language does the narrator use to communicate his message?
3. Compare the opinions of Cline with those of the speakers in the video. What facts do the speakers use to support their opinions?
4. How did the hurricane change Galveston? How did it change Isaac Cline's life?

Activities

1. With a partner, write down your ideas about the presentation of the video. What do you learn from the still pictures? What do the moving pictures show? Why do you think both forms of media are used?
2. What tools do people use today to track hurricanes or tornadoes? Make a poster showing how weather tracking and warnings have changed since 1900. Research information online or in magazines (search keyword: weather tracking). Your poster should include charts, photographs, illustrations, and facts.

Name ______________________________ Date ______________________

UNIT 3 Courage

CNN Video

A Teenager's Brave Journey Brandy Mobley is 16 years old. She was born without arms and legs. In this video, you will see the courageous way in which Brandy lives her life

Before Viewing

Who do you know that is brave? What qualities do brave people have? Write the words below in the Word box of the Word Squares activity. Use a dictionary to help you understand the words.

bravery independent gifted
self-reliant self-determined courageous

Word:	Sentence:	Word:	Sentence:
Meaning:	Symbol:	Meaning:	Symbol:
Word:	Sentence:	Word:	Sentence:
Meaning:	Symbol:	Meaning:	Symbol:
Word:	Sentence:	Word:	Sentence:
Meaning:	Symbol:	Meaning:	Symbol:

While Viewing

First Viewing

Watch and listen carefully to see how Brandy behaves in the video. Listen for verbal messages, or the words, that are used to describe Brandy.

Second Viewing

Watch the people around Brandy. How do they act around her? Look for nonverbal messages, or how people behave. Do they show her respect?

Third Viewing

1. As you watch the video, think about sentences that you could write to describe Brandy, using the words from the Word Squares activity.
2. Listen for verbal and nonverbal messages. Are there any new words that you can add to your Word Squares activity?

After Viewing

Discussion

1. What does the filmmaker want you to know about Brandy? What is the filmmaker's purpose in making this video?
2. What influence or effect does the video have on its viewers? Do people feel sorry for Brandy? Do they admire her?
3. Explain what you liked or disliked about the presentation of the video.

Activities

1. Complete the Word Squares activity. Write the meaning of each word. Then write a sentence using the word. Finally, draw a symbol to help you remember the new word.
2. Work with a partner. Using your word squares, compare your perceptions about Brandy. Discuss what you learn about her from the video clip.
3. Write a letter to a friend describing Brandy and her life. Make comparisons between your life and her life. What do you like or admire about her? Why? Is she someone you would like to know? Why or why not?

Name ______________________________ Date ____________________

UNIT 4 Discoveries

CNN Video

Exploring Space Astronauts travel to and explore space in space shuttles. This video clip presents details about the Space Shuttle program. It also features Mae Jemison, the first African-American woman in space.

Before Viewing

Work with a partner. Read the four statements below. Decide if the statements are true or false. Write your answers. Then check your work after you have watched the video.

1. A telescope in space can give us a view of distant places. True or false?
2. People can float in space. True or false?
3. Scientists cannot work in space. True or false?
4. Space crews are able to repair satellites. True or false?

While Viewing

First Viewing

This video includes many science words. As you watch, note any words or phrases you do not understand.

Second Viewing

Use a Sunshine Organizer to help you understand the video clip. Write the name of the video clip in the circle. Think about possible answers to the questions as you view the video.

WHO?
WHAT?
HOW?
Exploring Space
WHEN?
WHY?
WHERE?

Third Viewing

1. As you watch the video, record your answers to the questions on the Sunshine Organizer.
2. Use your dictionary or ask your teacher to clarify any words or phrases that you still do not understand.

After Viewing

Discussion

1. How do people travel in space? What do they do in space?
2. What images from the video helped you understand (or interpret) space travel? How did the moving pictures help you understand the events?
3. Who is Mae Jemison? What do you see her doing in the video?

Activities

1. Use the Venn Diagram to compare and contrast the video "Exploring Space" with "Mae Jemison, Space Scientist" on page 267 of your textbook.
2. Would you like to travel in space? Write a paragraph outlining why you would or would not like to travel in space.
3. Go back and check your true and false answers from the *Before Viewing* section. Correct any false statements.

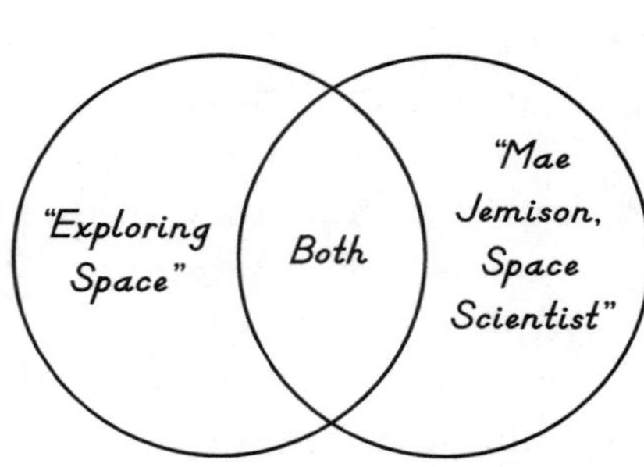

Name ______________________ Date ______________________

UNIT 5 Communication

CNN Video

Sharing Cultures Jenny Nattingly is 16 years old. She is living with a host family in China. This video clip shows how she learns to fit into a new culture.

Before Viewing

Interview a student who is from another country. Use the questions in the Two-Column Chart to find out about his or her first day in the United States. Write his or her answers in the second column.

Questions	Answers
When did you arrive?	
How did you feel?	
Did you experience any problems?	
What were they?	
Did positive things happen?	
How do you feel now?	

While Viewing

First Viewing

Watch and listen to learn the basic facts about the video clip. Note as many things as possible on the Storyboard.

Second Viewing

Fill in the Storyboard with details about Jenny's life in China. Then write one question you have about the video clip.

1. First, ______	2. Second, ______
3. Third, ______	4. Fourth, ______
5. Fifth, ______	6. Finally, ______

Third Viewing

1. Watch and listen for details that describe China and the people in the video clip.
   Jenny is ________. (happy, sad, smart)
   China is ________. (busy, fun, interesting)
2. Ask your teacher to clarify any questions you have.

After Viewing

Discussion

1. What important information is presented in this video? What do you learn about Jenny? What do you learn about China?
2. What did Jenny do to fit into the new culture? What did Jenny's host family do to help her fit in?
3. Connect your experiences to the video. What do you do to fit into a new place or culture?

Activities

1. Review your interview with a student from another country. Present the responses to the class.
2. In small groups, produce a video or an audio program about what it is like to move to the United States. Include recordings or videotapings of your interview. If you choose to videotape your interview, try to include still pictures or photographs. Share your program with the class.
3. Work with a group. Act out a skit that shows a first day at a new school. Present your skit to the class.

Name ______________________ Date ______________

UNIT 6 Frontiers

CNN Video

Frontiers In the 1850s, the Penn family settled in Texas. This video clip explains how their family farm changed and became part of a Texas state park.

Before Viewing

What is on a farm? What animals live there? What do people do on a farm? Complete the Cluster Map with a partner.

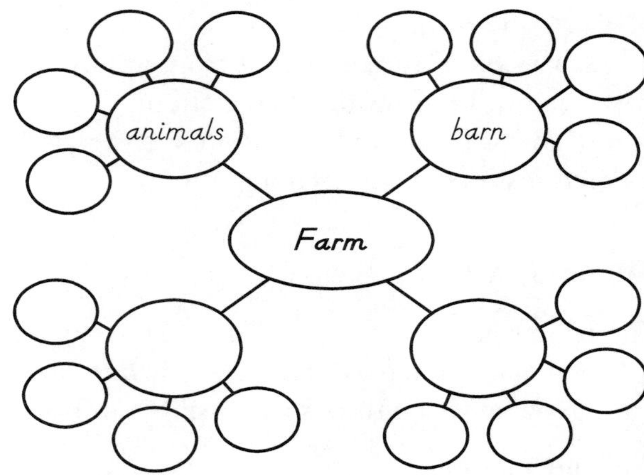

While Viewing

First Viewing

Look for pictures of old and new things in the video. Take notes as you listen for important dates and events.

Second Viewing

Organize ideas and events on the Timeline. Fill it in with important dates and events.

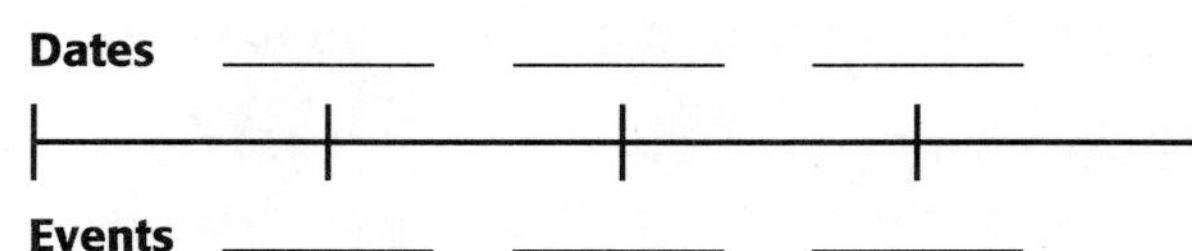

Third Viewing

1. Listen carefully to learn about how the Penn family farm has changed.
2. Add more notes to your Timeline.

After Viewing

Discussion

1. Use your Timeline to summarize the video. What are the main events in the story of the Penn family farm?
2. What does the filmmaker want you to know about the Penn family?
3. Does the filmmaker use the shots and pictures effectively? What meaning does the filmmaker want to communicate?

Activities

1. Review your Timeline. Retell the story of the Penn family farm to a partner.
2. Find out about farms in your state. Do research at your school or local library. Learn about what was farmed in your state. Find out what is still grown on farms in your state. Write a short report on how farming has changed in your state.
3. Do you think farms will continue to change? Do research to support your opinion. Present your ideas and research to the class.

Video Answer Key

UNIT 1 CHALLENGES

Before Viewing
Answers will vary.

While Viewing

First Viewing
The main idea of the video is Shackleton's adventure. Possible details include: information about the ship, the conditions they faced, and the men themselves.

Second Viewing
Answers will vary.

Third Viewing
Answers will vary.

After Viewing
Discussion
1. The filmmaker's purpose is to inform and entertain.
2. Shackleton is shown to be courageous.
3. Venn Diagram:

"Antarctic Survival": Frank Hurley was the ship's photographer.
"Antarctic Adventure": The story includes details about the ship.
Both: Shackleton was brave and courageous.
It was a dangerous adventure.
The trip was in the South Atlantic.
Shackleton rescued his men.

Activities
1. Students' work will vary.
2. Students' summaries will vary but should include the main events from the video.
3. Students' work will vary.

UNIT 2 CHANGES

Before Viewing
Students' work will vary but should include a discussion about what it is like before and after a natural disaster.

While Viewing

First Viewing
Students' summaries will vary but should include one or two of the main ideas of the clip.

Second Viewing
Isaac Cline worked for the government. His job was to warn people about storms. His wife and child died in the storm. After the storm, he worked even harder at tracking storm systems. One man says that Cline thought he knew it all. Another man says Cline did all that he could.

Third Viewing
Answers will vary.

After Viewing
Discussion
1. The narrator persuades the viewer to understand the challenges that Isaac Cline faced. He thought he knew everything. He did all that he could.
2. Answers will vary but should include these words: *deadly, phenomenon, terrible.*
3. One man interviewed in the video said Isaac Cline thought "he knew all there was to know." Another man said that it was easy to say a distant storm was not going to come. Cline did not have the tools to track these types of storms accurately.
4. Galveston was destroyed. Isaac Cline studied hurricanes for the rest of his life.

Activities
1. The still pictures show what Galveston looked like before and after the storm. The moving pictures show the ocean and interviews. The two forms show the old and new events.
2. Satellites and airplanes are two tools used to track storm systems. Research projects will vary.

UNIT 3 COURAGE

Before Viewing
Answers will vary.

While Viewing

First Viewing
She can teach things to other people. Her life is not a punishment.

Second Viewing
The people around Brandy like her. They laugh with her. She teaches them important lessons. People smile around Brandy. They respect her.

Third Viewing
1. Students' work will vary but may include:
   Brandy is independent.
   Brandy is self-reliant.
   Brandy is determined.
   Brandy is gifted.
2. Answers will vary.

After Viewing
Discussion
1. The filmmaker wants to inform you about a brave person with a disability.
2. People do not feel sorry for her. People who watch the video admire Brandy.
3. Answers will vary.

Activities
1. Answers will vary.
2. Students' work will vary.

UNIT 4 DISCOVERIES

Before Viewing
1. T
2. T
3. F
4. T

While Viewing

First Viewing
Answers will vary but may include *satellite, Hubble Telescope, Space Shuttle, Mir Space Station.*

Second Viewing
Students' work will vary.

Third Viewing
Students' work will vary.

After Viewing
Discussion
1. They travel in space shuttles. They perform experiments in space.
2. Answers will vary.
3. Mae Jemison is a scientist, an astronaut, and the first African-American woman in space.

Activities
1. Venn Diagram:

Video: about the space program, history of space travel, the successes and failures in the U.S. space program
"Mae Jemison, Space Scientist": includes facts about where she grew up, her education
Both: general information about the space program; information about Mae Jemison

2. Answers will vary.
3. Answers will vary.

UNIT 5 COMMUNICATION

Before Viewing
Students' work will vary.

While Viewing

First Viewing
Answers will vary.

Second Viewing
Jenny rides a bike in China. She is a young American. She was a little nervous at first.
Students' questions will vary.

Third Viewing
1. Possible answers:
   China is growing. It is involved in capitalism.
   Jenny likes Chinese food.
2. Students' questions will vary.

After Viewing
Discussion
1. Possible answers: Jenny likes China. China is a dynamic and complex nation.
2. Jenny is learning Chinese. Her foster family is trying to help her with her meals.
3. Answers will vary.

Activities
1.–3. Answers and projects will vary.

UNIT 6 FRONTIERS

Before Viewing
Answers will vary but may include a listing of animals (cows, pigs, horses) and activities (take care of animals, grow crops).

While Viewing

First Viewing
Answers will vary but may include old things: barns; new things: skyscrapers, Dallas.

Second Viewing
Timelines should include:
mid-1850s: Penns came to Texas;
1859: Penn built home for family;
1970: Penn family sells farm; Texas Parks Department builds park.

Third Viewing
1–2. Answers will vary.

After Viewing
Discussion
1. The Penns bought the farm. They lived on it. They sold it. The farm was made into a park for the public to see. It shows the country's history.
2. The Penns were a farm family. They wanted to share their farm.
3. The filmmaker wanted to show what a farm was like over 150 years ago.

Activities
1.–3. Answers and projects will vary.

Activity Book Answer Key

UNIT 1 • CHAPTER 1

Build Vocabulary
page 1

A.
1. f 3. e 5. d
2. c 4. a 6. b

B.
1. C 2. P 3. X

C.
1. C D E F 2. S T U Z

D.
1. applause 4. fable
2. challenge 5. surprise
3. desert 6. trotted

Writing: Punctuation
page 2

1. "One large orange juice, please," she said to the man.
2. He said, "That's two dollars."
3. Kathy said quietly, "Oh no."
4. "I have only one dollar," she said.
5. "I am sorry," the man said.
6. Kathy asked, "What is the price of one small juice?"
7. The man smiled and said, "One dollar."
8. Kathy smiled back and said, "Give me one small juice, please."

Elements of Literature
page 3

A. Students should circle *showers* and *flowers.*

B.
1. play 3. sun
2. race 4. winner

Word Study
page 4

A.
1. climber 3. driver
2. writer 4. dancer

B.
1. dancer 3. climber
2. driver 4. writer

C. Answers will vary.

Grammar Focus
page 5

A.
1. The camel practiced ballet.
2. She worked for long months.
3. They moved away.
4. She rode a horse.
5. She laughed.
6. They won the race.

B. Students should circle *rode* and *won.*

C. Answers will vary. Students should include the past tense form of these verbs: *ask, talk, do.*

Grammar Focus
page 6

A.
1. I did not walk the dog after supper. I didn't walk the dog after supper.
2. You did not do your homework after school. You didn't do your homework after school.
3. After they cleaned the house, they did not go to the park and play. After they cleaned the house, they didn't go to the park and play.
4. When the soccer game was over, we did not go straight home. When the soccer game was over, we didn't go straight home.

B.
1. Yesterday, I went to the park. What did you do yesterday?
2. I went for a bike ride. Did you see a lot of people at the park?
3. I did not see a lot of people. I only saw Pedro. Where did you ride your bike?
4. I rode my bike by the lake. Did you want to come?

From Reading to Writing
page 7

Answers will vary.

Across Content Areas
page 8

1. This article is about horses.
2. Students can identify any two of the following headings: "Size," "Legs and Hoofs," "Teeth."
3. Students can identify any two of the following labels: *Forehead, Cheek, Neck, Chest, Knee, Mane, Shoulder, Back, Thigh, Tail.*
4. You would look under the heading, "Teeth."
5. Answers will vary.

UNIT 1 • CHAPTER 2

Build Vocabulary
page 9

A.
1. shelter 5. sliver
2. worthless 6. pause
3. focus 7. handful
4. flammable

B.
1. able, aid, area
2. lark, letter, lure
3. rash, rosy, rustle
4. merry, mistake, moss
5. earth, emblem, excite

Writing: Capitalization and Punctuation
page 10

A. The type of birch tree that Brian found grows from Alaska across Canada to Labrador. It also grows in parts of the United States, such as Minnesota, Oregon, and Colorado. In the past, Native Americans made canoes from its bark. Today, birches are used to make products such as ice cream sticks and broom handles.

B.
1. period
2. question mark
3. period
4. exclamation point
5. period
6. question mark

Elements of Literature
page 11

A.
1. The forest was as dark as a cave.
2. The moon was like an apricot-colored balloon.
3. The stars twinkled like distant fireflies.
4. A sailboat glided as gracefully as a swan.
5. Our sleeping bags seemed as soft as the clouds.

B.
1. a skyscraper
2. a whisper
3. a beautiful butterfly
4. putting together a puzzle
5. night and day
6. a bass drum

Word Study
page 12

A. Possible compound words: sunflower, sunlight, sunroom, daylight, daytime, underwater, understand, bedtime, bedroom, headlight, headwater, headstand, headroom, lunchroom, lunchtime

B.
1. moonlight 4. rainbow
2. campfire 5. footprints
3. flashlight

Sentences will vary.

Grammar Focus
page 13

A.
1. was 3. was 5. were
2. were 4. were 6. was

B.
1. He was a teenager alone in the woods.
2. The birches were beautiful and their bark was useful.
3. The only food was wild berries.
4. The hatchet was sharp.
5. The sparks were tiny red coals of heat.

Grammar Focus
page 14

A.
1. was 3. was
2. Were 4. were

B. Students' sentences should include the verb forms *was not, were not, wasn't* and *weren't.*

From Reading to Writing
page 15

Answers will vary.

Across Content Areas
page 16

1. Possible response: The purpose of the chart is to show what can be placed in a one-person survival kit.
2. What, How Many, Purpose
3. whistle, mirror
4. It can be used for eating, scooping, and digging.
5. 2
6. Possible response: There are many matches in the kit so someone can easily start a fire in case of emergency.
7. Answers will vary. Students should state if they would want their survival kit to be similar or different. They should give one or more reasons to support their responses.

UNIT 1 • CHAPTER 3

Build Vocabulary
page 17

A.
1. accept 2. raw 3. hide

B.
1. b 3. a 5. c
2. d 4. e

Writing: Spelling
page 18

1. relentlessly 4. terribly
2. dully 5. angrily
3. fatally 6. scarcely

Elements of Literature
page 19

A.
1. twin sister 4. not anxious
2. figure-skating lessons 5. middle age
3. angry 6. hid her face

B. Answers will vary. Students' sentences should include personification.

Word Study
page 20

A.
1. immediately 4. early
2. quietly 5. finally
3. safely

Students should correctly use the adverbs in their sentences.

B.
1. brightly 4. impatiently
2. lazily 5. suddenly
3. greatly

Grammar Focus
page 21

A.
1. masts, sails, nouns
2. dangerous, daring, adjectives
3. stumbled, fell, verbs
4. slowly, steadily, adverbs
5. tossed, quivered, verbs
6. Days, weeks, nouns

B. Sentences will vary.

Grammar Focus
page 22

A.
1. tents, equipment, and lifeboats (words)
2. food, water, and shelter (words)
3. fished, slept, and waited (words)
4. would drift north and take them to safety (phrases)
5. started breaking up and suddenly split (phrases)
6. Ernest Shackleton and two of his men (phrases)

B.
1. Shackleton formed a crew, and the expedition set sail.
2. The beginning of the end came on Sunday, and the end came on Wednesday.

3. They walked for three days, and they traveled less than two miles.
4. The ice was solid underfoot, and it gave them water to drink.
5. The men reached Elephant Island, and they rested.

From Reading to Writing
page 23

Answers will vary.

Across Content Areas
page 24

Animals on the land: insects only; Animals along the coasts: 45 kinds of birds, including the emperor penguin and other penguins; several types of seals, including Weddell seal, fur seal, and elephant seal. Possible quotation: "Weddell seals dive as deep as 2,000 feet (609.6 meters)."

UNIT 1 • CHAPTER 4

Build Vocabulary
page 25

1. *Panda* should be circled.
2. 1. and 2. should be circled.
3. /pan' d[schwa]
4. in the mountains of China and Tibet
5. The panda at the zoo is cute.

Writing: Capitalization and Punctuation
page 26

A.
1. Yang's mother asked, "Why do you have to stomp your feet?"
2. "Sorry, I do not understand Japanese," the girl said.
3. I told the teacher, "He took my ballpoint pen."
4. Yang felt less lonely when the boy said, "My name is Matthew."

B.
1. "Yingtao is my last name," Yang explained.
2. "I was speaking Chinese," Yang told the girl.
3. The secretary said, "We have a number of Asian-Americans in this school."
4. The boy smiled and said, "I am glad you were not hurt."

Elements of Literature
page 27

A.
1. direct 3. indirect 5. direct
2. indirect 4. direct 6. indirect

B. Answers will vary. Possible responses:
1. nervous 2. frowned

Word Study
page 28

A. registration form, information, formal; family name, family tree, familiar

B.
1. family name 4. family tree
2. formal 5. familiar
3. information 6. registration form

Grammar Focus
page 29

1. dependent 5. dependent
2. independent 6. independent
3. independent 7. independent
4. dependent 8. dependent

Grammar Focus
page 30

A.
1. When Yang's family arrived, the school year was almost half over.
2. After Yang started to walk fast and stomp his feet, his parents complained.
3. As soon as the teacher came into the room, Yang stood.
4. While she lived in China, Second Sister was surrounded by friends.
5. Before he left China, Yang had learned to swim.

B. Answers will vary. Students should write three complex sentences about their school experiences.

From Reading to Writing
page 31

Answers will vary.

Across Content Areas
page 32

1. Beijing
2. Pacific Ocean
3. Taiwan and Japan
4. Answers will vary but should include three of the following: Vietnam, Laos, Myanmar, Nepal, Bhutan, India, Pakistan, Tajikistan, Kyrgyzstan, Kazakhstan, Mongolia, North Korea.
5. Answers will vary but should include two of the following: Bangladesh, South Korea, Japan, Taiwan.

UNIT 1 • CHAPTER 5

Build Vocabulary
page 33

A.
1. 3 3. 2 5. 4
2. 1 4. 4 6. 2

B. Students should write four sentences using the word *spring*. Each sentence should use a different definition of *spring*.

Writing: Spelling
page 34

1. there 4. there 7. they're
2. their 5. their 8. their
3. there 6. They're

Elements of Literature
page 35

A.
1. b 2. a 3. a

B. Answers will vary. Students might answer that Martha wanted to know why the principal was acting as he was. They might also answer that Martha was motivated by respect for herself.

Word Study
page 36

A. Students should underline the root words *like, do, accept,* and *create* in the chart under the column **Larger Words.**

B.

act
1. actor 2. react 3. action

play
4. replay 5. playing 6. display

sign
7. significance 9. signify
8. resign

present
10. presentation 12. presentable
11. represented

Grammar Focus
page 37

A.
1. could not participate
2. could study
3. could play
4. could afford
5. could not look

B. Answers will vary.

Grammar Focus
page 38

A.
1. Martha couldn't believe the board wanted to charge fifteen dollars for the jacket.
2. Couldn't her teachers help Martha with her problem?
3. Martha couldn't decide how to ask Grandpa for the money.
4. The principal couldn't let Martha lose the scholarship jacket.

B. Answers will vary. Students should write questions based on their own ideas.

From Reading to Writing
page 39

Answers will vary.

Across Content Areas
page 40

Students should use the Venn Diagram to compare and contrast how they are alike and different from Martha.
Each student should write two sentences describing how the student and Martha are the same.
Each student should write two sentences describing how the student and Martha are different.

UNIT 2 • CHAPTER 1

Build Vocabulary
page 41

1. pigments
2. carbon dioxide
3. glucose
4. chlorophyll
5. excess
6. deciduous
7. disintegrate

Writing: Punctuation
page 42

1. At the end of the day, I rushed home.
2. During spring vacation, I went to the zoo.
3. At the end of the summer, we went camping.
4. During the movie, he fell asleep.
5. As the day was ending, I realized I forgot to take my dog for a walk.
6. In the early morning hours, she was busy studying for her test.
7. As time went on, he began to enjoy his math class.
8. After a spring rain, a rainbow might appear.

Elements of Literature
page 43

A.
1. Plants take water from the ground and carbon dioxide from the air.
2. Plants use sunlight to turn water and gas into glucose.
3. Plants use glucose to grow.
4. Plant releases oxygen into the air.

B.
1. Chlorophyll disappears from leaves.
2. Stored glucose is trapped inside.
3. Cells get bigger during the fall.
4. Bottom cells form a seal between the leaf and tree.
5. Top cells begin to dissolve and form a tear-line.
6. Leaves fall from the tree.

Word Study
page 44

A. (Students should say pronunciations aloud.)

B. Unscrambled letters: paragraph, geography

C. Possible responses:
1. biography, the history of a person's life
2. elephant, the largest animal that lives on land
3. phrase, a small group of words
4. photographer, a person who takes photographs

Grammar Focus
page 45

A.
1. like 3. do 5. sings
2. has 4. crawls

B.
1. My mother does not drive to work.
My mother doesn't drive to work.
2. Barbara does not do very well in math.
Barbara doesn't do very well in math.

Grammar Focus
page 46

1. Does she eat meat?
2. Do they speak Spanish?
3. Do you have lunch at noon (almost) every day?
4. Does she like math?
5. Do they listen to classical music?
6. Does he play in every game?
7. Does it rain a lot in Florida?

From Reading to Writing
page 47

Answers will vary.

Across Content Areas
page 48

Answers will vary. Student responses should reflect an understanding of what each audiovisual resource can be used for.

UNIT 2 • CHAPTER 2

Build Vocabulary
page 49

1. c **3.** f **5.** d
2. a **4.** e **6.** b

Writing: Punctuation
page 50

1. After I finished my dinner, I studied for my math test.
2. After we won the game, the coach yelled, "Great job!"
3. At the surprise party, everyone shouted, "Happy birthday!"
4. Linda and Pablo are going to study for the test together.
5. Before I go to the park, I have to take out the garbage.
6. When my brother interrupted me, I screamed, "Leave me alone!"
7. As I was leaving for school, my mother said, "Have a nice day."

Elements of Literature
page 51

Students should underline: The training began almost two years ago.
Answers for sentences will vary. Sentence should be in present tense. It should relate to the setting and events of the excerpt.

Word Study
page 52

A.
1. certainty; the condition of being certain
2. difficulty; the condition of being difficult
3. sixty; six times ten
4. honesty; the quality of being honest
5. loyalty; the quality of being loyal

B.
1. difficulty
2. certainty
3. honesty
4. loyalty

Grammar Focus
page 53

A.
1. Next year, the ship will sail from England to Virginia.
2. The settlers in Jamestown will build new homes.
3. Elizabeth's brother will join her next year.
4. Many mosquitoes will bite Elizabeth this summer.
5. In winter, the mosquitoes will die.

B. Answers will vary. Sentences should include the words *will study, will go, will eat, will read.*

Grammar Focus
page 54

1. they won't sail to Africa.
2. Will Elizabeth stay behind?
3. six ships won't sink
4. Will the colonists build houses in Jamestown?
5. Will a new baby be born?

From Reading to Writing
page 55

Answers will vary. First paragraph should be written in past tense and tell about what happened in the past year. Second paragraph should be written in future tense and tell about what might happen in the future.

Across Content Areas
page 56

The events in order are:
June 1, 1609: Nine ships sailed from Plymouth.
(no date): A hurricane struck.
August 11, 1609: We landed in Jamestown. Mosquitoes bite me.
August 12, 1609: We will begin to build our house.
(no date): A new baby will be born.

UNIT 2 • CHAPTER 3

Build Vocabulary
page 57

1. b **3.** f **5.** a **7.** g
2. c **4.** d **6.** e

Writing: Punctuation
page 58

1. Why do sheep leave the flock?
2. Do your work before you go to the game.
3. Some sheep like to stray from the flock.
4. What is Miguel doing today?
5. Is it time for school?
6. Can you help me with my math homework?
7. I think it is a good idea.
8. Do you think it is going to rain today?

Elements of Literature
page 59

1. winter; some time after 1920
2. southern part of the United States, probably Texas; after 1991
3. big city; after 1994

Word Study
page 60

A. It's, Its, its, It's

B. Answers will vary. The second and third sentences should include the possessive form *its.* The fourth and fifth sentences should include the contraction *it's.*

Grammar Focus
page 61

1. If I get an A, my mother will bake a cake.
2. If the weather is too cold, we can't go to the mountains.
3. If he does a good job, he will feel proud.
4. If the sidewalk is icy, he might slip.
5. If he does poorly on his test, he will feel upset.
6. If they walk quickly, they will reach their campsite by nightfall.

Grammar Focus
page 62

1. If I walk to school, I will not arrive on time.
2. He will be able to buy a bicycle if he saves some money.
3. If I eat breakfast, I will have energy for the rest of the morning.
4. She will go to the party if she finishes her homework.
5. If Gabriel goes to the computer camp, we will miss him this summer.
6. Jennifer will be a good soccer player if she practices.
7. If I visit New Mexico, I will not be able to go to the party.
8. Pablo will learn a lot if he listens to his grandfather.

From Reading to Writing
page 63

Answers will vary. All sentences must pertain to a conversation about "And Now Miguel."

Across Content Areas
page 64

Answers will vary. Paragraphs should include the main idea in the chart (preferably as the first sentence). Main details of the paragraphs should be the details in the chart.

UNIT 2 • CHAPTER 4

Build Vocabulary
page 65

1. bewildered **6.** flawless
2. bouquet **7.** halfheartedly
3. sturdy **8.** recited
4. gasp **9.** appropriate
5. inquisitive **10.** possession

Writing: Punctuation
page 66

1. When we returned from shopping, my father asked, "Did you buy anything at the store?"
2. My mother said, "Yes, I bought a gold bracelet."
3. My father replied, "May I please see it?"
4. Then my father said, "This is very nice."
5. Then my little brother said, "You forgot to ask me if I bought anything."
6. "Excuse me, but did you buy anything young man?" my father said.
7. Tommy smiled and said, "I bought a pack of gum with my own money."

Elements of Literature
page 67

A. Answers will vary. Possible responses:
1. The narrator is unhappy because she does not want to be there.
2. The narrator thinks her family is strong.
3. The narrator and her family members were nervous about meeting their passenger.
4. The narrator likes her new family member. She changes her mind.
5. The narrator is surprised at her feelings. She feels affection for the new family member.
6. The narrator thinks her family is not as strong as she had previously thought.

Word Study
page 68

A.
1. priceless; without a price
2. hopeless; without hope
3. bottomless; without a bottom
4. fearless; without fear
5. careless; not careful

B.
1. hopeless **4.** fearless
2. bottomless **5.** careless
3. priceless

C.
1. The teacher checked José's test and found that it was flawless.
2. I was so tired after running in the race that I was breathless.
3. My dog is homeless until my father fixes the doghouse.
4. I was nervous going to the dentist, but the whole examination was painless.

Grammar Focus
page 69

A.
1. adjectives: new, many
 New sentence should be the same except the adjectives should be replaced.
2. adjective: large
 New sentence should be the same except the adjective should be replaced.
3. adjective: fresh
 New sentence should be the same except the adjective should be replaced.
4. adjective: silver
 New sentence should be the same except the adjective should be replaced.
5. adjective: small
 New sentence should be the same except the adjective should be replaced.
6. adjective: large
 New sentence should be the same except the adjective should be replaced.

B. Answers will vary. All adjectives chosen should make sense as modifiers.

Grammar Focus
page 70

A. A shy student entered the small classroom today. She wore a red skirt and a blue sweater. Her brown eyes were hidden behind the thick lenses of her glasses. Her two long braids moved from side to side as she walked. The teacher looked up and smiled at her. The noisy class was suddenly silent. The students were all eager to meet their new classmate.

B. Answers will vary. Students should write six sentences about things around them. Each sentence should include at least one adjective that describes the thing.

From Reading to Writing
page 71

Answers will vary.

Across Content Areas
page 72

Answers will vary.

UNIT 2 • CHAPTER 5

Build Vocabulary
page 73

1. a **4.** b **7.** a
2. b **5.** b **8.** b
3. a **6.** b

Writing: Capitalization
page 74

1. When we go to South Dakota, we are going to see Mount Rushmore.
2. I went to the movie with my friend, Sarah Parker.
3. In my geography class, we are learning about the Great Plains.
4. When we went to New York City, we saw the Statue of Liberty.
5. After school, we will be going on a field trip to a museum.
6. My mother and father are taking the family on a vacation to Florida.
7. My history teacher, Mr. Hanson, gave us a surprise quiz at the end of his lecture.

Elements of Literature
page 75

A.
1. a **2.** a **3.** b **4.** b

B.
1. b **2.** d **3.** a
4. c **5.** e

Word Study
page 76

A.
1. sadness, the condition of being sad
2. neatness, the condition of being neat
3. fairness, the condition of being fair
4. illness, the condition of being ill
5. goodness, the condition of being good
6. thoughtfulness, the condition of being thoughtful

B.
1. adjective: *ill*
   Sentence should include the noun *illness.*
2. adjective: *neat*
   Sentence should include the noun *neatness.*
3. adjective: *fair*
   Sentence should include the noun *fairness.*
4. adjective: *kind*
   Sentence should include the noun *kindness.*
5. adjective: *thoughtful*
   Sentence should include the noun *thoughtfulness.*

Grammar Focus
page 77

1. We are packing our bags.
2. My cousin/he/she is sleeping in our house
3. I'm speaking to my friend
4. We are writing in our journal
5. she is visiting her home town
6. the elders/they are telling stories
7. I am studying
8. my brother/he is playing basketball
9. Pablo/he is working on the computer
10. I'm riding the bus (to school)

Grammar Focus
page 78

1. Is she riding her bicycle?
   She is not riding her bicycle.
   She isn't riding her bicycle.
2. Are they swimming today?
   They are not swimming today.
   They aren't swimming today.
3. Am I going to a party tomorrow?
   You are not going to a party tomorrow.
   You aren't going to a party tomorrow.
4. Are we wearing uniforms to school?
   We are not wearing uniforms to school.
   We aren't wearing uniforms to school.
5. Is he going on a field trip?
   He is not going on a field trip.
   He isn't going on a field trip.

From Reading to Writing
page 79

Answers will vary.

Across Content Areas
page 80

A.
1. Lumbee **5.** Blackfoot
2. Cherokee **6.** Navajo
3. Iroquois **7.** Seminole
4. Pueblo **8.** Paiute

B.
1. Lumbee
2. Paiute
3. Three: Lumbee, Cherokee, and Iroquis
4. Five: Blackfoot, Paiute, Seminole, Navajo, and Pueblo.

UNIT 3 • CHAPTER 1

Build Vocabulary
page 81

A.
1. frightens **5.** scream
2. barking **6.** wild
3. tough **7.** afraid
4. strangers

B.
Under "Related to Sounds": barking, scream
Under "Related to Feelings": frightens, afraid
Additional response will vary, but should fit the categories.

Writing: Spelling
page 82

1. There are only ten days left until my birthday.
2. Before school starts I need to go to the store to buy some supplies.
3. I spent most of my weekend studying for my math test.
4. Soon I will have to decide what colleges I want to start applying to.
5. My mother says she wants me to go to the store.
6. I will go to my friends' birthday parties.

Elements of Literature
page 83

A.
1. in
2. jaws
3. exact rhymes

B. Answers will vary. Students' responses should rhyme with the sentences provided.

Word Study
page 84

A.
1. My father doesn't know what time he will be home from work.
2. He says he'll bring pizza for dinner on his way home.
3. I may not eat the pizza because I don't like the kind my father is bringing home.
4. After we eat, it'll be time for me to do my homework.
5. My father sometimes helps with math problems that I can't understand.

B.
1. cannot **4.** do not
2. it is **5.** I would
3. I have

Grammar Focus
page 85

A.
1. over **4.** into
2. above **5.** on
3. under **6.** over

B. Answers will vary. Make sure students' responses correctly use prepositional phrases of place.

Grammar Focus
page 86

A. Answers will vary. Make sure students' responses correctly use prepositional phrases of place.

B.
1. I cannot wait to attend the birthday party at my brother's house.
2. The party is for my sister that lives in Chicago.
3. I have to pick her up at the airport before the party.
4. The last time I saw her was at my brother's wedding.
5. My sister and I are taking a trip to Mexico.

From Reading to Writing
page 87

Answers will vary.

Across Content Areas
page 88

A. Answers will vary. Cluster maps should include frightening things that can be seen, and frightening things that can be heard.

B. Poems will vary. Poems should use ideas from cluster maps. They should have similar rhymes or exact rhymes.

UNIT 3 • CHAPTER 2

Build Vocabulary
page 89

1. bitter **5.** struck
2. disaster **6.** headed
3. suffered **7.** ignored
4. tugged

Writing: Punctuation
page 90

1. Maria said, "I have a lot of homework to do tonight."
2. "It looks like it is going to rain all day long," replied William.
3. My father shouted, "Billy, it is time for dinner!"
4. "When I get home from work, start painting the house," Fernando said.
5. Martha whispered, "Little Jimmy is sleeping, so we need to be very quiet."
6. The coach bellowed, "Everybody played a great game."
7. "If we study hard, the test should not be too difficult," Elizabeth said.

Elements of Literature
page 91

The first thing you need to do is mix water and flour to make the pizza dough. Second, spread the pizza dough into a flat and round circle to make the crust. Third, spread pizza sauce over the crust. After the pizza sauce is on the crust, sprinkle cheese over it. Then top the pizza with your favorite pizza toppings. After everything is on the pizza, bake it for ten minutes. The last step is to eat and enjoy.

Word Study
page 92

A.
1. I told Manuel that I wanted to go to a movie with him.
2. I think my family is going to take a vacation to China this summer.
3. My father and mother are going to visit my uncle John in California.
4. In school today we studied the Bill of Rights.
5. Maria and Nancy are going to go to a computer camp in Illinois.
6. I saw Phillip when I went to the grocery store.

B. The following should be checkmarked and underlined: dr. marshall, magna carta, atlantic ocean, texas, new york yankees.

Grammar Focus
page 93

A.
1. take off **4.** get up
2. stop by **5.** set out
3. call up **6.** turn in

B. Answers will vary. Make sure students' sentences correctly use two word verbs.

Grammar Focus
page 94

A.
1. took off **4.** turned in
2. stopped by **5.** took off/set out
3. called up **6.** set out/took off

B.
Answers will vary. Make sure students' sentences correctly use two word verbs.

From Reading to Writing
page 95

Answers will vary.

Across Content Areas
page 96

Answers should list the types of information to be found in the various resources.

UNIT 3 • CHAPTER 3

Build Vocabulary
page 97

Drawings will vary but should show meaning of words.
Related words
for *cottage:* cabin
for *hiding:* covering
for *shock:* surprise
for *satchel:* backpack
for *comb:* brush
for *suitcase:* container

Writing: Spelling
page 98

A.
1. The sick patient usually slept until noon.
2. Mr. Wong swept the kitchen floor with a straw broom.
3. She left the party earlier than her friends.
4. The long snake crept across the desert sand.
5. Jack spent most of his free time reading books.
6. They often sent letters to their family in Mexico.
7. The computer kept a record of all the books that are in the library.

B. Answers will vary. Make sure students' sentences correctly use the irregular past tense verbs.

Elements of Literature
page 99

A.
1. Answers will vary. Students should indicate the words *fun, my favorite, surprise, I feel thankful, they care about me.*
2. Answers will vary. Students might write that the writer's tone shows joy, thankfulness, excitement, surprise.

B. Answers will vary. Make sure the students' word choice reflects tone.

Word Study
page 100

A.
readiness playfulness

B.
enjoyment assignment

C.
1. argument **4.** assignment
2. playfulness **5.** agreement
3. happiness

Grammar Focus
page 101

A.
1. The town theater is small, but the theater in the city is huge.
2. Carlos is not very patient, but he is very intelligent.
3. Mom's pasta was overcooked, but her chicken turned out just right.
4. The library is closed now, but it will be open tomorrow morning.
5. It is too hot to go running, but we go swimming in the lake instead.

B. Answers will vary. Students' answers should show contrast from first sentence part in compound sentence.

Grammar Focus
page 102

A.
1. He liked to learn. But he had never been to school.
2. Sari had to walk two miles. But she knew some short cuts.
3. Sleeping takes up a lot of time. But it is not a waste of time.
4. Daisy thought she had found gold. But she had found fool's gold instead.
5. It is very cold outside. But he didn't put on a coat.

B. Answers will vary. Make sure students use but correctly to show contrast.

From Reading to Writing
page 103

A. Answers will vary.

Across Content Areas
page 104

Answers will vary depending on which holidays students choose to write about.

UNIT 3 • CHAPTER 4

Build Vocabulary
page 105

1. meaning 1 **5.** meaning 2
2. meaning 1 **6.** meaning 2
3. meaning 2 **7.** meaning 1
4. meaning 2 **8.** meaning 1

Writing: Capitalization
page 106

A. Words that should be capitalized are underlined.

George Washington decided that the president's house should be built in Washington, D.C. In 1800, President John Adams became the first president to live there. The house changed over the years. It had been rebuilt and repaired. It had even been painted. But each time it was painted, it was painted white. In time it became known as the White House. Another famous building in Washington, D.C., is the United States Capitol Building, where the Senate and the House of Representatives work.

Elements of Literature
page 107

A.
1. He loves the land. He is sad that camps of soldiers are taking it away.
2. Answers will vary.
3. Answers will vary. Students may answer *sadness, anger.*

B. Answers will vary.

Word Study
page 108

A.
1. figurative language
2. literal language
3. literal language
4. figurative language
5. figurative language
6. literal language
7. figurative language
8. literal language

B. Images will vary.

Grammar Focus
page 109

A.
1. smaller **3.** taller **5.** lovelier
2. simpler **4.** cheaper **6.** easier

B.
1. faster
2. more descriptive
3. more interesting
4. longer
5. more intelligent
6. cheaper
7. easier

Grammar
page 110

A.
1. the lightest
2. the most entertaining
3. the smallest
4. more beautiful than
5. sturdier than
6. the most intelligent

B.
1. sturdiest **4.** easiest
2. narrower **5.** smallest
3. lighter **6.** most entertaining

From Reading to Writing
page 111

Answers will vary.

Across Content Areas
page 112

1. alphabetical
2. because there is an illustration on that page
3. last name
4. page 24
5. brakes

UNIT 3 • CHAPTER 5

Build Vocabulary
page 113

1. rose **5.** baby
2. potatoes **6.** peace
3. lion **7.** eyes
4. drum

Writing: Punctuation and Capitalization
page 114

1. They stamped their feet very hard; they bellowed fearfully.
2. Chickens and ducks ran into bamboo bushes to hide; fish jumped frantically in the ponds.
3. Our watchdog crawled under a bed; he whined.
4. The houses were gone; the sheds were destroyed.
5. Now it was safe for us; it was also safe for the animals.
6. The fire would keep predators away; it would keep us warm.
7. There wasn't much space in the garden; we were hemmed in by fallen trees.
8. Tank's beating heart comforted me; little by little, I fell asleep.

Elements of Literature
page 115

A. Answers will vary. Possible responses:
1. Mario's mother is at the door. She found out about what he did and will discipline him.
2. Luisa and the girl will become friends.
3. Someone is calling Anne to offer her a job.

B. Answers will vary. Students may note that sunnier, milder weather might foreshadow happy events. Stormier weather might foreshadow trouble.

Word Study
page 116

A.
1. daytime **4.** football
2. bookstore **5.** backpack
3. flowerpot **6.** bedroom

B. Answers will vary. Sentences should include any three of the following words: *daytime, bookstore, flowerpot, football, backpack, bedroom.*

Grammar Focus
page 117

A.
1. us **4.** us **7.** me
2. them **5.** them **8.** him
3. it **6.** you

B. Answers will vary. Sentences should include the pronouns *it, me, him.*

Grammar Focus
page 118

1. Aldo and I had an argument over cars and the environment.
2. Aldo drives big cars and likes them.

3. I walk to work because I believe walking is the best way to travel. The argument between Aldo and me never ends.
4. Aldo's car uses a lot of gas, but ours uses very little.
5. I don't agree with Aldo's opinion about cars, and he doesn't agree with mine.

From Reading to Writing
page 119

Answers will vary. Students' responses should use the writing techniques listed.

Across Content Areas
page 120

1. dogs, horses
2. cats, goldfish
3. turkeys, chickens (Answers will vary for the second part of the question.)
4. Answers will vary, but they should fit the categories indicated in the Venn Diagram.

UNIT 4 • CHAPTER 1

Build Vocabulary
page 121

A.

1. d.	**3.** g.	**5.** b.	**7.** h.
2. a.	**4.** e.	**6.** c.	**8.** f.

B. Answers will vary.

Writing: Capitalization
page 122

A.

1. I asked, "Do you have a book about elephants?"
2. OK
3. "Are there any books about bugs?" I inquired.
4. The librarian said, "Yes, we have books about all kinds of animals."
5. OK
6. OK
7. I said, "Thank you for all your help."

B. Answers will vary, but the first word of dialogue in each sentence should be capitalized.

Elements of Literature
page 123

A. Venn Diagrams will vary.
B. Paragraphs will vary.

Word Study
page 124

A.

1. Serena used a video in her oral presentation about libraries.
2. Most cities in the U.S. have a library where you can borrow books.
3. I opened the window and, presto! a bird flew in.
4. The public can attend all meetings of the town government.
5. My brother wants to study optics in college.
6. After class, you are free to do what you want, but in this class you may not chew gum.

B. Answers will vary.

Grammar Focus
page 125

A.

1. This is the sweater that makes me itch.
2. Please return the books that belong to me.
3. I bought the cake that has the shape of a bird.
4. The student that has the best grades will win the scholarship.
5. The library that is near my house is not open on Sunday.

B. Relative clauses will vary, but they should begin with *that* and the subject of the relative clause.

Grammar Focus
page 126

A.
1. shirt **2.** CD **3.** book
B.
1. No. **2.** Yes. **3.** Yes. **4.** No.

From Reading to Writing
page 127

Answers will vary.

Across Content Areas
page 128

1. Because they are fiction.
2. Information about Carnegie and his library.
3. It would not have information about public libraries and libraries outside the United States.
4. *Libraries Through the Ages* would have the best information. Its title suggests that it has information about the history of libraries. It is nonfiction.

UNIT 4 • CHAPTER 2

Build Vocabulary
page 129

Words About Mountains: slope, altitude, descend, frozen, crater, ridge
Words About Ancient Ruins: preserved, mummy, artifacts, statues, textiles, pottery

Writing: Punctuation
page 130

A.

1. What is your name? question
2. My name is Dalva. statement
3. Where is the gym? question
4. It is over there. statement
5. Please give me my book. command
6. Who is he? question
7. His name is Youssouf. statement
8. Put the book on the table. command

B.

1. What are you doing this weekend?
2. I am going to go to my aunt's house.
3. OK
4. I would like to, but I am busy this weekend.
5. Do you want to go next weekend?

Elements of Literature
page 131

Students' work will vary but should include the use of first-person pronouns.

Word Study
page 132

A.

1. described	**5.** divided
2. folded	**6.** dropped
3. included	**7.** reduced
4. slipped	**8.** chopped

B. Answers will vary.

Grammar Focus
page 133

A.

1. It is important to get an education.
2. It is fun to learn about computers.
3. It is easy to use the Internet.
4. It is important to work hard.
5. It is great to make new friends.
6. It is difficult to meet new people.
7. It is necessary to save money.
8. It is interesting to learn new subjects.

Grammar Focus
page 134

1. was
2. will be/might be
3. must be
4. might be
5. would be/might be

From Reading to Writing
page 135

Students' work will vary.

Across Content Areas
page 136

B.

1. It is about the loss of oxygen as you climb a mountain.
2. Breathing/ Keeping Warm
3. Keeping Warm
4. It gets colder and there is less oxygen.

UNIT 4 • CHAPTER 3

Build Vocabulary
page 137

A.

1. c	**3.** b	**5.** g	**7.** e
2. f	**4.** a	**6.** d	

B. Answers will vary.

Writing: Spelling
page 138

A.

1. repairing	**6.** looked
2. dripping	**7.** claiming
3. shopped	**8.** mapped
4. parking	**9.** mopped
5. tipped	

B. Answers will vary.

Elements of Literature
page 139

A. Character maps will vary.
B. Paragraphs will vary.

Word Study
page 140

A.

1. c	**3.** a	**5.** g	**7.** d
2. e	**4.** f	**6.** b	

B. Answers will vary.

Grammar Focus
page 141

A.
1. Once **3.** After **5.** Finally
2. Before **4.** Then **6.** Soon
7. A year ago, he left the swordmaster.

B. Answers will vary.

Grammar Focus
page 142

A.

1. Once there was a young girl.
2. About two years ago, she decided to learn to ice skate.
3. Before she could learn, she had to buy ice skates.
4. So then she went to the store and bought skates.
5. The next thing she did was take ice-skating lessons.
6. She soon learned how to skate without falling down.
7. After two months of lessons, she was a good skater.
8. Two years later, she began to compete in skating contests.
9. She finally became a champion skater.

B. Sentences will vary, but each sentence should contain an adverb to show time.

From Reading to Writing
page 143

Checklists will vary.

Across Content Areas
page 144

A. Cluster maps will vary.
B. Drawings will vary.
C. Sentences will vary.

UNIT 4 • CHAPTER 4

Build Vocabulary ***page 145***

A.

1. b	**3.** f	**5.** c	**7.** g
2. d	**4.** h	**6.** a	**8.** e

B. Answers will vary.

Writing: Spelling
page 146

1. thief	**6.** OK
2. OK	**7.** OK
3. OK	**8.** vein
4. freight	**9.** pierce
5. receive	**10.** OK

Elements of Literature
page 147

A. Students' work will vary but should show sentences with past tense.
B. Stories will vary but contain flashbacks.

Word Study
page 148

A.
1. movement; happening
2. without shape
3. able to be seen

B. Answers will vary.

Grammar Focus
page 149

A.
1. Although Liz was very young, she decided to try out for the team.
2. Although I do like snacks, I will try it.
3. I liked reading this novel although I prefer history books.
4. Although you do not want to stop reading, you have to clean your room.
5. She did not win the race although she tried very hard.
6. Although math is my best subject, it is not my favorite.
7. Martina never came to the party although she said she would come.
8. Although my parents enjoy cooking, they do not cook very well.

Grammar Focus
page 150

A.
1. OK
2. Answers will vary, but a correctly punctuated independent clause should be added.
3. Answers will vary, but a correctly punctuated independent clause should be added.
4. Answers will vary, but a correctly punctuated independent clause should be added.
5. Answers will vary, but a correctly punctuated independent clause should be added.

B. Sentences will vary, but should contain *although* and correct punctuation.

From Reading to Writing
page 151

Checklists will vary.

Across Content Areas
page 152

1. the article
2. the article
3. the chart

UNIT 5 • CHAPTER 1

Build Vocabulary
page 153

1. frowned
2. knob
3. windy
4. thin piece
5. ate a lot quickly
6. looked quickly
7. cold
8. tomorrow
9. turn down
10. unhappy

Writing: Capitalization
page 154

1. Aunt Hilda and Uncle Enrique live on a farm.
2. On the farm Uncle Enrique works hard.
3. He is also a doctor at Newtown Clinic.
4. At the clinic, his name is Doctor Enrique Chavez, but everyone calls him Doctor Enrique.
5. Fortunately, Uncle Enrique enjoys having two jobs.
6. Aunt Hilda has one job.
7. She works at Western University.
8. There, they call her Professor Chavez.

Elements of Literature
page 155

Marco went to the airport with his sister, Alejandra. They got there very early. They waited until their brother's plane landed. When the plane landed, they went to meet him. They saw so many people. Finally, Marco/he saw his brother. He waved at him. His brother waved back. They all hugged.

Word Study
page 156

A.
1. uncomfortable; not comfortable
2. unwrap; to take off wrapping
3. unable; not able to
4. unprepared; not ready or not prepared
5. unusual; not usual, rare
6. untie; to take apart a knot or tied rope
7. unaware; not aware of

B.
1. imbalance; out of balance; not in balance
2. immature; not mature, childish
3. impatient, not patient, in a hurry
4. imperfect; not perfect, flawed
5. impractical; not practical
6. improper; not proper, wrong
7. improbable; not probable, unlikely

Grammar Focus
page 157

A.
1. has learned
2. has set
3. have finished
4. have decided
5. have talked
6. have decorated
7. has snowed
8. has returned
9. have mailed
10. have eaten

B.
1. My mother has baked snacks for my friends.
2. He has finished reading the book.
3. They have walked all the way home.
4. We have learned how to ice skate.
5. The children have asked for ice cream.

Grammar Focus
page 158

A.
1. Has she visited them?
2. Have they waited for them?
3. Has she stayed long?
4. Has he called her?
5. Have they worked here?

B.
1. He hasn't played baseball
2. She hasn't exercised.
3. They haven't reduced the time limit.
4. She hasn't talked to him.

From Reading to Writing
page 159

Students' work will vary but should show correct use of quotation marks and punctuation in dialogue.

Across Content Areas
page 160

1. sunny
2. warm front
3. snow
4. cold front
5. rain
6. cloudy

UNIT 5 • CHAPTER 2

Build Vocabulary
page 161

1. The water gushed out of the faucet.
2. She looked bewildered and confused.
3. She was a strong and powerful child.
4. The dog was scared and trembling in a corner.
5. The vines are growing on the trellis.
6. She searched her pockets quickly and feverishly for the money.
7. She waved and used other gestures to get his attention.
8. He was nervous and stammering to explain his excuse.
9. They used yarn and needles for crocheting the sweaters.
10. She transformed from a young girl to a beautiful woman.

Writing: Punctuation
page 162

1. 1
2. 2
3. 4
4. 3
5. 1
6. 2
7. 1
8. 4

Elements of Literature
page 163

Students' work will vary but should show the mood and action of the characters.

Word Study
page 164

A.
1. The bird flew swiftly into the treetops.
2. The crowd cheered wildly when their team won.
3. The baby walked slowly.
4. The rain poured constantly.
5. My aunt greeted me warmly.
6. He asked the question softly.

B.
1. rapidly
2. instantly
3. painfully
4. sadly
5. quickly
6. gladly

Grammar Focus
page 165

A.
1. The man was shoveling snow off my driveway.
2. I felt the cool breeze that was blowing through my hair.
3. They were going out to eat in a restaurant.
4. We are forming a club for opera lovers.
5. Diego was trying to get to sleep early.

B.
1. My brother was walking by the lake.
2. Elaine was brushing her hair in her bedroom.
3. They were walking to school in the morning.
4. The race car was zooming around the track.
5. The bluebirds were nesting in the box.

Grammar Focus
page 166

A.
1. Was she walking with her friend?
2. Was he helping the teacher?
3. Were they eating at the table?
4. Was she pouring water in her hands?
5. Was she listening to her speak?
6. Was she running away?

B.
1. She wasn't eating with her fork.
2. He wasn't helping the girl.
3. She wasn't running outside.
4. She wasn't listening to her teacher.
5. They weren't expecting her to learn.
6. She wasn't spilling water.

From Reading to Writing
page 167

Answers will vary.

Across Content Areas
page 168

Students' work will vary. Students should show that they know how to use audio-visual resources to get information for reports.

UNIT 5 • CHAPTER 3

Build Vocabulary
page 169

A. Students read for general comprehension.

B. Answers will vary. Words that would typically be thought of as "scientific" are: stapes, malleus, incus, cochlea.

C. Answers will vary.

Writing: Punctuation
page 170

1. The sounds that you hear at home—the television, the kitchen, and cars on the street—all move through your ear.
2. Can you see—I mean—hear me?
3. The ear—and its many parts—allows you to hear many different sounds.
4. The plucking causes the rubber band to move back and forth—or vibrate—very quickly.

Elements of Literature
page 171

A. Answers will vary. Sentences should explain why students feel their eyesight is important.

B.
1. cornea
2. retina
3. cornea
4. retina
5. the innermost layer of the eye that receives light
6. Hyperopia
7. when you can clearly see objects that are far away, but you cannot clearly see objects that are close
8. when you can clearly see objects that are near, but you cannot clearly see objects that are far away

Word Study
page 172

A.
1. d
2. f
3. b
4. h
5. j
6. a
7. i
8. c
9. g
10. e

B. Students' sentences will vary.

Grammar Focus
page 173

A.
1. walks
2. likes
3. enjoys
4. practice
5. wants
6. explain
7. plans

B.
1. The middle ear has three small bones.
2. The outer ear funnels the sound to the middle ear.
3. The cells in the inner ear excite nerve cells.
4. Our two ears hear things differently.

Grammar Focus
page 174

A. I am in a rock group. There are three other people in my group. We have guitars, drums, and keyboards. We have fun at big concerts. We have traveled all over the world. Our drummer is great. She has many fans. She does a wonderful job at every performance.

B.
1. is
2. are
3. are
4. is
5. do
6. has
7. has
8. are

From Reading to Writing
page 175

Answers will vary.

Across Content Areas
page 176

A. Venn Diagrams should show different information for the following:
"Hearing: The Ear": vibrations, molecules, sound engineers
"How We Hear": care for the ear
Both: structure of ear, balance

B.
1. structure of ear, balance
2. care for the ear

UNIT 5 • CHAPTER 4

Build Vocabulary
page 177

Words About Characters: features, superheroes, aliens; mutants
Words About Process: springboard, concept, sketch

Writing: Punctuation
page 178

1. Let's see what happens when I do this. Kaboom!
2. He fell off the table. Splat!
3. Get away from me. Yuck!
4. Let's get him! Run!
5. Hey, wait for me!
6. Here they come. Oh no!

Elements of Literature
page 179

First, find the browser you want to use.
Find the search box on the screen.
Then, type in your subject.
It is best if you choose your subject carefully.
Then you can find your facts quickly.
When you are done, the research paper is truly yours.

Word Study
page 180

A.
1. A Californian is a person from the state of California.
2. A physician is a person who practices medicine.
3. An electrician is a person who fixes electrical things.
4. A Bostonian is a person from the city of Boston.
5. A Georgian is a person from the state or country of Georgia.

B.
1. electrician
2. Georgian
3. Californian
4. physician
5. Bostonian

Grammar Focus
page 181

1. If you talk in class, you get in trouble.
2. My mother gets nervous if she drinks coffee.
3. If you study hard, you get better grades.
4. If the backpack is green with stripes, it's mine.
5. My ears hurt if I listen to loud music.

Grammar Focus
page 182

1. it's my sister
2. I don't go out
3. I don't get the money
4. if she makes soup
5. if she sings

From Reading to Writing
page 183

Students' work will vary but should show steps in a process.

Across Content Areas
page 184

Students' KWL charts will vary but should show research used.

UNIT 6 • CHAPTER 1

Build Vocabulary
page 185

1. b
2. g
3. a
4. c
5. f
6. e
7. d

Writing: Punctuation
page 186

A
1. ?
2. .
3. !
4. !
5. ?
6. .

B. While walking in a dark forest, we spotted a baby bear on a hill. I was scared! Sure, it was too small to hurt a human. But when you see a baby bear, you need to ask yourself a question. Is there a mother bear nearby? A big, strong mother bear can hurt a human. She can be dangerous if you are somewhere between her and her baby. After we spotted the baby, we walked calmly and quietly through the forest. We didn't look at the baby or make any quick moves. We wanted the mother to know we were no threat to her cub. I was glad when we were out of the forest.

Elements of Literature
page 187

Square 1
Sacagawea
Native American guide, interpreter
She carried a baby on her back, translated.
strong, tough, brave, smart, friendly

Square 2
Thomas Jefferson
President (NB: though text doesn't say so)
Fascinated by the West; wants to know more
Curious, intelligent, decisive

Square 3
Meriwether Lewis
Explorer, captain, expedition co-leader
Chosen to lead; chose a co-leader
Brave, generous, smart

Square 4
William Clark
Explorer, captain, expedition co-leader
Chosen to co-lead, brought his boyhood friend and slave; didn't free York
Brave, smart, ungenerous to York

Square 5
York
Slave, boyhood friend of Clark
At Clark's side often; would sacrifice his life; not freed
Brave, loyal, eventually disappointed

Word Study
page 188

Answers will vary. Possible responses:
1. The students took a long stroll.
2. What a wonderful view this is!
3. The gentle wind was refreshing.
4. The sailboat slowly crossed the large lake.
5. The campers hiked up the steep road.
6. Our old house is on this street.
7. The kids ran back home for lunch.
8. The storm never ended during our vacation.
9. The school acquired several new computers.

Grammar Focus
page 189

A.
1. Appositive: the math teacher
   Noun being renamed: Mr. Hanson
2. Appositive: my sisters
   Noun being renamed: Shelley and Catherine
3. Appositive: Frederick
   Noun being renamed: The coach
4. Appositive: my parents
   Nouns being renamed: Mario and Liz
5. Appositive: Mr. Tildon
   Noun being renamed: The principal

B. Answers will vary.

Grammar Focus
page 190

A.
1. Luigi, my best friend, is from Italy.
2. My friends, Mario and Stephan, will be joining us for dinner.
3. My sister, Julia, plays the flute.
4. Mrs. Lopez, our teacher, went to school with my father.
5. My grandparents, my mother's parents, have lived with us for a long time.

B. Answers will vary, but should contain appositives and correct punctuation.

From Reading to Writing
page 191

Answers will vary.

Across Content Areas
page 192

1. The Mississippi
2. Pike's Early Life
3. Death as a Hero
4. Exploring the Mississippi

UNIT 6 • CHAPTER 2

Build Vocabulary
page 193

A.
1. confident
2. impractical
3. perturbed
4. indignant
5. embarrassed
6. serenely
7. despair

B. Sentences will vary, but each one should use a vocabulary word correctly.

Writing: Punctuation
page 194

1. OK
2. One of my brothers went to college; the other did not.
3. OK

4. Some days I feel like playing soccer; other days I do not.
5. Today I will work; tomorrow I will rest.
6. OK
7. I am planning to use the money to buy a bike; the rest I will save.

Elements of Literature
page 195

1. scary
2. happy
3. serious
4. adventurous

Word Study
page 196

A.
1. The ship was invisible in the fog.
2. The cold weather is intolerable!
3. The campers were unprepared for rain.
4. Rain in the desert is uncommon.
5. It is impossible for me to go to the movie.
6. My decision was unwise after all.

B.
1. a meal that is not good for you/not healthy
2. a chess player who has not played much/does not have much experience
3. a voice that you cannot recognize/do not know
4. water that is not clean/not pure
5. a customer who cannot wait calmly/is not patient
6. a toy that does not cost much/is not expensive

Grammar Focus
page 197

A.
1. We had started our trip when Mom said, "Wait! I forgot my bag."
2. When summer came and the beaches opened, she had learned how to swim.
3. Patricia didn't really like the earrings that her husband had bought the day before.
4. When we finally got to the restaurant, it had closed.
5. The old house had belonged to my grandmother, but now it belonged to me.

Grammar Focus
page 198

1. Question: Had Rajan heard the news before he arrived home?
2. Negative (full form): Dad had not planned the trip that we took. Negative (contraction): Dad hadn't planned the trip that we took.
3. Negative (contraction): The game hadn't started when we found our seats.
4. Negative (full form): The roller coaster had not stood still for a second before it raced down the tracks.
5. Question: When I finally caught a fish, had Gina left? Negative (full form): When I finally caught a fish, Gina had not left. Negative (contraction): When I finally caught a fish, Gina hadn't left.
6. Negative (contraction): We hadn't reported the fire when fire trucks arrived.
7. Question: Had it stopped raining before the plane took off?
8. Question: Had Jimmy practiced the drums for a week before Jerry bought earplugs?

From Reading to Writing
page 199

Answers will vary.

Across Content Areas
page 200

A. Storyboards will vary.
B. Answers will vary.
C. Summaries will vary, but information in the summary should be from the storyboard.

UNIT 6 • CHAPTER 3

Build Vocabulary
page 201

1. i
2. b
3. e
4. g
5. j
6. d
7. f
8. c
9. a
10. h

Writing: Capitalization and Punctuation
page 202

1. John F. Kennedy was once the President of the United States.
2. I want to visit North Dakota next summer.
3. Bill is going to have dinner with us next Tuesday.
4. The third Monday in January is Martin Luther King Day.
5. Is the holiday in May Memorial Day or Labor Day?
6. The big river between Illinois and Iowa is the Mississippi River.
7. Did you see Mount Rushmore when you went to South Dakota?
8. My grandparents are visiting Mark and me this weekend.
9. The Sears Tower in Chicago was once the tallest building in the world.

Elements of Literature
page 203

1. to persuade
2. to inform
3. to entertain

Word Study
page 204

A.
1. b
2. e
3. f
4. a
5. c
6. d

B.
1. f
2. c
3. b
4. e
5. a
6. d

Grammar Focus
page 205

All sentences should contain a dependent clause with *that.*

Grammar Focus
page 206

A.
1. Answer should have an independent clause added to the dependent clause.
2. OK
3. Answer should have a dependent clause added to the independent clause and *that.*
4. Answer should have a dependent clause added to the independent clause and *that.*
5. OK
6. OK

B. Answers should contain an independent clause and a dependent clause with *that* in each sentence.

From Reading to Writing
page 207

Answers will vary.

Across Content Areas
page 208

1. 19
2. He was arrested in a protest in North Carolina.
3. He was arrested protesting against laws he thought were unfair.
4. Possible answer: Yes; He fought for what he believed in.
5. There were riots in 130 United States cities and a national holiday was named after him.
6. Yes; important civil rights laws were passed during his lifetime.

UNIT 6 • CHAPTER 4

Build Vocabulary
page 209

1. triumph
2. restrict
3. denied
4. liberty
5. proposed
6. eliminate
7. valiant
8. struggle
9. vowed
10. pleaded

Writing: Spelling
page 210

A.
1. shelves
2. inches
3. watches
4. hisses
5. faxes

B.
1. lives
2. beaches
3. thieves
4. taxes
5. knives

Elements of Literature
page 211

A.
1. If I win this election
2. I will
3. use of the same letter in many words—work, worry, weak, wealthy; listen, loudest, learn, likes; respect, rest, relax, retire, responsibilities, requests

B. Answers will vary, but paragraph should reflect the same patterns of repetition found in the original speech.

Word Study
page 212

A. Answers will vary, but they should include adjectives describing the noun in the center of the web.

B.
1. Sentence should contain the noun *movie* along with adjectives from word web.
2. Sentence should contain the noun *pizza* along with adjectives from word web.
3. Sentence should contain the noun *mountains* along with adjectives from word web.
4. Sentence should contain the noun *song* along with adjectives from word web.

Grammar Focus
page 213

A. Sentences will vary, but should show contrast.
B. Possible responses:
1. He is sad about leaving, yet he is happy to move to California.
2. She is a fast reader, yet she is a slow writer.
3. It is bright outside, yet it is dark inside.
4. It is clear that you understand how to tie a knot, yet it is not clear that you can do it.

Grammar Focus
page 214

A. Answers will vary, but should show contrast or similarity depending on the conjunction provided.

B.
1. My father likes to cook, and he cooked tonight.
2. He made my favorite kind of pizza, but/yet he burned it.
3. He also made a dessert, but/yet he forgot to serve it.
4. After dinner my family went to a movie, and I went with them.
5. The movie was pretty good, but/yet I thought it was too long.
6. I was tired when we returned home, but/yet I didn't go to bed.

From Reading to Writing
page 215

Checklists will vary.

Across Content Areas
page 216

1. 1
2. Alaska, Delaware, North Dakota, South Dakota, Vermont, Wyoming
3. They have small populations.
4. California
5. Answers will vary.
6. New York